THE MEANINGS
OF TEACHING

An International Study of
Secondary Teachers' Work Lives

Edited by
Allen Menlo and Pam Poppleton
Statistical Analysis and Technical Editing by
LeVerne S. Collet

BERGIN & GARVEY
Westport, Connecticut • London

Library of Congress Cataloging-in-Publication Data

The meanings of teaching : an international study of secondary
  teachers' work lives / edited by Allen Menlo, Pam Poppleton ;
  statistical analysis and technical editing by LeVerne S. Collet.
      p.   cm.
  The nine-country study reported in this book has been carried
out by member teams of the Consortium for Cross-Cultural Research
in Education.
  Includes bibliographical references and index.
  ISBN 0–89789–586–X (alk. paper)
  1. High school teachers—Cross-cultural studies.   2. High school
teaching—Cross-cultural studies.   I. Menlo, Allen.   II. Poppleton,
Pam.   III. Collet, LeVerne S.   IV. Consortium for Cross-Cultural
Research in Education.
LB1777.M464   1999
373.11—dc21   98–51219

British Library Cataloguing in Publication Data is available.

Library of Congress Catalog Card Number: 98–51219
ISBN: 0–89789–586–X

First published in 1999

Bergin & Garvey, 88 Post Road West, Westport, CT 06881
An imprint of Greenwood Publishing Group, Inc.
www.greenwood.com

Printed in the United States of America

The paper used in this book complies with the
Permanent Paper Standard issued by the National
Information Standards Organization (Z39.48–1984).

10   9   8   7   6   5   4   3   2   1

Contents

Illustrations

TABLES

Preface

This book will describe how secondary school teachers in nine countries have experienced several aspects of their work and how their experiences have affected the quality of their professional lives. Since the study providing this information was conducted during the late 1980s and the early 1990s, its findings can also be used to construct a picture of what it was like to be a secondary school teacher in different parts of the world during that time. The similarities and differences discovered between the countries give rise to greater understanding of the teachers' perspectives, implications for the improvement of teaching and schooling, and to social science knowledge. The results of the study will also enable teachers in any country to compare their experiences with those of teachers in several other countries and thereby develop a cross-cultural perspective on their work, which will in turn promote a sense of international professional identity.

Some aspects of the study have already been available to the academic community in the form of papers given at international conferences and articles published in learned journals. The findings, interpretations, and implications reported here go well beyond earlier reportings. The number of countries involved is greater as are the particular dimensions on which they are compared; also, a more sensitive form of analysis is used. The book will also present the work in a more integrative and accessible manner than has previously been available to a wide range of colleagues in schools, universities, and related settings.

The nine-country study reported here is one of a series of comparative studies on secondary teachers' working lives which have been carried out by member teams of the Consortium for Cross-Cultural Research in Education. Each team comprises faculty or faculty and student members located within a university or research-institute setting in each country. At the time of this writing, twelve member teams are engaged in a twelve-country comparative study of *The Influence of Recent Educational Change on the Dynamics of Teachers' Working Lives*. Members of the consortium for cross-cultural research in education, their locations, and the team directors are as follows:

University of Michigan (United States), Allen Menlo*

University of Sheffield (United Kingdom), Pam K. Poppleton*

Hiroshima University (Japan), Akira Ninomiya*

National Institute of Education (Singapore), Wong Kooi Sim (relocated), Guat Tin Low*

University of Warsaw (Poland), Wieslaw Wisniewski (deceased), Renata Siemienska Zochowska*

University of Haifa (Israel), Lya Kremer-Hayon*

University of Windsor (Ontario, Canada), Colin Ball (retired), Noel Hurley; and Dalhousie University, (Nova Scotia, Canada), J. B. Roald and H. J. Murphy*

Russian Academy of Education (Moscow), Boris Gershunsky*

Johann Wolfgang Goethe-Universitat (Frankfurt, Germany), Hans-Joachim Lissmann*

University of Tasmania (Australia), John Williamson

Hungarian Institute for Educational Research (Budapest), Tamas Kozma

Asian Centre for Organization Research and Development (New Delhi, India), Jaya Indiresan

University of Utrecht, Theo Wubbels; and Vrije University in Amsterdam, Hans Vonk (the Netherlands)

University of South Africa (Pretoria), Johan Booyse

Universidade Federal do Rio Grande do Sul (Brazil), Maria das Gracas Furtado Feldens

Universite Cheikh Anta Diop, Dakar (Senegal), Babacar Fall

Chinese Academy of Sciences (Beijing), Kan Shi

The Consortium is a research partnership that has grown from a membership of three countries in 1981 to seventeen currently. It was cofounded by this book's two editors and a third colleague, Dr. Hans-Joachim Lissmann, of the Johann Wolfgang Goethe-Universitat in Frankfurt, Germany, and it was initially known as the Frankfurt–Michigan–Sheffield Cross-Cultural Study Program. A small grant from the University of Michigan made it possible for the three cofounders to participate in face-to-face planning sessions at each other's institution. The planned purpose of the enterprise continues to be the

*Teams participating in the nine-country study.

generation of social science knowledge about teaching and schooling and the translation of that knowledge into improved understandings of educational systems and processes as well as action implications for the improvement of education within and across the national settings involved. The Consortium has always been a proponent of the search for deeper and broader meanings of teaching and an advocate for the use of these meanings in creating a work life for teachers that allows the fullest expression of their potential in society. In carrying out this interest, its work has been supported financially by private and government sources and the universities involved. New team memberships have come about through emergent professional contacts, which have developed partly through meetings held at international conferences, and partly through research travel and the considerable technological developments in communication that have taken place over the past ten years.

Over time, the core academic interest of the Consortium has become more clearly defined as teaching in the secondary sector, including the quality of the teaching life and all matters relevant to the continuing professional development of teachers and the roles of the providers of teacher education. Within the Consortium there has always been a common study available for member teams who wish to be involved in a demandingly collaborative venture in cross-cultural comparative research within the core area of interest. At the same time, some teams have also conducted studies in line with the Consortium's core interest, but highlighting their own emphasis, style, and methodology.

The Consortium provides a friendly context for those who wish to pursue comparative studies related to teaching and teacher education. It has already built an international database that is serving to encourage and increase the number of studies in this area by other workers. A Consortium library containing over eight hundred books, dissertations, journal articles, and conference papers bearing information on the areas of teacher work life and cross-cultural research is located at the University of Michigan team offices. Over the years, teams have not only worked together on the same projects but they have arranged and hosted, in their own countries, the data collections of other teams who had initiated solo projects.

The directors of all teams constitute a directorate that as a loosely knit body engages in discourse regarding general and specific issues in the conduct and management of current projects, the planning of future projects, and the presentation and dissemination of findings. Allen Menlo and Pam Poppleton, who began academic collaboration in 1965, have shared the leadership in the overall Consortium since its origination. Participative discussion and consensual decision making are pursued via face-to-face meetings at conferences, team-on-team visits, and electronic and regular mail. The Consortium's central E-mail address, cccre-um@umich.edu, provides a means of reaching the directors of all teams simultaneously. The promotion of inclusion and open communication and the development and maintenance of an organizational identity are continuing efforts. The latter is not without difficulty in an organization whose units are separated by international distances which tend to create an abstractness of imagery for its members. Though, as seems to be the case with all living systems, the sharing of superordinate goals and a strong commitment to a collaboratively systematic process have been important contributors toward both a positive experience and a sense of progress. It is quite interesting that the cultural differences between members have functioned more as a gentle source of cross-cultural learning, world-mindedness, mutual appreciation, and challenge, rather than as obstacles to communal efforts. Indeed, we have found that working together in a loosely bounded academic organization can provide a rich, continuing agenda of interpersonal, intergroup, and international insights.

There is a seemingly endless list of individuals, groups, and organizations to be personally contacted and thanked for their support and assistance in completing this study. In this publication we wish to formally thank the following for their expressed belief in the importance of the Consortium's work and their generous grants, awards, and other forms of support and assistance: the University of Michigan School of Education; the University of Sheffield Division of Education; the Robert Sage Foundation; the Economic and Social Research Council of the United Kingdom; the Michigan State Department; The British Council of Education; Phi Delta Kappa Standing Conference on Studies in Education; the Michigan Education Association; The Michigan Federation of Teachers.

1

Introduction to the Consortium's Study

Pam Poppleton and Allen Menlo

BACKGROUND AND OBJECTIVES

This chapter first traces the events that drew the attention of members of the Consortium for Cross-Cultural Research in Education to the need for an international comparative study of the work lives of teachers. After identifying, discussing, and operationalizing all of the variables in the study, a set of objectives was presented, which served as an action agenda for the research. The broad implementation of this study—moving it from conceptual to actual—required the consideration of several procedural and substantive issues; each of these is identified and discussed. Then, to place this study in a broader context of other studies of a similar nature, four other such studies and their theoretical and methodological issues are described. Finally, there is a review of the forthcoming chapters that will give form and substance to these issues and considerations.

Background to the Study

During the last thirty years, there has been a shift in the broad range of educational provision and policy in the United States, Canada, Australia, Europe, and in most developed countries, as a result of profound structural changes in industry and new technologies. Changes have also occurred in population patterns and demographic trends. These have had a dramatic effect on the demand for school employment, leading to shifting patterns in the employment of teachers and higher unemployment trends in general. Governments began to claim that schools were responsible for falling educational standards and economic decline, while the notion that the more a nation spent on education, the more the economy would thrive was called into question. In some cases, teachers were blamed for the ills of nations by promoting child-centeredness in learning through mixed-ability teaching and by the neglect of basic skills. At the secondary-school level, the rapid development of new technologies highlighted the need to increase the proportion of young people pursuing further education in order to acquire new skills for use in an increasingly competitive world. The higher incidence of social problems in the secondary schools led to difficulties in the recruitment of teachers, which in turn produced a gradual deprofessionalization of the teaching force. A report published by the Organization for Economic Cooperation and Development (OECD) in 1990 described the period as one of profound dissatisfaction among teachers and a deterioration in the relationships with their employing authorities. Teaching quality became a major concern of governments, whose focus was on maintaining an adequate supply of competent and highly motivated teachers.

By the mid-1980s, educationists in a number of countries were expressing anxieties about the implications of the reforms, both real and pending, for teachers and their schools, and wished to place them in an international context so that the nature and scope of the dynamics and issues could be more fully understood. Accordingly, a decision was taken in 1985 by several teams of the Consortium for Cross-Cultural Research in Education to mount an international study of teachers' work lives. In this study, three major components of the work lives of teachers from different countries would be compared: their classroom practices, their roles and responsibilities, and their work conditions. Also three major indicators of the quality of their work lives would be compared: their overall job satisfaction, the centrality of their work in their lives, and their experience of job-related stress. Teachers from the different countries would be compared by the effect of their practices, roles and responsibilities, and work conditions on their work-life quality. Further, they would be compared by the ways their own personal and demographic characteristics entered into the nature of their work lives and its quality. By 1990, work was completed by colleagues in the United States, England, West Germany, Singapore, and Japan. By 1992, these researchers had been joined by colleagues from four other countries: Israel, the Soviet Union, Canada, and Poland. All had agreed to a common set of objectives and collected data using a common questionnaire.

Objectives of the Study

The preceding pages provide a brief overview of the education issues that served as a major source of motivation to conduct the present study and have defined the major constructs that appear to be embedded in these issues. With the issues and constructs in mind and with a belief in the potential of cross-cultural comparative inquiry to surface new understandings about the issues, the aforementioned nine-country-based research teams of the Consortium set forth the following objectives to guide the study in each of their countries.

1. To study the perceptions of teachers working in public sector, secondary comprehensive schools about three major factors (working conditions, teaching practices, and professional roles, relationships, and responsibilities) of their work lives.

2. To study the perceptions of the teachers about three major indicators of their work-life quality, particularly their overall job satisfaction, work centrality, and job-related stress.

3. To study the relationships of the three major work-life factors of teachers and their personal characteristics to the quality of their work lives.

4. To examine similarities and differences between teachers from different countries regarding the foregoing factors, indicators, and relationships.

5. To consider the similarities and differences as sources of formulated knowledge.

6. To consider implications for educational policies and practices for the improvement of education within and across the nine countries.

The achievement of these objectives posed several technical issues and conceptual considerations, which will be identified and discussed briefly in the remainder of this introductory chapter and in more detail in later chapters.

CONCEPTUAL ISSUES

During the past thirty or so years, comparative education as it was conceived in the 1960s has met a number of epistemological challenges. Noah and Eckstein (1969) appeared to equate the study of comparative education with the application of the scientific process to research in education. This emerged as the attempt to use cross-national data to test propositions about the relationships between education and society and between teaching practices and learning outcomes. This is the positivist position in which "only empirical statements about education are scientific and only scientific statements are meaningful" (Epstein, 1988). The challenges have come from cultural relativism associated with the anthropological school (Mallinson, 1975), from ethnomethodology (Zimmerman, 1978), and more recently from the rise of pluralism and postmodernity (Cowen, 1996), all of which reject the positivistic assertion of invariant relationships between education and aspects of society and the existence of cultural universals. It follows that different methodologies are associated with positivism and relativism respectively, which Epstein (1988) regards as mutually incompatible views. For positivists, he says "the very purpose of comparison is to generalize across cultures" and this requires a standard methodology. Postmodernists, on the other hand, would deny the existence of universal cultural features, arguing that the "major research traditions which have been employed in comparative education are often fundamentally deficient in the ways they conceive culture [and] ignore the multiplicity of cultural values and forms within a given milieu" (Welch, 1993; Liebman & Paulston, 1994).

Just as different countries were involved in the Consortium's study, so too were different researchers who, as well as reflecting the cultures of their countries, reflected also academic cultures, which are by no means homogeneous. In pursuing educational research, academics are constantly grappling with new ideas and, in the process of evaluating them, forming new perspectives that give access to different kinds of knowledge and different ways of searching for it. Therefore, there has to be a negotiated settlement between researchers before the action begins. In practical terms, such negotiations arise at the point of deciding upon an appropriate methodology for a comparative study and are generally expressed in terms of quantitative versus qualitative methods, a range of which are available to the researcher. In the case of our study, it was recognized from the outset that such a large-scale study must lay emphasis on the quantitative dimension, while not ruling out the collection of qualitative data based on interviews, to aid interpretation of the survey results.

Moving this international–cross-cultural study ahead required the consideration of several substantive issues. Each of these is now identified, discussed, and related to the present study.

Types of Research

The researcher in the international field quickly becomes aware that making international comparisons employs much the same family of methods, both quantitative and qualitative, as most other types of research. However, there are a number of different terms used to describe studies which appear to have much in common, and it may be appropriate at this point to attempt a little ground clearing of the terms used.

Comparative research is an umbrella term for a variety of studies that compare social groups, organizations, or nation-states on one or more criteria that are of interest to the researcher. It is used mainly, though not exclusively, to refer to cross-national comparisons as reflected in the content of articles published in the major journals of comparative education and directed at an international audience. However, it may include comparisons between regions in any country defined according to geographic, systemic, socioeconomic, or other relevant criteria.

Cross-national research is one form which, according to Kohn (1989), may be distinguished from other types of comparative research by the broad range of comparisons that can be made of political and economic systems, cultures, and social structures. He distinguishes four types of cross-national research: those in which the nation is the *context* of study, those in which it is the *object* of study, those in which it is the *unit* of study, and those that are *transactional* in nature. While admitting that it may be difficult in practice, to distinguish "nation as context" from "nation as object," generally, the former would be interested in how certain social institutions or groups operate in different contexts (e.g., Broadfoot, 1981). Research in the latter category would be more interested in extending our knowledge of the country or countries involved, such as a study of the provision for special education in Britain and France in which the type of provision may be related to country-specific cultural features.

In cross-national research, there is a sense in which the nation is always the unit of analysis, but analyses may depend on the degree of precision that the researcher is seeking concerning the national features that are the subjects of study. For instance, a study of education under different administrative systems in the England and the former Soviet Union was primarily interested in the issue of the centralization–decentralization of control (Poppleton, Gershunsky, & Pullin, 1994). This meant considering a number of dimensions on which the form of administration was presumed to operate and a statement of hypotheses against which the outcomes of the study could be tested. As Kohn remarks, this "requires much better data than are generally available in multi-nation data sources" (1989, p. 23).

Cross-cultural research may be cross-national or may involve comparisons between subcultures within, or across countries. It attempts to describe the varieties of social behavior encountered in different cultural settings: to analyze their origins and to identify those that are similar across cultures. The search for universals in human behavior and development has been one of the prime motivations for undertaking cross-cultural studies. It has been supposed, for example, that a culture of teaching exists that is independent of setting or occupants and may be seen to have universal characteristics. Waller (1932) considered that teaching did something to teachers so that there was something "teacherish" about them. Lortie (1975) identified the characteristics of presentism, conservatism, and individualism as elements in the teacher culture arising from the teachers' absorption in the immediate demands of the classroom, resistance to and even a reluctance to consider changes in what and how they teach, and emphasis on the autonomy that delimits the boundaries of their interactions with colleagues. However, over a period of twenty years or so, there has been a trend away from conceptualizing the teaching culture as a relatively static and homogeneous social entity to recognizing considerable diversity in both its form and content (Hargreaves, 1994).

All these studies were unicultural and North American in origin, but the existence of national differences (if found) can help to point up features in one system that might otherwise be taken for granted, and many aspects of one country's education can be illuminated by systematic comparison with education in other countries. Thus, cross-cultural research may be a rich source of both universals across cultures and particulars within each culture (Brislin, Lonner, and Thorndike, 1973).

Advantages of a cross-cultural perspective over a unicultural one is that each culture acts as a testing ground for the universality of research findings; and cross-national comparisons from the findings of each of the nine countries represented here should present the opportunity to extract understandings and develop recommendations that have a broader and more reliable base than those developed from single country studies. However, it has to be acknowledged that few recommendations for change have been developed directly from first-hand, cross-cultural findings (Boyd & Menlo, 1984; Nisbet & Broadfoot, 1980). Indeed, Gallimore (1985) holds that no simple translation between models applicable in one setting to models applicable in others can yet be made. The Laboratory of Comparative Human Cognition (1986) recommends continued cross-cultural research in which translation principles are formulated and then tested through carefully studied efforts at diffusion of findings within and across cultures. Today, when the tendency to borrow freely from the practices of other countries in order to solve their own problems seems to be endemic among politicians, such careful studies are badly needed.

The Consortium's study is both cross-national and cross-cultural in taking account of the teachers' culture in the context of nine countries. As we have seen, the study is based on the teachers' perceptions of their work lives via self-report questionnaires and semistructured interviews in which social perceptions were an important element. We can use these data in order to provide us with an interpretation that will encompass the richness of everyday experiences and help us to understand the relevance of political and economic systems to the cultures and social structures within educational systems.

International Studies. Other categories have been used to describe the study of systems and the structures developed to uphold those systems, whether in education or some other aspect of political and social life. The term *international studies* was introduced into education by the Comparative and International Education Society to cover studies that "describe, analyze or make proposals for a particular aspect of education in one country other than the author's own" (Postlethwaite, 1988). International studies of this kind play an important role in developing international awareness and understanding and stimulating practical help and support by the "haves" for the "have nots."

Competing Research Paradigms

In the course of the development of the social sciences, a number of contested research paradigms have evolved that have particular relevance in studies of education and comparative education, where they fuel the debate about the use of appropriate methodologies.

In the context of the comparative study of *classroom-anchored* research, Ginsberg and Klopfer (1996) defined and described positivist, interpretivist, and critical science approaches in terms of their conception of theoretical knowledge, their conception of the social world, and the role of their scientists in this social world as they influence choices in policy research. A positivist study would certainly employ quantitative methods of analyzing data from questionnaire, interview, or direct observations. An interpretivist study would employ qualitative methods based on the elicitation of accounts from the experiences of key persons which could be subjected to a number of checks to establish the validity of the data by such methods as triangulation, checking against other respondents, or examining documentary evidence. A critical science approach may use both quantitative and qualitative methods in the search for understanding the relationships between context and social perception as people strive to make sense of their social worlds. We may summarize the competing paradigms as positivistic versus interpretivist, and a critical science that shares elements of both by using quantitative or qualitative methods insofar as the aim is to search for regularities or for meanings.

How did these competing research paradigms affect the choices made in the Consortium's research? We were interested in the work-life perceptions of teachers as an occupational group as a way of gaining access to the quality of the teacher's work lives in different contexts that could be studied. This demanded a positivistic, macrostudy using quantitative methods in the form of a self-report questionnaire. But we were also interested in the meanings that the teachers attached to their experiences, which might be very different in different countries even though the experiences themselves could be very similar. Obtaining such perceptions and perspectives would be the job of the interpretative, microanalysis, and both would need to be taken into account in order to make the comparisons complete.

Replication

It has been strongly recommended by Robinson and Levin (1997) that greater use should be made of replication as a means of assuring the significance and generalizability of findings from educational research. They refer particularly to studies in which the same research design is repeated with new sets of participants in order to see if the original study's results will occur again and are not limited to the unique characteristics of a single sample. If a researcher is interested in phenomena related only to teachers, then new samples of teachers with different characteristics might be studied to determine the extent to which the array of patterns and relationships discovered for teachers with one set of personal and environmental characteristics is similar to or different from that of teachers with another set of characteristics. It is in this way that cross-cultural research has an inherent potential for functioning as replication. In our study, the values, traditions, and norms of each country are the characteristics that differentiate each sample of teachers from the other eight samples. Thus, it would seem that the findings that are replicated in nine different countries have passed one rather rigorous test of significance and generalizability.

International Borrowing

In practice, where cross-national differences are found to exist, the things that account for their existence are often not clear, whether they be national in origin, cultural, or products of particular social and economic systems. The problem in all kinds of comparative study is how to account for the differences (and similarities) once they have been identified and to assess their significance for contemporary decision making.

The problem of international borrowing is particularly acute in educational comparisons, for they are often undertaken with policy implications in mind. There is a widespread belief, especially among politicians, that we have much to learn from the educational practices of other countries. This is a specially seductive belief in an age of reform when often the simplest solution to one's own problems seems to be the wholesale transfer of teaching methods from A to B, without any consideration of their appropriateness in the context of B. For instance, Kenneth Baker, Secretary of State for Education, asserted at the 1987 North of England Conference that "the systems elsewhere in Western Europe seem to succeed much better than ours in keeping more of their young people in full-time education and for longer. One reason must be that these systems offer more young people qualifications which are worthwhile and respected in their own society. This message emerges clearly from HMI's recent report on education in the Federal Republic of Germany" (Phillips, 1989). As a result, a fresh emphasis on similar schemes of vocational training were to be introduced.

Yet Michael Sadler, Head of the Board of Education in 1900, had warned

In studying foreign systems of education we should not forget that the things outside the school matter even more than the things inside. We cannot wander at leisure through the educational systems of the world like a child strolling through a garden and pick off a flower from one bush and some leaves from another and then expect that if we stick what we have gathered in the soil at home, we shall have a living plant. (Phillips, 1989)

Arguments about the wisdom or folly of educational borrowing run right through comparative educational thought from its origins until the present day. It may be, however, that we have much to learn about the unwise adoption of wholesale policy transitions from one cultural context to another and about employing the processes of sensitive, creative adaptation of research findings and teaching–schooling processes of one country to another.

Culture and Cultural Diversity

Teachers' perceptions of their work are reflected through the medium of the occupational culture of teaching (Hargreaves, 1980), expressed as personal concerns at one level and as professional ones at another. These are important intervening variables between the micro and macrolevels of analysis that can be studied both within and between countries. Such studies are cross-cultural as well as cross-national in character.

But is there a culture of teaching that transcends national boundaries, and should we search for universals in a pluralistic world? If diversity is a characteristic of cultures, can national cultures be said to exist in a form in which comparisons are possible? In 1987 an international study reported an investigation into "The Meaning of Working" (MOW International Research Team, 1967), which was carried out in thirteen countries. The responses of diverse occupational groups were gathered in regard to the quality of their work experiences. From the seven countries for which appropriate data were available, four stable patterns of meaning emerged: an *instrumental* pattern, in which work was undertaken largely to obtain income; an *expressive* pattern, in which work was regarded as an instrument of self-expression; an *entitlement* pattern, in which work was regarded as a right rather than a duty; and a *contact* pattern, in which work was undertaken primarily for the social contact opportunities. From large multioccupational samples, all countries showed elements of all four patterns, but it was possible to define a modal pattern for each country. German respondents were found to score highest on the *instrumental and expressive* dimensions; Americans and Japanese on work as *low entitlement*; while the modal pattern for the Israelis and Yugoslavs was the *expressive* dimension. All four patterns occurred equally in the Belgian and Dutch national samples. When the combined samples were broken down into ten occupational groupings, teachers were unique in showing lowest instrumentality and entitlement combined with highest expressive work centrality associated with duty and contact patterns. Thus, there does appear to be evidence of a common orientation to work among teachers of different nationalities and different subcultures within them, and, over a period of twenty years or so, there has been a trend away from conceptualizing the teaching culture as a relatively static and homogeneous social entity to recognizing considerable diversity in both its form and content. In research conducted in Canada and England, Hargreaves (1994) identified four broad forms of teacher culture, which were defined as individualism, balkanization, collaboration, and contrived collegiality and which serve as "powerful psychological referents for every aspect of teaching work . . . in classroom, staffroom, subject department" as well as teachers' relationships with colleagues, governors, and administrators. By influencing ways of behaving in all these contexts, they define what is "teacherish" about teaching.

A Framework for Comparative Education Analysis

Bray and Thomas (1995) have recently given consideration to the classification of comparative studies and their analysis. Their approach is described in Figure 1.1. Three dimensions are used to classify comparative studies of which the geographic–locational dimension identifies seven possible levels of analysis; the second nonlocational geographic dimension identifies selected demographic groupings, and the third dimension shows selected aspects of education and society. It should be possible to locate every comparative study in one or more cells in the diagram. The shaded cell represents a research project comparing curriculum plans for all varieties of educational programs

Figure 1.1
A Framework for Comparative Education Analysis

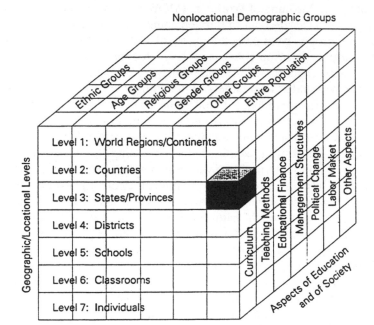

Source: From Mark Bray and R. Murray Thomas, "Levels of Comparison in Educational Studies: Different Insights from Different Literatures and the Value of Multilevel Analysis,"
Harvard Educational Review, 65:3 (Fall 1995), p. 475. Copyright © 1995 by the President
and Fellows of Harvard College. All rights reserved.

for the entire population in two or more provinces, where the unit of analysis
is the province.

Such a framework helps to clarify what is the main unit of analysis being
employed and to display the relative influence of micro and macrofactors in
making comparisons. It was developed to encourage and make possible multilevel analyses in an area that has been characterized by single level studies con-
centrating on, for example, individual students, classrooms, or schools, while
ignoring the fact that individuals are nested within classrooms, classrooms within
schools, schools within systems, and systems within countries (Kreft, 1993).
The statistical tools for such interpretations are complex, but whatever the
nature of the data, analysis should conform to the logic of the argument.

The Consortium's research compares the perceptions of selected samples
of secondary school teachers in nine countries about their working lives in
the period of 1987 to 1990, the unit of analysis being the country. Bearing in
mind the three dimensions just discussed, in the Consortium's study the major unit of analysis was to be the country; the demographic characteristics to

include age; gender and marital status of secondary school teachers; and those aspects of occupation and society (work satisfaction, work centrality, and job-related stress) thought to contribute to the quality of the teacher's working life.

OTHER COMPARATIVE STUDIES OF TEACHING

While there is no lack of research studies of teachers and their working lives, comparative and cross-cultural studies in this area are rare, and four examples of such studies since the 1960s follow. Their descriptions make it possible to acquaint the reader with other works related to the present study while throwing light on methodological problems and theoretical approaches.

The first, and the one nearest to our own study in conception, design, and methodology, was a 1970 study of "Teacher Role in Four English Speaking Countries," conducted by an international team of researchers in the United States, Great Britain, Australia, and New Zealand (Adams and Biddle, 1970). This was the decade of large-scale social surveys using interviews and laboriously constructed questionnaires (Verba, 1969).

The study was described as a fact-finding one based on the assumption that "before an ethology of educational systems can be developed, a certain amount of basic data has to be garnered. Nonetheless, the data are rich and diverse and provide not only a means for the testing of hypotheses subsequently, but ample basis for generating more" (Adams, 1970). Over 12,000 teachers were involved and the questionnaire yielded 131 dependent variables that could be tested against national and demographic differences. The major hypotheses examined were concerned with the relationship between the organizational properties of schools and demographic characteristics on the one hand, and two composite variables, job satisfaction–dissatisfaction and career commitment on the other. It was found that overall the age and sex composition of staff yielded the most significant findings. As age increased, job satisfaction decreased as did teachers' anticipation of withdrawal from teaching, this being the lowest in male-dominated schools. Organizational complexity was the strongest structural variable in predicting both job satisfaction and career commitment and was defined as the number of levels in the administrative hierarchy of the school and degree of subject-matter specialization.

The main thrust of the study, however, was to examine the incidence and nature of role conflict in the various countries, role conflict being what a person experiences "when he encounters mutually contradictory demands that are being placed upon him simultaneously." Teachers were asked to respond to a list of role expectations that they perceived might have been held for them by other teachers, their own consciences, parents, principals, and school officials. Role conflicts could be demonstrated within all of the countries and showed a good deal of similarity. American teachers occupied a midposition on most of the measures, though, with British colleagues, they showed greater conflict over the acceptance of nonprofessional duties (e.g., supervising clubs or school meals) and the practice of corporal punishment. In contrast, Australians and New Zealanders accepted nonprofessional duties as part and parcel of the teaching job and favored the use of corporal punishment. British teachers showed greatest conflict over the social promotion of students.

The problem of semantic differences in interpreting cross-cultural data is raised in these accounts. What, for instance, is the meaning attached to the term nonprofessional duties by teachers in the different countries? Unpaid involvement in extracurricular activities was an accepted part of the teacher's professional role in the 1960s in Britain yet by the mid-1980s it had become a key issue in industrial action. The explanation for the British teachers' low score on this item was explained by Adams as "what our respondents reported might represent their values rather than their practices" (1970, p. 58), and this distinction was later to be incorporated into the Consortium's study.

The study did not attempt to relate teachers' role conflicts to their job performance, classroom morale, or student achievement. But the International Association for the Evaluation of Educational Achievement is well known for its series of cross-national surveys of educational outcomes in a number of curriculum areas. It has been concerned with the basic curriculum areas of language, mathematics, and science, and its surveys have been a major factor in stimulating intense international concerns about the relative standing of achievement in the countries surveyed and the promotion of intense competitiveness between and within them.

While the surveys have generated important findings, questions about the influence of educational systems and policies on the one hand and classroom practices and learning strategies on the other have remained unanswered. They have not been neglected, however, as the possible effects of the macrocontext were addressed in "The National Case Study" (Passow, Noah, Eckstein, & Mallea, 1976) based on twenty-one countries, and of the microcontext by "The IEA Classroom Environment Study" (Anderson, Ryan, & Shapiro, 1989), which represents "a rare opportunity for a comparative examination of factors which may influence what may happen in classrooms which, in turn, may influence what students do and learn and how they feel." The CES was conducted in ten countries and designed in 1978 when enthusiasm for looking at the fine detail of classroom events via systematic observation and recording was at its height. Studies conducted within the process–product paradigm (Dunkin & Biddle, 1974) offered great promise of extending our understanding of the role played by teachers and pupil–teacher interactions in stimulating learning. In addition, a comparative study would attempt to identify factors present in one country's classrooms that might be absent in another's and point to particularly successful or unsuccessful practices. Because it is possible that different things *work* in different countries, note Anderson, Ryan, and Shapiro: "The need for naturalistic correlational studies is especially marked in international research." It was originally intended to continue the study into a second, experimental phase, but this proved not to be justified by the findings. "Of the more than 300 correlations with student achievement between the observational variables and student achievement . . . only 18 were statistically significant." The research concluded that differences in teacher behavior were not related in any systematic way to student achievement. Nowak (1989) has commented that "comparative, cross-historical, cross-cultural or cross-national studies often aim at the discovery of broad, possibly universally valid regularities applying to complex objects. The more complex are the objects of study, the more independent from each other are the antecedent conditions and . . . the more likely are such studies to fail."

It was always possible that the large scale of this study and the complexities of its procedures would miss the target. It is interesting, therefore, that a significant development in the 1980s was the growing interest in ethnographic methods and the burgeoning output of studies of teachers' lives and work, which aimed to capture the meanings that teachers attached to their experiences more sensitively than routine questionnaires and computer-based data analyses.

A methodologically eclectic study by Broadfoot and Osborn (1992), used self-report questionnaires and semistructured interviews combined with classroom observation in a study of French and English primary teachers' perceptions of their roles and responsibilities. Four hundred primary school teachers in each of the counties of Avon (England) and Bouches du Rhone (France) were chosen for their similar socioeconomic and geographic features, and equal numbers of teachers were selected in each case to represent four socioeconomic groups. A questionnaire planned jointly by the English and French researchers was given to the teachers after pilot trials and revision and was followed up by intensive interviews and observations of small subsamples of sixteen teachers in each cohort. Each of these teachers was asked to keep a diary of professional activities out of school during one week. "The aim of this intensive and qualitative fieldwork stage [was to] illuminate teacher perceptions in greater depth than is possible by questionnaire methods."

Some striking similarities and differences were found. Both groups felt a strong sense of responsibility to themselves, their consciences, and their pupils, but French teachers felt far less accountable than the British to parents, colleagues, and society in general and more accountable to the state. In terms of educational objectives, most of the influences perceived as important by French teachers came from the educational system itself, but outside the school, whereas English teachers felt that their work was strongly influenced by the institutional context in which they worked. They also expected more of themselves in their work and had more ambitious goals, worked more closely with parents, and were more likely to regard teaching as a vocation. This study revealed evidence of consistent national differences in the conceptions of professional responsibility held by teachers in the two countries, each reflecting deep-seated cultural assumptions.

Another two-country comparison of the teachers' perceptions of their roles—this time in disadvantaged schools in the England and the United States—illustrated the flexibility and impact of an interpretative approach to interview data (Poppleton, Deas, Pullin, and Thompson, 1987). This was an early study from the Consortium in which secondary school teachers retold their experiences of working "in an area like this," "in a school like this," and of "being a classroom teacher," and "being and becoming a professional teacher." There were many similarities, each group seeing themselves as core professional groups and as good teachers who took pride in providing conditions of continuity and stability for vulnerable children against great odds. Each group asserted its identity as classroom teachers as distinct from office workers, social workers, or administrators, but, the American teachers in particular called attention to the interference that they perceived from administrators. This study revealed more about subcultural influences within countries than large differences between them.

In general, the quantitative studies revealed national differences rather than similarities between countries, whereas the reverse tended to be true of the qualitative aspects of the studies. Is this an example of finding what one seeks? If one seeks, by either method, to reveal the existence and nature of teachers' perspectives on their work and professional roles, some will be rooted at a national level, and some in professional and local subcultures. The discovery and understanding of such differences and similarities requires the employment of a combination of research methods.

Returning to the competing research paradigms mentioned earlier, the distinction made between cross-national and cross-cultural studies is not clearcut, and a good case can be made for the use of both quantitative and qualitative methods of data collection and analysis to aid the processes of interpretation.

METHODS AND PROCEDURES USED IN THIS STUDY

This section provides a brief description of the data collected and the methods, procedures, and statistics used in the data analyses. A more detailed description of procedures and a series of comprehensive statistical tables that document the material presented in succeeding chapters appear in a technical supplement to this book described in the appendix. This supplement should prove particularly useful to persons who are themselves conducting cross-cultural research in education.

Variables to Be Studied

Figure 1.2 provides a picture of all the explorable variables and intervariable relationships within the overall study, as well as more detailed information on each variable and its role. The left-hand area displays the variables selected as the three major components of teacher work life, those things that

Figure 1.2
The Explorable Variables and Intervariable Relationships within the Overall Study

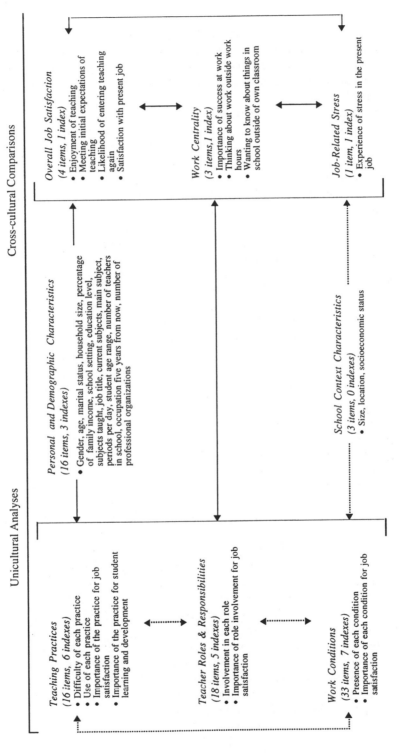

have highest salience within the daily professional experience of teachers: their teaching practices, their roles and responsibilities, and their work conditions. These are later referred to as domains: the *practice domain*, the *roles domain*, and the *conditions domain*. Items within each domain were grouped to form *indexes*.

In addition to the concepts of domain and indexes, readers will encounter the term *dimension*. Within each domain, respondents were asked to rate each item on a one to three scale to indicate the extent to which they perceived it to be present in their work and, again, according to the extent to which they perceived it to contribute to their job satisfaction. The two dimensions, the *amount dimension* and the *importance dimension*, are frequently used in reporting the findings of the study. The difference between these two ratings is also an important variable and is known as the *incongruity index*. The practice domain is somewhat different because it has four dimensions rather than two.

The upper left-hand block indicates that teachers were asked about four characteristics specific to each of their teaching practices (and therefore called *facet specific*): their extent of difficulty, use, importance for job satisfaction, and importance for student learning and development. The sixteen practices were then grouped and treated as five sets or indexes. The middle left-hand block shows that teachers were asked about two facet-specific characteristics of each of their eighteen roles and responsibilities; the extent of their involvement in each; and how important their involvement in each was for their job satisfaction. Indicated also is that the eighteen roles and responsibilities were grouped and treated as five indexes. The lower left-hand block points out that teachers were asked about the extent to which each of thirty-three conditions were present in their work and how important the conditions were for their job satisfaction. Also indicated is that the thirty-three conditions were grouped and treated as seven indexes.

The right-hand area shows the three major variables selected as indicators of the somewhat abstract, holistic, and nondimensional quality of work life: overall job satisfaction, work centrality, and job-related stress. Singly and together they communicate the emotional and attitudinal experience of work, and they can be regarded as *facet free*. The upper right-hand block speaks to the fact that the teachers' overall job satisfaction was assessed by asking four questions concerning the extent to which they enjoyed teaching as an occupation, how much it met their initial expectations, the likelihood of their entering teaching if faced with that decision again, and how satisfied they were with their present teaching job. The middle right-hand block indicates that the teachers' work centrality was assessed by finding out how important it was to be successful at work, how much they thought about their work outside working hours, and to what extent they wanted to know what was happening outside their own classrooms. The lower right-hand block shows that job-related stress stood as a single item, since this study was not intended to explore the source of stress, but only to include it as a third indicator of work-life quality. While some discourses about the experience of stress (e.g., Selye, 1974) do not treat it as necessarily having negative valence, we assumed that our teachers responded to its more usual meaning of a feeling of internal disequilibrium in reaction to negative experience.

The center area identifies two descriptive variables, one related here to the teachers in the study and the other to the schools in which the teachers worked. The seventeen personal and demographic characteristics of teachers that were selected for their relevance to the study are listed in the upper-center block, and the three context characteristics of the schools are identified in the lower-center block. Due to the variability across countries in the meanings and codings of teacher responses, only a small number of the twenty characteristics were used in cross-country comparisons; but the remainder were valuable for within-country purposes.

The two-way and one-way vectors shown as arrows in the figure identify an overall research agenda of explorable questions or hypotheses. In and of themselves, the vectors are not intended to be predictive of variable associations or directions of influence, although the Consortium studied directions of influence as determined by the purposes and logic of its study. Continuous-line vectors between variables identify those relationships that were analyzed as a part of this study. Broken-line vectors identify relationships that were not analyzed as a part of this study. The schema comprising Figure 1.2 has implicitly and explicitly provided a broad common focus for the Consortium's research teams. While the research questions regarded as being of interest have varied between countries and each has been free to establish its precise agenda in the broad scope of the project, it should be clear that this book is primarily concerned with the core comparative project.

Designing the Questionnaire

The first step was to design a common instrument in the form of a questionnaire. The facet-free and the facet-specific variables that then required operational definition are represented in Figure 1.2. Questionnaire construction was carried out by research team members from the Universities of Michigan and Sheffield, who met twice during a period of a year, once in each university.[1] During these meetings, questions of nomenclature, meaning, response stems, rating scales, and order of presentation of items were thrashed out.

Items were derived from three major sources. The first consisted of earlier cross-cultural studies based on teacher interviews conducted in Michigan, Sheffield, and Frankfurt and designed to elicit views on the factors encouraging and discouraging good practice in teaching (Lissmann, 1983; Menlo, 1985; Poppleton, Gray, Harrison, Lindsay, and Thompson, 1985). The second source was the research and theoretical literature on job satisfaction (Quinn & Shephard 1974; Locke, 1976; Kalleberg, 1977), on work centrality (Mannheim & Cohen, 1978), and on job stress (Kyriacou & Sutcliffe, 1978; Smilansky,

1984). The third source was the compendium of already developed survey instruments on the interpersonal and situational aspects of classrooms and schools. The final version of the questionnaire consisted of six parts comprising some ninety to one-hundred items depending on the slight variations in the demographic, personal, and school information required by the researchers in the different countries that were ultimately involved. The items actually analyzed are described in Figure 1.2.

Translating the Questionnaire

The next step was to confront the problems of translating the questionnaire into languages other than English, which were initially German and Japanese (Polish, Hebrew, and Russian being added later). This was accomplished by research colleagues in each country who were native language speakers, followed with back-translation by a native language speaker who also spoke English. However, it has long been recognized that the procedure may do no more than achieve a "spurious lexical equivalence" (Broadfoot & Osborn, with Gilly & Paillet, 1988). The real problem lies in achieving conceptual equivalence so that the literally equivalent words and phrases convey the same meaning in all the languages concerned. In Chapters 2 through 8 there are instances given where this requirement was not fully met even though pilot testing of the questionnaires was carried out in each case. This was particularly so where a practice or process was recognizable but did not exist in the same form in two or more countries. One example is *individualized learning*, which can be interpreted as independent study, discovery learning, or resource-based learning by some teachers and as setting individual exercises or offering individual opportunities to reply by others. Similarly, the interpretation of *counseling* varies from giving advice on personal problems to coaching, and curriculum (a term not used in a number of countries that get by on pedagogy and assessment). In these circumstances, interpretation of the questionnaire responses depended on spotting discrepancies and exploring meanings with colleagues from the countries concerned. It is not always possible to predict beforehand what these might be, and several solutions to the problem have been suggested in the literature on the *emic–etic* distinction, that is, the description of a phenomenon in terms of its own cultural units versus the use of a term or category in units that are external to the culture (Price-Williams, 1975). Since the emic viewpoint studies behavior from inside the target system and the etic viewpoint does so from outside the target system (Segall, Dasen, Berry, and Poortinga, 1990), it was advantageous to put both perspectives into operation by having a research team from each country involved. This provided the opportunity to build inclusion of all nine countries into the construction and modification of the questionnaire and the interpretation of teacher responses to it.

A device such as the semantic differential (Osgood, 1968) is an example of a measurement tool that may ease the task of reducing emic–etic conflict. It has been used in many comparative studies in education (e.g., Broadfoot & Osborn, with Gilly and Paillet, 1988; Menlo, 1979).

Compensating for Biased Ratings and Response Sets

A problem that is particularly critical in the case of comparative studies is the existence of a response set. Respondents may be influenced by a social desirability factor, that is, they may feel that it is more culturally acceptable for professionals to say that they undertake research or further study or that they specialize in some aspect of student welfare. In large, randomly drawn samples, such response tendencies tend to cancel each other out, but if they represent a deeply embedded cultural characteristic or norm confined to one country, they could produce bias in an internationally based study. This is a problem for researchers of comparative studies if they do not have intimate knowledge about the cultures involved at the interpretation stage.

Other forms of distortion in the data arise from the existence of another kind of response bias by one or more of the groups being compared. This could come from a reluctance to commit oneself by rating all items in the middle category, thus producing errors of central tendency or, alternatively, a tendency to rate in the extreme categories only (Chun, Campbell, & Yoo, 1974). It may be identified by placing the mean scores for each country in rank order on each separate item (or index) and observing the existence of a persistent country tendency (Adams, 1970).

Response sets and linguistic confusion can only partly be overcome by statistical treatment of the data. Even though all countries used identical items and rating procedures, the mean values derived from these items were unique to each dimension and to each country. Valid comparisons can only be made when effects are measured on the same scale, and those who are familiar with trying to equate an exam mark of 75 (where the mean is 60) with a mark of 75 (where the mean is 45) will readily appreciate the problem. The solution generally adopted in such circumstances is to take account of the distance of a mark from its own mean in standard deviation units and transform the two mark lists to a common mean and standard deviation so that they can legitimately be compared in the form of t-scores.

In this study, this procedure was applied to the ratings made by teachers within a country in order to subtract the biasing effect of individual tendencies by establishing the relative standing of items and indexes in terms of t-scores on each dimension for each index. In order to examine the differences between countries, however, it was necessary to compare the relative standing of countries in terms of their distance from the nine-country means on each dimension for the whole study sample. In this case, two-way analyses of variance were conducted to identify similarities and differences based on the summed original ratings. This yielded t-deviations from the nine-country mean in the dimensions of each domain.

Achieving Sampling Equivalence

In order to make meaningful comparisons, like must be compared with like and the more countries are involved, the more difficult this becomes. The ideal solution lies in specifying the target populations beforehand in each case and in drawing random national samples. This becomes problematic, however, when faced with comparing a small, predominantly urban country like Singapore with a huge multicultural and multifaceted country such as the old Soviet Union.

Many of the countries represented in our study, such as the United States, Canada, England, and Germany, had education systems based on local or regional authorities, and it was deemed appropriate to base a survey on a region where teachers could be shown to have similar characteristics to those in the whole nation. It was specified, however, that surveys should include industrial as well as rural areas and that the schools included should be comprehensive (or common) schools and include the age group eleven to sixteen wherever possible. From this base, researchers varied in the strategies they adopted for sampling. Some used schools as the unit, others teacher–networks or in-service departments. Singapore, Japan, and Israel were able to supply national samples while the other countries provided regional ones, and this variation in sampling must be kept in mind in interpreting the results (e.g., the relative size of the standard deviations on the various measures). The total sample consisted of 7,084 teachers.

Characteristics of the Samples

In this report of the study, only those demographic and personal questions yielding a sufficiently large number of responses from teachers in all countries, were used. These were questions on age, gender, and marital status. Other questions that did not yield sufficient responses from teachers in all countries were length of full-time teaching experience, years in present school, number of changes of school, subjects taught during career, and currently, highest level of qualification, occupational status, teacher training, membership in professional organizations, and teacher unions. Anticipated job change in five-years time and nature of the change, number of job applications made in the previous year, and school characteristics in terms of location, size, and age range of pupils also did not yield sufficient responses to be used. All this information proved to be extremely useful in interpreting single-country studies and may be called upon where appropriate in the process of interpreting international comparisons.

The Qualitative Data

While the quantitative data from the survey provided the core material for making comparisons, reliance on a single channel carries dangers. Lacey (1976) stated, "I feel very strongly that the world under investigation seen through one method of collecting data becomes enormously distorted by the limitations of that data and the available methods of analysis." In addition to the statistical information, we need also to recognize the embeddedness of attitudes and feelings in the professional culture and to be able to grasp the fine grain of work experience.

Two sources were used to obtain qualitative data. The first source was included in the questionnaire when respondents were asked to use the last page "to tell us anything more you wish to say about the matters relating to the questionnaire." Many took the opportunity to do so. The second source was the several prior semistructured interview studies where individual teachers or small groups of teachers would explore with researchers experiences such as the best and the worst times they had experienced in their teaching careers; what teaching experiences had made them feel enthusiastic about their work and what made them feel discouraged; what it was like for them when they started teaching; what advice they would now give to a young entrant to the profession; and what would most improve the quality of their professional lives as teachers. All interviews were recorded and transcribed, and the resulting data were available in order to check and illuminate the survey findings. In this way, the prior interviews contributed significantly to the interpretation of the meanings of teaching in this study (Lee, 1985; Evers & Engle, 1989; Menlo & Marich, 1988; Poppleton & Riseborough, 1989).

Strategies for Data Analysis

The first step in developing an appropriate analytic strategy is to determine the functional relationships among variables implied by the purposes of the study. For purposes of analysis, variables had been divided into five domains: (1) demographics, (2) roles, (3) conditions, (4) practices, and (5) quality of work life. The task was to use the research purpose of domain variables to assign them to one of three functional roles: dependent variable, independent variable, or moderator variable. An outline of the logic involved in determining the conceptual function of variables is implicit in our definitions of these functional roles. (Notice that we are interested in the primary function of variables; it should be understood that virtually all variables may serve secondary as well as primary functions.)

In general, a dependent variable functions as a measure of the outcomes of interest in a study. The term "outcome" suggests that changes in this variable are caused (or at least influenced) by other variables in the study. All variables in the roles, conditions, and quality of life domains can be thought of as dependent variables in this sense.

An independent variable functions as a measure of a major presumed cause of the variations we wish to observe in a study. Since country to country variations in the variables constituting the three domains listed above was a focal interest, country functioned as the independent variable in this study. In broad statistical terms, we were interested in assessing the effects of country (or culture) on each variable in the roles, conditions, practices, and quality of life domains.

A moderator variable measures organismic or structural characteristics that may change or moderate the effect of an independent variable on the dependent variables. In this study, differences in the distributions of variables in the demographic domain may explain some of the observed country-to-country differences in scores on the various dependent variables. Consequently, the effects of demographics should be controlled statistically when comparing any of the dependent variables across countries.

Conceptual Model. In a complex study such as this, the independent, moderator, and dependent variables frequently form a time-related chain of influence. A model of the hypothesized chain of influence in this study is described in Figure 1.3. As conceptualized in the model, quality of work life is determined by a time-related chain of influence running from the independent variable (country) through moderator variables (demographics) and mediating dependent variables (roles, conditions, and practices) to the ultimate dependent variables (quality of work life).

It is helpful to trace the flow of influence from left to right through the model. Country (and related economic and cultural factors) probably has a fairly direct influence on the demographic distribution of selected teachers. Teacher demographics, such as age, gender, and marital status, in turn, influence the specific job obtained by teachers: their assigned roles and responsibilities, the associated work conditions, and the teaching practices they use. All these mediate the combined effects of country and demographics, and pass that influence along in modified form to the quality of work life domain.

Notice that two types of dependent variables are identified in the model. Mediating dependent variables are "dependent" because we expect them to change as a function of country and demographics; they are "mediating" because we also expect them to influence quality of work life and thus pass on the mediated effects of demographics. Quality of work life measures are the "ultimate" dependent variables because they are both the last to be affected and our major interest. An important element of the model is the notion that demographics have both a direct and an indirect effect on the quality of work life.

We have mentioned previously that a major goal of the study was to explore country to country changes in the relationships among variables. Figure 1.3 identifies the specific relations to be examined; each relationship is identified by an arrow in the figure with a label indicating the chapter where it is discussed. As indicated by the figure, relationships among demographics, roles, conditions, practices, and quality of work life are analyzed by country.

Figure 1.3
A Conceptual Model of the Chain of Influence Connecting Variable Domains

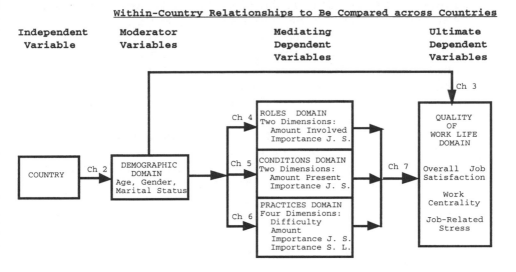

Variables Analyzed. The variables analyzed in the demographics, roles, conditions, practices, and quality of work life domains and were derived from teacher responses to items on the questionnaire. As shown in Figure 1.3, teachers responded to each roles and conditions item on two dimensions: (a) amount—how much of this role or condition was present in your job, and (b) importance J. S.—how important is the role or condition for your job satisfaction. Each item in the practices domain had four response dimensions: (a) difficulty—how difficult is the practice, (b) amount—how much do you use it, (c) importance J. S.—how important is it for job satisfaction, and (d) importance S. L.—how important is it for student learning. The analyzed variables included eight mean scores representing the average rating for all items in each domain dimension: role amount, role importance, condition amount, condition importance, practice difficulty, practice amount, practice importance J. S., and practice importance S. L. In addition, the analyzed variables included eight incongruence means representing the average difference between items on pairs of domain dimensions.

In each domain or domain dimension, items dealing with similar content were averaged to provide index scores. As shown in Figure 1.3, there were three demograhic indexes (age, gender, and marital status) and three quality of work life indexes (overall job satisfaction, work centrality, and job-related stress). There were also five roles indexes, seven conditions indexes, and six practice indexes. These are defined in other sections as indicated by the chapter labels in Figure 1.3.

Effect Size. Comparisons among means were used to answer many of the research questions in this study. Because of our large samples, differences between means that were too small to be of practical importance were often statistically significant. The effect-size statistic (Vockell & Asher, 1995, pp. 357–360) was developed to guard against overinterpretation of these trivial differences. Effect size is computed by dividing the difference in means by the best available estimate of the standard deviation of the scores concerned. An effect size of 0.30 or more is generally considered large enough to indicate practical importance. Since the means for all of our variables are expressed in t-score units, which have a standard deviation of ten, any difference in means of three or more points is both statistically significant and large enough to be educationally important.

Statistical Analyses. Although all items and indexes were analyzed, the presentation in this book is concentrated on the eight dimension means listed above and on the indexes from the amount dimension of relevant domains. The results reported come from four different types of statistical analyses.

1. A cross-tabulation of three demographic indexes (age, gender, and marital status) with country. The purpose here is to compare category percentages for each variable and combination of variables across countries.

2. A separate country by demographics ANOVA (analyses of variance) for each of the eight dimension means listed above. Since the intent here is to assess differences in the average amount and importance ratings of various demographic groupings across countries, the original ratings (raw scores) are analyzed. To permit an effect-size comparison, country means are presented as t-score deviations from the mean of all nine countries. However, because means are based on original ratings, interpretation of differences among them must take account of the potential biasing effects of culture and language discussed earlier in this chapter.

3. Multifactor, repeated-measures ANOVAs (see Winer, 1971, ch. 7) were computed using sets of index variables as the repeated factor. Separate ANOVAs were computed for the amount dimension of the roles, conditions, and practices domains, and for the three indexes in the quality of work life domain. Since our interest here is in comparing the relative standing of indexes across countries and demographics, original ratings were transformed to within-dimension t-scores prior to analysis. Consequently, differences in index means of three or more points are not only statistically significant and educationally important, but also free of cultural or linguistic bias. For this reason, these analyses account for a majority of the results reported in subsequent chapters.

4. In each country, a multiple regression analysis of each quality of work life index was computed using the thirty-five selected indexes and means from the first four domains of Figure 1.3 as predictors. The purpose here was to determine the amount of unique influence each domain, dimension, and index had on each quality of work life index.

A detailed description of the specific indexes in each domain dimension appears in chapters 2 through 8. Persons interested in a discussion of the technical merits of these procedures and analyses or a detailed presentation of the statistics behind the reported results should request a copy of the *Technical Supplement* described in the appendix.

CONTENTS OF CHAPTERS 2 THROUGH 8

Chapter 2 provides the reader with a brief historical picture of selected education-related events in each of the nine countries. Each sketch, constructed through the use of information from scholarly publications and interviews with practitioners, acquaints the reader with the climate of education in each of the countries for the time prior to the collection of data and in some cases beyond. To add to this picture, the distributions of gender, age, and marital characteristics of the sampled teachers for each country are presented and discussed for side-by-side comparison with each of the other countries.

In Chapter 3 the reader is introduced to the concept of the quality of teacher work life and to the three aspects of quality as designated in this study: overall job satisfaction, work centrality, and job-related stress. A rather extensive review of research-based and theoretical literature on each of these three aspects is presented, since the influence of all other variables on them is one of the major foci of the study. The results of comparisons between all nine countries on each of the three aspects of quality of work life are presented and discussed. As well, the similarities and differences between countries on how the teacher's gender, age, and marital status affect the three aspects of their quality of work life is clearly displayed and interpreted. Findings are followed by sociopsychological speculations, interpretations, and implications.

Chapters 4, 5, and 6 contain an introduction to the area of teacher work life (roles and responsibilities, work conditions, and teaching practices, respectively) being examined in the particular chapter. This introduction, plus a review of prior research and theoretical literature about the work life area, are intended to provide the reader with an image and understanding of it. Results and interpretive discussion are presented on the ways teachers in each of the nine countries engage in the work life area and how their gender, age, and marital status influence this engagement. What is finally considered through the presentation of simplifying graphics and accompanying discussion are the effects of the ways teachers in each of the countries engage in the work life area upon the three aspects of their work-life quality—overall job satisfaction, work centrality, and job-related stress. All of the foregoing is explored to identify the similarities and differences between the nine countries' teachers and to extract sociopsychological meanings and implications. These meanings and implications were free to emerge through the unique process of viewing teachers in each country in the context of comparison to their colleagues in each other's country.

Chapter 7, while dealing with the same concepts and variables as Chapters 2 through 6, has a distinctly different purpose. It identifies and clarifies for the reader what the country-to-country similarities and differences are in the influence of combinations of all previously identified variables on the three aspects of the quality of work life. It specifies the sets of roles, conditions, and demographic characteristics that are the major determiners of the teachers' overall job satisfaction, the centrality of teaching in their lives, and the stress they experience in their work. It also describes how much and in what ways these relationships vary or stay the same from country to country. In addition, it speaks to the question of the profitability of using a conceptual frame derived in one country to design and execute cross-cultural investigations.

Explanation of the complex analyses used to arrive at the important and interesting results are purposively toned down for the reader, and only the most relevant tables accompany the narrative. For the more curious reader, other tables are available in the *Technical Supplement.*

In Chapter 8, the editors, each from a different perspective, reflect on the meanings of teaching that can be drawn from this study. One perspective involves a close examination of all the similarities and differences between teachers of the several countries in the study's many dimensions of teaching and teacher work life. The consequences of this examination provide an interesting and insightful response to the long-standing question regarding the extent to which and ways in which there appears and does not appear to be a worldwide culture of teaching. Another perspective involves an understanding of the ways in which the structure of language used to translate research findings into meanings can render the findings so inert as to lower their potential for use, or so action prone as to increase their use potential. In the service of heightening the application of this study's findings, all major findings have been translated into and presented as action-prone meanings and implications.

NOTE

1. These visits were funded by the British Council.

REFERENCES

Adams, R. S. (1970). Perceived teaching styles. *Comparative Education Review, 14* (1), 50–59.

Adams, R. S.; and Biddle, B. (Eds.). (1970). Symposium on teacher role in four English speaking countries. *Comparative Education Review, 14* (1), 1–64.

Anderson, L. W.; Ryan, D. W.; and Shapiro, B. J. (Eds.). (1989). *The IEA classroom environment study.* Oxford: Pergamon.

Boyd, R. D.; and Menlo, A. (1984). Solving problems of practice in education: A prescriptive model for the use of scientific knowledge. *Knowledge, Creation, Diffusion, Utilization 6,* 59–74.

Bray, M.; and Thomas, R. M. (1995). Levels of comparison in educational studies: Different insights from different literatures and the value of multilevel analysis. *Harvard Educational Review, 63* (3), 472–490.

Brislin, R. W.; Lonner, W. J.; and Thorndike, R. M. (1973). *Cross-cultural research methods*. New York: John Wiley & Sons.

Broadfoot, P. M. (1981). *Constants and contexts in educational accountability: A comparative study*. Unpublished report to Social Science Research Council. Reading, England.

Broadfoot, P. M.; and Osborn, M. J. (1992). French lessons: Comparative perspectives on what it means to be a teacher. In D. Phillips (Ed.), *Oxford studies in comparative education: Vol. 1. Lessons of cross-national comparison in education* (69–88). Wallingford, UK: Triangle Books.

Broadfoot, P.; and Osborn, M.; with Gilly, M.; and Paillet, A. (1988). What professional responsibility means to teachers: national contexts and classroom constants. *British Journal of Sociology of Education, 9* (3), 265–287.

Chun, K.; Campbell, J. B.; and Yoo, J. H. (1974). Extreme response style in cross-cultural research: A reminder. *Journal of Cross-Cultural Psychology, 5* (4), 465–479.

Cowen, Robert. (1996). Last past the post: Comparative education, modernity and perhaps post-modernity. *Comparative Education, 32* (2), 151–170.

Dunkin, M. J.; and Biddle, B. J. (1974). *The study of teaching*. New York: Holt, Rinehart and Winston.

Epstein, Erwin H. (1988). The problematic meaning of "comparison" in comparative education. In Jurgen Schriewer (Ed.), *Theories and methods in comparative education*. Frankfurt am Main: Verlag Peter Lang.

Evers, T. B.; and Engle, J. M. (1989). *What teachers tell us about students and learning*. Paper presented at the Annual Meeting of the American Educational Research Association, San Francisco, CA, March 27–31.

Gallimore, R. (1985). *The accommodation of instruction to cultural differences*. Paper presented to the University of California Conference on the Educational Underachievement of Linguistic Minorities, Lake Tahoe, CA, May 30–June 1.

Ginsburg, Mark B.; and Klopfer, Leopold E. (1996). Choices in conceptualizing classroom-anchored research and linking it to improve educational quality in "developing" countries. *Research Papers in Education, 11* (3), 239–254.

Hargreaves, Andrew. (1994). *Changing teachers, changing times: Teachers' work and culture in the postmodern age*. London: Cassell.

Hargreaves, David. (1980). The occupational culture of teachers. In P. Woods (Ed.), *Teacher strategies: Explorations in the sociology of the school*. London: Croom Helm.

Kalleberg, A. L. (1977). Work values and job rewards: A theory of job satisfaction. *American Sociological Review, 42*, 124–322.

Kohn, Melvin. (1989). Cross-national research as an analytic strategy. In M. L. Kohn (Ed.), *Cross-national research in sociology*. Newbury Park, CA: Sage.

Kreft, I. (1993). Using multilevel analysis to assess school effectiveness: A study of Dutch secondary schools. *Sociology of Education, 66*, 104–129.

Kyriacou, C.; and Sutcliff, J. (1978). Teacher stress and satisfaction. *Educational Research, 21*, 89–96.

Laboratory of Comparative Human Cognition. (1986). Contributions of cross-cultural research to educational practice. *American Psychologist, 41*, 1049–1058.

Lacey, C. (1976). Problems of sociological fieldwork: A review of the methodology of Hightown Grammar. In M. Shipan (Ed.), *The organization and impact of social research*. London: Routledge and Kegan Paul.

Lee, Frances. (1985). *The analysis of 211 secondary and pre-university teachers' responses in the group interviews and individual written explanations.* Research report of the Department of Educational Psychology, Singapore Institute of Education, Singapore.

Liebman, M.; and Paulston, R. G. (1994). Social cartography: A new methodology for comparative studies. *Compare, 24* (3).

Lissmann, H. J. (1983). *Teachers' experience with good and poor instructional practice in a German school.* Paper presented at the annual meeting of the Society for Cross-Cultural Research, Washington, D.C., February 18–20.

Locke, E. (1976). The nature and causes of job satisfaction. In M. Dunnette (Ed.), *Handbook of industrial and organizational psychology.* Chicago: Rand McNally.

Lortie, D. (1975). *School teacher: A sociological analysis.* Chicago: University of Chicago Press.

Mallinson, Vernon. (1975). *An introduction to the study of comparative education.* London: Heinemann.

Mannheim, B.; and Cohen, A. (1978). Multivariate analyses of factors affecting work centrality of occupational categories. *Human Relations, 31*, 525–553.

Menlo, A. (1979). A comparison of school-related perceptions, attitudes, and values of teachers in three countries. *Resources in Education*, RIE Access No. ED164438.

Menlo, A. (1985). *A cross-cultural comparison of teachers' perceptions of good practice and associated factors in England, West Germany and the United States.* Paper presented at the annual meeting of the American Educational Research Association, San Francisco, CA, April 16–20.

Menlo, A.; and Marich, M. (1988). *Teacher wisdom as a source for the knowledge base of teacher education.* Paper presented at the Midwest Regional Holmes Group Conference, Chicago, IL, May 13–15.

Menlo, A.; and Poppleton, P. (1990). A five-country study of the work perceptions of secondary school teachers in England, the United States, Japan, Singapore, and West Germany. *Comparative Education, 26* (2–3), 173–182.

MOW International Research Team. (1967). *The meaning of working.* London: Harcourt Brace Jovanovich.

Nisbet, J.; and Broadfoot, P. (1980). *The impact of research on policy and practice in education.* Aberdeen, UK: Aberdeen University Press.

Noah, H. J.; and Eckstein, M. A. (1969). *Toward a science of comparative education.* New York: Macmillan.

Nowak, Stefan. (1989). Comparative studies and social theory. In M. L. Kohn (Ed.), *Cross-national research in sociology.* Newbury Park, CA: Sage.

OECD. (1990). *The teacher today.* Paris: OECD Publications.

Osgood, C. E. (1968). On the strategy of cross-national research into subjective culture. In Charles Osgood (Ed.), *The social sciences: Problems and orientations, 6*, 5–37. The Hague: UNESCO.

Passow, A. E.; Noah, H. J.; Eckstein, M. A.; and Mallea, J. R. (1976). *The national case study: An empirical comparative study of twenty-one educational systems.* New York: John Wiley & Sons.

Phillips, D. (1989). Neither a borrower nor a lender be? The problems of cross-national attraction in education. *Comparative Education, 25* (3), 267–273.

Poppleton, P.; Gray, J.; Harrison, B.; Lindsay, G.; and Thompson, D. (1985). *Aspects of care in schools: The teachers' perspectives.* Sheffield, UK: USDE Papers in Education, University of Sheffield.

Poppleton, P.; Deas, R.; Pullin, R.; and Thompson, D. (1987). The experience of teaching in "disadvantaged" areas in the United Kingdom and the USA. *Comparative Education, 23* (4), 303–315.

Poppleton, P.; Gershunsky, B. S.; and Pullin, R. T. (1994). Changes in administrative control and teacher satisfaction in England and the USSR. *Comparative Education Review, 38* (3), 323–346.

Poppleton, P.; and Riseborough, G. (1989). Teaching in the mid-1980s: The centrality of work in secondary teachers' lives. *British Educational Research Journal, 16* (2), 173–182.

Postlethwaite, T. N. (Ed.). (1988). *The encyclopaedia of comparative education and national systems of education.* Oxford: Pergamon Press.

Price-Williams, D. R. (1975). *Explorations in cross-cultural psychology.* San Francisco: Chandler and Sharp.

Quinn, R. P.; and Shephard, L. V. (1974). *The 1972/73 quality of employment survey.* Ann Arbor, MI: Survey Research Center.

Riseborough, G.; and Poppleton, P. (1991). Veterans versus beginners: A study of teachers at a time of fundamental change in comprehensive schooling. *Educational Review, 43* (3), 307–334.

Robinson, D. H.; and Levin, J. R. (1997). Reflections on statistical and substantive significance, with a slice of replication. *Educational Researcher, 26* (5), 21–26.

Segall, M. H.; Dasen, P. R.; Berry, J. W.; and Poortinga, Y. H. (1990). *Human behavior in global perspective: An introduction to cross-cultural psychology.* New York: Pergamon Press.

Selye, Hans. (1974). *Stress without distress.* Toronto: McClelland and Stewart Limited.

Smilansky, J. (1984). External and internal correlates of teachers' satisfaction and willingness to report stress. *British Journal of Educational Psychology, 54*, 84–92.

Verba, Sidney. (1969). The uses of survey research in the study of comparative politics: Issues and strategies. In S. Rokkan, S. Verba, J. Viet, and E. Almasy (Eds.), *Comparative survey analysis.* The Hague: Mouton.

Vockell, Edward L.; and Asher, J. William. (1995). *Educational research* (2d ed.). Englewood Cliffs, NJ: Prentice Hall.

Waller, W. (1932). *The sociology of teaching.* New York: John Wiley & Sons.

Welch, A. (1993). Class, culture and the state in comparative education: Problems, perspectives and prospects. *Comparative Education, 29*, 293–313.

Winer, B. J. (1971). *Statistical principles in experimental design* (2d ed.). New York: McGraw-Hill.

Zimmerman, Don H. (1978). Ethnomethodology. *American Sociologist, 20*, 6–15.

2

The Countries and Teachers

Milan Marich and Kenneth Vern Stenlund

This chapter is divided into two sections. In the first part the reader is presented with a thumbnail sketch about each country's educational context. As the various countries are structured differently in regard to social, economic, political and educational aspects, we provide only a brief description of the important educational events that may have relevance for the results of this study. We also include an account of changes that have occurred in each country since the time the survey was completed that may have implications for the working lives of teachers.

To present a short sketch of recent educational developments for each country, it was crucial to get information from individuals who represented their individual countries and who were in the mainstream of education-related events. These individuals were in a position to explain relationships between education and other social, political, and economic perspectives. Each of these professional educators is acknowledged early in the chapter for their contributions regarding education in their respective counties. The information provided was then used in writing the first section of this chapter.

The second part of the chapter provides a broad-based assessment regarding the distribution of major demographic characteristics across the nine countries who participated in the study. Although considerable demographic information was collected through the questionnaire, it was decided to report only those data which were fully available for all the countries studied so that meaningful cross-national comparisons could be made. Of these, three were selected: gender, age, and marital status. These were variables likely to have influence on teacher responses relative to items measuring work conditions, roles and responsibilities, teaching practices, and quality of work life. It is important also to remember that each country is subject to historical, social, and economic forces that shape the demographics of those who enter and remain in the teaching profession. Thus, it is helpful to understand the dynamic interplay of gender, age, and marital status in relation to the historical, social, and economic forces.

ABOUT THE COUNTRIES

A number of professional educators contributed valuable information for this section of the chapter. The information was utilized in presenting the short sketches. A special acknowledgement is given to the following persons for their assistance.

- Ulrich Basselli, Gesamtschule Sulzbachtal (Germany).
- Foo-Pang Yan Gek, teacher (Singapore).
- Boris Gershunsky, Russian Academy of Education (Russia).
- Helmut Hartmann, Martin Luther Gymnasium (Germany).
- Lya Kremer-Hayon, University of Haifa (Israel).
- Hans-Joachim Lissmann, Johann Wolfgang Goethe–Universitat (Germany).
- Akira Ninomiya, Hiroshima University (Japan).
- Pamela Poppleton, University of Sheffield (England).
- Wong Kooi Sim, National Institute of Education (Singapore).
- Marta Zahorska, Institute of Sociology, University of Warsaw (Poland).

The following discussions of the general characteristics of each country are presented in alphabetical order.

Canada

Canada has been a relatively stable country in the post–World War II period with education remaining on the back burner until the 1970s. Individual provinces are by and large responsible for educational planning and regulation, and over the last thirty-plus years many initiatives have been undertaken throughout all of these jurisdictions. In Ontario, educational reformists argued for "open classroom-based" physical environments as a new era of education dawned in the early 1970s. Times were stable for the teaching work force, and this period saw widespread hiring of teachers as shortages became the norm.

The advent of more powerful teacher federations and union organizations escalated salaries, positioning the teaching profession as one of choice for many university graduates entering the 1980s. Much debate centered around new teaching methodologies, including "whole language" programs, which have been advanced in many sections of the country. During the 1980s and

1990s several government-led commissions, including the Smith Inquiry, have investigated the need for educational reform, given Canada's declining ability to compete in many world markets. These investigations have focused attention on issues such as the need for core-based curricula and the place of schools in preparing students for the marketplace.

The 1990s have been a very turbulent time for Canadian teachers in relation to decades past. In Ontario, salaries were frozen by the Labor government of the early 1990s for a three-year period, and the current government has been victimized by public-servant strikes and walkouts due to increasing layoffs and firings. Included in this latter group of civil servants are teachers. Recent events in Quebec vis-à-vis the vote on separation from Canada has caused much concern within all spheres of Canadian culture, including the teaching profession. Canada is at a time in its history when change is perceived as needed; however, educators share a feeling of impotence in affecting meaningful change. This has resulted in decreasing morale within the profession and a fear of the future in many quarters. Several provinces are currently in an oversupply position in relation to available teacher pools, while the existing work force approaches retirement age.

Canada is currently experiencing the type and scope of uncertainty within its educational community never seen before. Governments across the land are demanding more and more "accountability" and responsibility from teachers for student success. Yet these demands are framed by a context in which record numbers of marriages are failing, with many of the surviving families forced into a two-income situation in order to make ends meet. These are the times for teachers who are faced with increasing behavior problems and larger-than-manageable classroom numbers. Into this difficult dynamic a new generation of younger teachers will soon emerge in Canada, as the current work force bows to early retirement inducements or withdrawal due to disenchantment.

England

In reviewing the school setting during the twenty-year period following World War II, little changed in the secondary schools in England. On the other hand, between 1976 and 1996, little stayed the same, and the last twenty years is marked by many concerns and controversies. Today, schools are currently faced with a reform program that includes not only a national curriculum but also changes in many facets of educational life. The reform movement brought about changes in school governance, management and funding, the roles of local authorities, student testing and school inspection, pedagogy, teacher training, and the conditions of work and employment of teachers. As so aptly stated by Ball (1992), "It is easier to capture the scope of change by listing those things that remain the same—except I can't think of any."

With the election of successive Labor governments and the widespread espousal of the principle of equality of opportunity, the tripartite system of

grammar, technical, and secondary modern schools were progressively aban-
doned by the local education authorities in favor of all-through comprehensive schools; progress, though, was slow. The compulsory school attendance
age was raised from fifteen to sixteen in 1972 as a result of the social and
economic pressures of providing a skilled work force, but it was still apparent
that the school system had great difficulties in coping with the burden of
expectations placed upon it.

As the public expressed more and more anxieties about falling educational
standards, a series of public meetings collectively called "The Great Debate"
were initiated by the then Labour government in order to determine what had
gone wrong and to collect suggestions for improvement. One issue identified
was that Britain was not competing successfully enough in world markets;
the answer seemed to lie in a wholesale revision of education and vocational
training that could be more in line with the needs of a technology-based industry and commerce. The Education Act of 1944, with its emphases on education according to need, aptitude, and ability, was eventually succeeded by
the Great Reform Act of 1988. This act placed emphases on choice and diversity, and a consumer-led rather than producer-led educational system emerged.

A good deal of cynicism occurred during the Great Debate, but the concerns that emerged (e.g., accountability, a core curriculum, teaching quality)
became the themes in the so-called age of educational reform in the 1980s
and 1990s. The status of teaching as a profession was challenged publicly,
and the status of teachers as employees was attacked by a government that
removed their bargaining rights after a period of industrial unrest (1983–1986).

The educational reforms may be separated into four major areas of which
two were central to the setting up of a national curriculum. These specified
that (1) the subjects to be studied by all pupils in state schools from the ages
of five to sixteen (English, mathematics, and science) were given core subject
status tightly defined and prescribed; (2) the levels of attainment to be achieved
would be designated in these subjects as well as the methods of assessment to
be carried out by the teachers; (3) the control of financing education was to
be taken away from the local authorities and given to each individual school;
and (4) the governance of schools, where responsibility for decision making
and effective management would be shared by enlarged governing bodies,
was embodied in law. Schools were given greater autonomy, but the principle
of accountability was invoked through involving parents and other represen-
tatives of the community on school boards. The first two measures were instituted to ensure a standardization of the curriculum and the management of
academic standards. In addition, they were to be centrally controlled.

Modifications continued as the Reform Act was implemented, and the period starting in the mid-1980s was one of upheaval in English schools
(Poppleton, 1988). In no other period have teachers and schools been studied
so intensively and so closely scrutinized by official bodies. This has caused a
great deal of reform initiative in the area of teacher training, which continues

to the present time. All these reforms greatly impacted the teaching profession and produced low school morale. It was not surprising when many teachers left the profession altogether, feeling rejected and bitter.

West Germany

From the end of World War II until 1989, Germany was divided both politically and physically into two separate countries. When the German survey was conducted in 1987, the Berlin Wall was still in place, and the German survey was carried out in the West German state of Hesse.

The position of the teacher will be better appreciated against a brief historical account of schooling in the state of Hesse in the last two decades given by Lissmann and Gigerich (1990). During this time, the major educational reform was the introduction of comprehensive schools, or *Gesamtschulen*. The integrative Gesamtschulen developed to replace the traditional school system in which pupils of differing abilities and capabilities were separated at the age of ten. Instead, all were to be integrated, the idea being that students could profit from being taught in heterogeneous learning groups until the age of sixteen.

This concept of schooling and teaching reflected two trends in the sociopolitical life of West Germany in the 1960s and early 1970s. First, there was a perceived need for highly skilled workers in the economy, and the traditional school system did not seem capable of performing this task. The failure was described as *Bildungskatastrophe*. Second, it was felt that a society which had invested so much into a new school system ought to reflect political and scientific discussions on the conditions of social and individual emancipation. New schools were designed and built. Young teachers were recruited soon after finishing their examinations. However, a strong opposition hindered school development by campaigning on issues of basic school achievement raised by the new movement. The government offered the additive Gesamtschule as a kind of compromise, while wishing still to retain something of the traditional school system.

After a decade of political discussion and research, the government tried to phase out comprehensive schooling, and further reform was discontinued. According to a number of educators, the feeling was that all types of education were competing for students under conditions of declining numbers and the "founding euphoria" of the Gesamtschulen in the early 1970s was followed by a quieter phase of "resignation" (Hartmann, 1996). More recently, a new school law in 1992 broadened the roles and responsibilities of the teachers whose tasks were now defined as "educating, teaching, counseling and taking care of the pupils." This is largely attributed to social changes such as "changed childhood, single-parent families, and loss of values." However, the new law does not appear dramatically to have changed the situation. Also, the impact of the unification of the two Germanies and the associated financial problems can be felt directly in larger classes, longer hours of schooling, and less money to support the system.

The attempts to reform the school system have influenced generations of students and, in general, have had more positive than negative results. But the backlash of the reform has had consequences for the working conditions of Hessian teachers. They have become less highly motivated and less prepared to support innovations. It was apparent that the rise and fall of the reform has left traces in the job consciousness and job satisfaction of teachers. It is important to remember, however, that the effects of such changes vary in the different states or *Länder*. For example, a new type of comprehensive school has been introduced in Saarland known as the "Team, Small-Group Model" where teachers have had to learn to cooperate with one another, to treat pupils as "partners" rather than students, and to work together in small teams. Some parents have now started to describe this new school model as "equalizing" schools.

Israel

Kremer-Hayon and Goldstein (1990) wrote "the history of education in Israel is fraught with dilemmas and conflicts which stem from specific political, social and demographic conditions." It is most appropriate to acknowledge that Israel, established as a new state in 1948, does not enjoy the benefits of a long educational tradition. If one views this as a disadvantage, it can certainly be also viewed as an advantage—the advantage being that educational traditions do not interfere with the introduction of educational innovations. Obviously teachers in Israel are likely to encounter difficulties not met by teachers in countries with longer educational traditions.

The Israeli educational system has undergone a relatively large number of changes in the last two decades. One clear trend has been the decentralization of the system, which previously was characterized as centralized. This was a pure top-down approach with educational decisions being made by officials in the central office in Jerusalem, which were then communicated to the school principals who were expected to implement them. A salient example is the external system of matriculation exams and how they functioned. The exams were sent to all schools on the same day and then returned to be evaluated anonymously by teachers who were not connected with the schools. Passing of the exams was a condition to get a graduation certificate, which was a condition to enroll in the university. This system resulted in high anxiety for both pupils and teachers and is in the process of change.

With the abundance of new programs and curricular materials introduced, teachers indicated feelings of being stressed as a result of their inability to cope with the many changes required. Teachers were required to change both attitude and behavior. Another additional source of stress was a national need to develop high intellectual skills, and this became a high priority in the Israeli educational scene. This specific need stemmed from the fact that the country is poor in natural resources, so that the creation and export of knowledge, especially in the field of technology, becomes an important economic source of income. Developing high intellectual skills is a difficult task, but it was further compounded by the relatively large number of illiterate immigrants arriving in the country. What is occurring in Israel currently is that the multicultural composition of the Israeli pupil population exceeds to a relatively large degree that of other countries. These and other demands in the intellectual as well as the social sphere create a difficult educational challenge with which Israeli teachers are expected to cope.

Japan

The background to the Japanese study is best represented by an account given by Ninomiya and Okato (1990). They indicated that during the 1980s, Japan devoted a great deal of energy and thought to what reforms and improvements were needed and how they should be implemented at the national level. A National Council on Educational Reform was established at the Prime Minister's Office in 1985, and a request was issued to discuss the basic guidelines of the "third educational reform." The rationale for this was that the educational system had been faced with so many difficult and unusual problems. There needed to be an effort to find ways to cope with the internationalization of Japan, the coming age of information, and the idea of a learning society or lifelong education.

The report submitted by the National Council on Educational Reform advocated for the improvement in the quality of teachers, and a variety of reform programs were recommended. These related to the introduction of in-service training for beginning teachers, a systematic procedure of in-service training for all teachers, the introduction of a more flexible teacher certification system, and improved procedures for appointing new teachers in order to attract competent people who are working in other areas. As a result of a revised law in 1988, teacher training reforms were implemented. It is believed that the training of more highly motivated and competent teachers is one of the greatest and most important tasks of teacher education policies in Japan.

It must be noted that reform was not predicated on failure in the educational achievement of Japanese students who have emerged as international leaders in their achievements in mathematics and science. The two particular problem areas of credentialism and the examination system were the focus for some of the reforms. Both reflected the highly centralized and controlled nature of public school education, which resulted in intense and closed competition regulated by restricted entry to elite institutions. As a result, this created the development of *juku* or cram schools along with private schools providing alternatives to the state system.

In 1989, Shields stated, "Schooling in Japan is a huge sorting machine characterized by meritocracy and competition; a hierarchical and pyramidal structure with elite universities at the top and prestige differentiation on every level." Because of tensions resulting from this system, problems of delinquency, truancy, physical punishment by teachers and bullying by students resulted. The academic competition became the cause for growing violence and dysfunction in many schools. Consequently, educational reform in Japan tended to emphasize moral education in the curriculum and changes in both initial and in-service teacher education. A compulsory in-service training program was introduced to prepare Japanese teachers for changing conditions.

Ninomiya (1996) added information about two new educational reforms. The first involves curriculum reforms that aim to develop the so-called "new" abilities among Japanese children. These are the abilities to think critically, to think independently, to think spontaneously, and to be creative instead of placing emphasis on the memorization of knowledge. Consequently, it was recommended that the roles and functions of teachers should be shifted from instructors to facilitators; this new concept would then have great impact on the teacher training and in-service programs. Teachers would need to become familiar with new ways of instructional leadership and class management. The children would also be encouraged to get involved with community services and volunteer activities so that they can develop their abilities to think and act spontaneously. The second of the reforms is a five-day week to be introduced for the schools which would help to develop the new curriculum program. Formerly, the Japanese school occupied so much time that children had no free time for themselves or for families to enjoy together. It remains to be seen if this reform will have any impact on the juku system.

Poland

After World War II, and with communism now in effect in Poland, the education system was modeled after a communist model. The idea originally was to create a change in the social consciousness of the Polish people. With this ideological approach, the curriculum of the school system and the organizational structure of the educational system were greatly influenced. Curriculum was quickly ideologized, and teachers stressed the memorization approach rather than other teaching strategies like inquiry or problem-solving approaches. The school system established by the government did focus however on educating the entire population. An important goal was to eliminate illiteracy. What actually occurred after World War II was that education became the specific domain of the state. This state of affairs still remains—the educational system is almost entirely financed, managed, and controlled by the Polish state.

A turning point in the Polish educational system was in 1989, when many reforms were introduced as a way to create a democratic state. As a result, one of the necessary elements of the reforms was a fundamental transformation of the educational system. Schools had to be organized around both the requirements of a democratic state and the conditions in a free-market economy. The Polish education system had been criticized for excessive centralization and bureaucratization. What had been instituted by the government was a system of values that the schools passed on, but in many respects it was contradictory to the corrections generally accepted in Poland. The schools also attempted to promote socialist and communist values which in many cases were alien and even hostile to the majority of Poles.

Even though there have been reforms in the educational system, the Polish government has been concerned more with economic reforms. As a result, not enough attention has been paid to the reform of the educational system. Changes did get introduced in 1990 by the new Education Act, but the changes in organizational and financial aspects of the education system are still not sufficient.

One of the first moves of the reformers was the demonopolization of the system. Since the 1950s, the only organizers of education who had any weight were those associated with the state. In 1989, the first nonpublic schools were registered, and it was once again possible for private persons and associations to create schools. Between 1989 and 1995, nonpublic schools were developing very dynamically. Despite there being only a small percentage of pupils attending these schools they have become a significant addition to the state-owned school system.

Decentralization of education also occurred, with elementary schools passing into the hands of local authorities. This process was started in 1992 and completed in 1996. Teachers in the past were obliged to follow only one program and teach it on the basis of only one textbook. Now they can choose from among several programs and several textbooks. A reform of the so-called "program base" was also initiated, which would enable a more flexible creation of programs, not excessively burdened with unnecessary information. Unfortunately, to this day this reform has not been completed.

Attempts have also been made to initiate changes in the authoritarian interpersonal relationships in schools through some legislative moves. In democratizing and socializing the schools, the rights of the parents, as well as the range of students' rights, were addressed. School councils were created, which included teachers, parents, and pupils. These councils today have quite broad capacities and are a consultative and supervisory body with respect to school management.

The reforms identified do not encompass all the transformations to which the Polish education system is being subjected at the present time. Some other significant changes are the secondary- and tertiary-level education that is being developed; local communities becoming an important partner for the educational system; and the dramatically increasing role of the church.

As one views the Polish schools and their teachers, there are some constant reappearances of certain problems. For the decided majority of teachers, the need to carry out reforms in the education system is irrefutable. Nevertheless,

the lack of a broader discussion on the possible variations in education reform is the reason why there is not a clear vision of the transformations. The
teachers have a tendency to perceive the remedy for all ailments as increasing
their material status and receiving greater inputs from the budget for the schools.
Other sources of financing, such as local authorities (in the case of schools
taken over by them) and tuition fees from the parents (in the case of civic
schools), are treated as a potential threat of external interference. It is true,
though, that the small capabilities of the teachers' community to cope with
these types of pressures and their great vulnerability due to their atomization
and particularly their tragic financial situation makes these threats a reality.

The education policy that has been carried out since 1989 is not clear to the
teachers; it has also been subjected to very harsh criticism. There is a tendency
among Polish citizenry to view all movements made by the authorities as a
way of saving on education, not as a way of making a vision of the school's
future a reality.

Studies of teachers' dissatisfaction in Poland are gaining more significance.
The attitudes in the teacher community are relatively negative and a bad prognos-
tic for reforms. If the attitude of teachers toward the transformations remains
negative, and the involvement of teachers in the reforms remains only on paper,
in implementation, these reforms will not work. For over forty years, the
Polish school was dominated by slogans of "democracy," "self-government,"
and "partnership," and they all contained the adjective "socialist"—which
changed the meaning of these terms by 180 degrees. This shadow of "socialist democracy" still hangs over the Polish school, and it will continue to be
there as long as the teachers do not find it in their interest to remove it.

Singapore

In describing the historical context to the Singaporean study, Sim (1990)
indicated that, over the last decade or so, the Ministry of Education in Singapore
has been progressively attempting to devolve responsibility to school personnel, especially to principals. Yip (1982) commented that "it is the declared
policy of the Ministry of Education to decentralize the management of Education." This literally meant that the principal was to assume a more powerful role
as greater autonomy and responsibility were transferred to this position. Since the
school curriculum was the substance of the school and central to schooling,
the principal became the "professional head" with full responsibility.

Since 1983, the Institute of Education has been conducting professional
programs for the preparation of prospective school leaders at various levels.
After consulting with other countries, the principals submitted a significant
report in 1987. The report, known as "Toward Excellence in Schools," recommended that some schools should go independent and that formal pastoral
care and career guidance programs be established in schools. These recommendations have been favorably received by the Minister and were system-

atically implemented. It is conceivable that the changes will affect conditions of work and roles and responsibilities as well as classroom practices. It is quite likely that all of this will affect teachers' job satisfaction and work centrality.

According to many educators in Singapore, recent policy changes have truly affected teachers and their teaching. A few of the important changes are as follows:

- Increased promotional prospects for teachers were introduced in 1995 when 2,456 teachers were promoted to the level of education officers. This appears to be a device that enables classroom teachers and others to be promoted without having to take on additional duties. It is to be conducted via a yearly promotion exercise based on performance criteria, including assessment of the teachers' "currently estimated potential," which determines the highest appointment level of work a teacher is capable of doing, and a high score on "helicopter quality," which is the ability and drive to look at a problem from a higher vantage point with simultaneous attention to relevant details.
- New pay scales were introduced with the aim of making the teaching profession more attractive and reducing the high resignation rate. With more secondary schools being built on new housing estates, more teachers were required. There was also an attempt to attract midlevel professionals to teaching. It is still too early to say how successful these strategies have been.
- Secondary schools were ranked to stimulate more competition and to provide parents and pupils data to make informed decisions.
- Pastoral care systems were to be extended to all primary schools by 1998.

United States

When the modern school system appeared in the United States in the nineteenth century, women dominated the profession. It is speculated that this early feminization of the profession was due to several causes. School systems were unable to attract and maintain the presence of male teachers only. The school year was lengthened, which deterred men from the profession due to their major involvement in agriculture. Improved certification and instructional demands requiring additional training, continuing school reforms, and the opportunity to pay lower salaries to females also reduced the number of males from the profession (Rury, 1986). This feminization of teaching continued for a period of time despite a desire to attract and retain men in the teaching profession, despite a prevailing belief that adolescent males should be provided male role models at the secondary level, and despite the belief that discipline problems would not be as problematic for male teachers as for female teachers. There were also distinct regional differences in social and economic conditions in nineteenth-century America that were impacted further by ethnic, religious, and political forces. Males moved more to roles in commerce, agriculture, manufacturing, and professional areas, and urban schools became increasingly staffed by females.

The decades after World War II were filled with constant criticism of what had occurred in education in the United States. There were many educational perspectives regarding missions and what the focus should be in the schools. By 1950, the postwar Baby Boom left the United States with an acute teacher shortage, causing complaints about the feminization of the teaching profession in the United States to fade (Ravitch, 1964; Hodgson, 1976). However, the postwar economic boom caused men to pursue other careers, and teaching in the United States then became more clearly identified as "women's work." The federal census of 1950 indicated that well over three-quarters of U.S. teachers were female. Tougher certification and training for U.S. teachers made teaching as a part-time job nearly impossible, thus limiting accessibility to the profession (U.S. Bureau of the Census, 1950). During the early years of the 1950s, the future of secondary education became a national issue. Educators raised questions about the quality of the high school curriculum, and there was a growing concern about the country losing out to the Soviet Union in education.

A new wave of criticisms and attacks occurred during the early 1960s, and many of the concerns of the 1950s became subdued. The 1960s focused on pressure to eliminate school segregation and to provide for the children of poverty. In addition, new studies emerged on school effectiveness. One such major study was a report on Equality of Educational Opportunity (Coleman et al., 1966). New developments continued, and an environment of protest developed in the schools, reflecting protests against the Vietnam War. In addition to the civil rights movement and concerns over urban poverty, the 1960s were marked by the unionization of teachers. Schooling had become a national priority, and teachers' salaries and working conditions improved. This resulted in a rise in the number of men teachers in the profession. In the 1970s, the issue of declining high school test scores became a major worry.

As in other countries during the 1980s, the general public became heavily involved in a range of national issues facing education. The public became more cognizant of issues, such as all children having an equal opportunity to receive a high quality education, the claimed low academic performance of students, misbehaviors in the schools as a result of drug use and violence, and the poor skills of workers who were continually falling further and further behind in the changes occurring in the technology field. Since there was so much criticism about the quality of high schools, hundreds of reports and studies were published. A follow-up of all this was that numerous recommendations related to more time spent in school, more credits required for graduation, and more required courses were submitted, and many actions were taken. High schools were urged to treat students as more mature individuals rather than creating efforts to control them. Reports called for more and better teachers and suggested that more money would be needed to attract quality people.

It appears that the 1990s have continued the emphasis of reforms during the 1980s. Currently, there is widespread concern over academic standards and school financing. These concerns have impacted on education in almost every state as citizens are demanding progress in educational reform.

The Soviet Union

The Soviet Education Congress held at the end of 1988 was an event of great importance for the Soviet school. Thousands of teachers participated and agreed that secondary and high school pupils do not meet the country's present or future demands. Their position was that the schools had impressed the rest of the world with their social dynamics and humanitarian qualities, but now, the teachers indicated, schools had lost their academic standing and had failed to react quickly to the demands of social changes, the quickened tempo of scientific and technological change, and the country's economic development. The economic backwardness compared to that of other developed countries in technology output was mainly due to the lack of qualifications and knowledge on the part of Soviet specialists and workers. This fact made the people extremely dissatisfied with the modern school. Students of Soviet educational policy have pointed to the schools' remarkable stability and continuity from the days of the Russian tsars through the Soviet socialist era and the collapse of the economic and political system in 1991 (Grant, 1992; Jewell, 1990).

Although major educational reforms were lacking, changes did take place. In the 1980s the pace of change quickened. A 1984 policy, the Reform of the General and Vocational School, aimed to extend the period of compulsory education and reduce the differences between academic and vocational programs. In addition, improvements were made in teacher training at both initial and in-service levels, salaries increased for educational workers, and support was given for teachers' social authority. Even though all this was to improve teacher status and attract high-caliber people into the profession, it did not fundamentally address the central problem, nor did it give teachers greater autonomy in their professional levels. Though salaries had increased for teachers, they were still less than the middle level in the country. President Yeltsin promised in 1991 that teachers would earn more and be on the same level with engineers and other workers, but this is still not realized today. As a result, teachers very often strike or protest.

Mikhail Gorbachov, made General Secretary of the Communist Party in 1985, introduced Perestroika and Glasnost as the guiding principles of the state. It was hoped that the atmosphere of openness and discussion that was occurring would impact education. The new strategies introduced were expressed in terms of education in a number of different ways, and some brought new problems. Ideas like differentiation and individualization were introduced, but Soviet teachers did not seem ready for these changes. Consequently, there was a great need to educate the teachers for all these new initiatives, and the retraining of the teachers was given a high priority.

Schools were encouraged to diversify the traditional curriculum to meet local needs and to teach as they saw fit, but without the resources to do so. In a report of school teachers being interviewed in 1989, "It was found that teachers were faced with a number of insufferable paradoxes in their professional lives. The teachers stressed that they had to differentiate without being elitist, increase standards without resources, develop individualized courses with no teaching aids or textbooks, and develop individualists who maintain a commitment to socialist principles. Obviously, the teachers repeatedly voiced their frustrations" (Poppleton, Bolton, Pullin, & Riseborough, 1990). The educational system was dominated by the Communist Party until 1991 and even then was still in a bureaucratic bind. In spite of the limited freedom granted to schools, teachers were unable to take advantage of this freedom after decades of being told what to do.

The trend toward greater autonomy is reflected in the encouragement of schools by the Ministry of Education to decide upon their own "educational credo." Schools are now allowed to develop an educational emphasis that will characterize the school, similar to the American magnet schools. Along with this change, the emergence of community schools is most apparent.

As the Soviet teachers now have more freedoms in schools and for themselves, they will need to focus in on solving the problem of how to use this freedom without enough resources, such as financial support, technical equipment, and textbooks. As Soviet teachers forge ahead with the many demands being placed on them for continued reform, the future is still unclear.

ABOUT THE TEACHERS

As previously mentioned, in describing the teachers who engaged in the study, the three demographic characteristics of gender, age, and marital status were selected, since data on these variables were fully available from all the participating countries.

In order to simplify subsequent analyses, collapsed versions of the age and marital status responses were used. Age was collapsed into three categories: up to 34 years of age; 35 to 49 years; and 50 years and older. Researchers in one or two countries felt that asking teachers to identify themselves as divorced or widowed would be an intrusion of privacy, and so marital status was collapsed into two categories: unmarried and married. Sampling procedures are fully described in Chapter 1. Variations in response numbers relative to the total number of teachers (N) are the result of teachers failing to provide information within specific demographic categories. For example, only 6,985 of the 7,084 teachers surveyed indicated their gender status. Similarly, ninety-eight responses were missing for the age variable, resulting in a total of 6,986 for this category. Finally, the marital status variable had 126 missing responses, which resulted in a total of 6,958.

As the demographic responses from separate countries were reviewed, many interesting observations were immediately apparent. For example, Japan, with 1,287 respondents, represents the largest teacher block surveyed of all the countries that participated, accounting for 18.4 percent of total respondents. The Soviet Union had 1,186 teachers surveyed, which was the second highest total, representing 17 percent of the total number of teachers surveyed. Israel and Canada had the lowest percentage of teachers in the study, with Israel's sample consisting of 345 teachers or 4.9 percent of the total, and Canada's 372 respondents or 5.3 percent of the total.

What follows now is information relative to the three main variables of age, gender, and marital status in the overall sample. Then, a country by country profile is provided as further background for the information contained throughout this book. Statements reflect the data in Table 2.1.

Table 2.1
Country Rankings of Gender, Age, and Marital Status: Percentages of Country Sample for Each Category

Rank	Teacher Gender		Teacher Age Category			Marital Status	
	Female	Male	Up to 34	35 to 49	50 and Up	Unmarried	Married
1	USSR 82.5	Japan 76.1	Singapore 52.9	Germany 72.5	US 26.6	Singapore 37.3	Israel 83.1
2	Poland 75.1	Germany 64.2	Japan 45.1	Canada 63.4	Japan 19.2	Poland 30.5	Germany 78.9
3	Singapore 68.1	Canada 62.4	USSR 43.6	US 62.3	USSR 17.5	Japan 28.3	US 76.6
4	Israel 67.2	US 57.0	England 34.8	Poland 60.2	Germany 16.4	England 25.6	USSR 75.5
5	England 45.0	England 55.0	Israel 33.0	Israel 52.1	Canada 15.7	Canada 24.9	Canada 75.1
6	US 43.0	Israel 32.8	Poland 25.0	England 51.1	Israel 14.9	USSR 24.5	England 74.4
7	Canada 37.6	Singapore 31.9	Canada 20.9	Singapore 39.8	Poland 14.8	US 23.4	Japan 71.7
8	Germany 35.8	Poland 24.9	Germany 11.2	USSR 38.9	England 14.1	Germany 21.1	Poland 69.5
9	Japan 23.9	USSR 17.5	US 11.2	Japan 35.7	Singapore 7.4	Israel 16.9	Singapore 62.7

Note: Data in this table are derived from the detailed cross-tabulation tables in Appendix C of the *Technical Supplement*.

Gender

In viewing the total sample with regard to gender, 52.8 percent of the respondents were female teachers, and 47.2 percent were male. The methodology inherent to this study was not designed to balance the percentage of participants by gender, yet these figures reflect a relative gender balance within the total sample of teachers. In some countries, gender differences may be due to the level of teachers' salaries by comparison with other occupations and/or specific cultural factors that result in one gender having a predominant status within the teaching profession for that particular country. These are the types of factors that might explain in part why Germany and Japan had the lowest numbers of female teachers within their overall teacher work force and within this sample as well. Of the nine countries surveyed, six had almost half of the teachers interviewed as female with a range of 43 percent at a low (United States) to a high of 82.5 percent (Soviet Union). In talking to teachers from a variety of global locations it is clear that the demography of teaching as a profession attaches to it different cultural meanings and importances around the world. Country by country, gender percentages help to delineate the various roles of men and women in the educational community within these specific locations.

Age

The age variable also showed some interesting differences across the countries surveyed. Almost half of the total teacher sample (49.7%) fell into the middle age group, 35 to 49 years, with Germany having a total of 72.5 percent of teachers within this category, the highest among all nations. For all nine countries, only 16.7 percent of the total were teachers 50 years or older, and in this category the Americans had the highest single concentration, with 26.6 percent of those surveyed in this age range. Finally, approximately one-third (33.6%) of teachers surveyed were in the youngest category with an age range up to thirty-four years old. Two Pacific rim countries, Japan and Singapore, scored highest in this age group, with 45.1 percent and 52.9 percent respectively. The Soviet Union also had a high percentage of "younger" teachers, with 43.6 percent of respondents falling into this category.

Given this information, it is apparent that the teacher participants as a whole reflect a "middle-aged" sample, predominantly neither old nor young as delineated through our categories. For most of the countries surveyed, this accurately reflects the general state of their respective teacher work forces.

Marital Status

Of the teachers interviewed from all countries, the overwhelming majority (73.3%) were married, with the largest percentage seen in Israel at 83.1 percent. The largest percentage of unmarried teachers was from Singapore (37.3%) which, perhaps not coincidentally, also represented the youngest group of teachers as previously noted. The only other country reporting more than 30 percent unmarried was Poland, at 30.5 percent.

It is predictable that, given the age distribution as previously noted, most of the teachers surveyed were at a time in their lives when marriage in any of the countries would most likely have already taken place. Of course, some teachers who reported being married may or may not be engaged in a traditionally held form of marriage, as this may vary across cultures and time. However, the data collected does provide some clue about marriage's contribution to the meaning of teaching generally and within nine broad cultures.

DEMOGRAPHIC PROFILES BY COUNTRY

In attempting to detail demographic information, the decision was made to resist the temptation of including a multiplicity of graphs and numbers as a form of presentation. However, Table 2.1 has been included in this chapter for ease of reference; the reader may look to other chapters and to various appendices for more analytic information on the relationships of demographics to other phenomena. What follows is a summary of demographic highlights that provides the reader with key information from specific countries as they relate to participants within the study.

The countries are presented alphabetically. Some countries receive more consideration than others at certain points in this reporting because of the nature of the data generated within that specific country in relation to other data collected. Any unusual or anomalous demographic data are presented as well.

Canada

Canada had the second smallest sample (N = 372), consisting of 37.6 percent females and 62.4 percent male teachers. The latter on a percentage basis is the third highest male sample in the study. Similar to the Americans and Germans, the Canadians had a high percentage of teachers (62.4%) falling into the 35 to 49 year age range. As with the majority of countries, the Canadians had over a 70-percent married rate, with 75.1 percent of teachers responding that they were married at the time of the survey. Like the English teacher group, this sample is fairly well balanced and does not possess any single distinguishing characteristic to set it apart from the other countries studied.

England

The English sample (N = 684) consisted of 55 percent males and 45 percent females, numbers which closely resembled the American percentages. However, unlike the U.S. sample, the English had a higher concentration of younger teachers, with 34.8 percent of their sample falling under the age of thirty-five, ranking the English fourth on this index of all countries surveyed. A total of 74.4 percent of the English teachers were married, a fairly standard response relative to the other countries. In total, the English demographic statistics were quite consistent with the averages across all samples and did not distinguish themselves in any unusual way. That is, when compared to other participating countries the English were in "balance" on all three main variables.

Germany

The German sample (N = 678) consisted of 35.8 percent females and 64.2 percent males, the latter statistic placing Germany as the second highest country in relation to male respondents. This may have cultural implications, where education (especially at the secondary level) has historically been a male-dominated field. The single distinguishing demographic consideration for this data set can be seen in the age variable, where 72.5 percent of the teachers fell in the age range between 35 to 49. This ranked the Germans as first within this age range, indicating a predominantly middle-aged work force within this sample. However, as with the Americans, the combined age categories of 35 to 49 and 50 and older account for 89 percent of the total German sample, meaning that this is another teacher group that leans toward an older composition. Like most other countries, a relatively high percentage of the German teachers were married, with 78.9 percent included in this category.

Israel

The country with the smallest sample was Israel (N = 345), where 67.2 percent of the respondents were female and 32.8 percent male. The age variable was fairly flat, with 52.1 percent between the ages of 35 and 49. However, the interesting demographic variable for this sample can be seen in the married–unmarried category. The Israelis were far and away the highest scoring country within this variable, as 83.1 percent of the teachers indicated that they were married and only 16.9 percent were not. Certainly, this should not be a surprising finding given some of the cultural and religious uniqueness that has formed this country. In a country that has historically had to fight for survival while surrounded by perceived adversaries of the state of Israel, a closeness associated with marriage and family has developed.

Japan

The Japanese demographics reveal some interesting anomalies relative to the other countries studied. The large number of respondents (N = 1,287) consisted of 23.9 percent females and 76.1 percent males, making this the highest concentration of male teachers within the entire group of teachers studied. Based on this sample, it would seem that males dominate the profession within this country at least at the secondary level. Certainly, this statistic will impact the learning experiences of students within this country since the perspectives brought into a majority of classrooms will be provided by males. And, in an educational culture historically run by males, it appears as if the cycle is continuing, with women occupying only one in four teaching positions at the secondary level. Another distinguishing demographic variable can be seen in the age section, where 45.1 percent of the teachers fell under the age of thirty-five, making Japan the second youngest teacher sample of all countries studied. Finally, 71.7 percent of the respondents were married, which follows a fairly consistent pattern across the majority of countries studied.

Poland

There were 75.1 percent females and 24.9 percent males in the Polish teacher sample (N = 630) and this placed Poland second in percentage of female teachers sampled. The age variable is again fairly well distributed, with a teacher sample dominated by the 35 to 49 age group (60.2% of all responses). What is interesting in the Polish data is the fact that only 69.5 percent of the respondents were married, a statistic that is somewhat surprising given the high number of female teachers. Within the traditional culture that one associates with Eastern Europe, it would seem that a high concentration of female teachers would have a higher marriage percentage. Such was not the case in the Polish sample, where more than 30 percent of the teachers indicated that they were not married.

Singapore

The gender percentages from Singapore reflect almost a complete reversal from those previously reported from the Japanese sample. Singapore recorded the third highest concentration of female teachers with 68.1 percent while males accounted for 31.9 percent of the sample. Of particular interest in this teacher group is the age demographic. It reveals a very young teacher work force relative to the other eight nations studied, wherein almost 53 percent of teachers were under the age of thirty-four. Singapore was the only country which scored more than 50 percent within this age category. In addition, only 7.4 percent of the respondents were over the age of fifty. In total, the Singapore teachers were a relatively young group, and this statistic has meaning relative to one of the other major variables examined, marital status. One might expect that a younger teacher population would have a lower marriage percentage, and such is the case with the Singapore sample. Only 62.7 percent of respondents were married, which is considerably lower in relation to percentage responses from the other countries. The Singapore teacher group was different from most of the other nations studied in all of the three major variables reported.

United States

The U.S. sample consisted of 57 percent males and 43 percent females (N = 882). Of the total group of teachers interviewed the majority (62.3%) fell within the age range between the ages of 35 to 49. Of particular interest in the American sample is the fact that teachers aged thirty-five or older made up almost 90 percent of the sample, making the American teachers the oldest group interviewed in the entire nine-country survey. It is a statistic that reflects the overall teaching population in the United States, one in which a generation of teachers is advancing toward retirement and is further along this road than any other country. Finally, 76.6 percent of the American teachers were married, and 23.4 percent were listed as unmarried.

Union of Soviet Socialist Republics

The Soviet sample was dominated with female respondents. Of the total sample (N = 1,186), females accounted for 82.5 percent while males only 17.5 percent, making this the highest concentration of female teachers among all sample groups. This may have a historical link in a culture that has seen many wars and uprisings throughout its history—with males' active military engagemants, it has been left to Soviet women to educate the children. The cycle of female leadership in the educational context appears to be intact. The Soviet sample size was the second largest in total numbers only to Japan. As for the age variable, the Soviet teachers comprised 43.6 percent of the sample under the age of thirty-four and another 38.9 percent under the age of forty-nine. The sample had 75.5 percent of the teachers married, a fairly average number across most countries studied.

SUMMARY

The demographic components presented in this study are representative of a rich mix of cultures and variables within the countries studied. While some of these variables are quite consistent across the entire teacher sample (such as the marriage statistic) others fluctuate within a relatively wide spectrum (such as age distribution). How these variables might impact teacher perceptions and attitudes is open to study and will be examined within the context of further chapters in this book. In presenting the highlights of the demographic data, we hope we have provided an initial snapshot of the persons being studied—both overall and in the context of their own countries.

REFERENCES

Ball, Stephen J. (1992). *Changing management and the management of change: Educational reform and school processes, an English perspective.* Paper presented at the annual conference of the American Educational Research Association, San Francisco, CA, April 20–24.

Coleman, J. S.; Campbell, E.; Hobson, C.; McPartland, J.; Mood, A.; Weinfeld, F.; and York, R. (1966). *Equality of educational opportunity*. Washington, D.C.: U.S. Government Printing Office.

Grant, Nigel. (1992). Education in the Soviet Union: The last phase. *Compare, 22* (1), 69–79.

Hartmann, H. (1996). Consultative correspondence from Rimbach, Germany.

Hodgson, G. (1976). *America in our time: From World War II to Nixon*. New York: Vintage Books.

Jewell, Mark E. (1990). *The effects of current Soviet educational reform on shaping research relevant to practice*. Paper presented at the annual meeting of the American Educational Research Association, Boston, MA, April 20.

Kremer-Hayon, D.; and Goldstein, Z. (1990). The inner world of Israeli secondary school teachers: Work centrality, job satisfaction and stress. *Comparative Education, 26* (2–3), 285–298.

Lissmann, J. J.; and Gigerich, R. (1990). A changed school and educational culture: Job orientation and teacher satisfaction at the Gesamtschulen in the state of Hessen, West Germany—Some international comparisons. *Comparative Education, 26* (2–3), 277–284.

Ninomiya, A. (1996). Personal communication with author, April 9.

Ninomiya, A.; and Okato, T. (1990). A critical analysis of job-satisfied teachers in Japan. *Comparative Education, 26* (2–3), 249–258.

Poppleton, P. (1988). Teacher professional satisfaction: Its implications for secondary education and teacher education. *Cambridge Journal of Education, 18* (2), 5–16.

Poppleton, P.; Bolton, N.; Pullin, R.; and Riseborough, G. (1990). Perestroika and the Soviet teachers. *New Era in Education, 71* (3), 93–97.

Ravitch, D. (1964). *The troubled crusade: American education since 1945*. New York: Basic Books, Chaps. 1 and 2.

Rury, J. L. (1986). Gender, salaries and career: American teachers 1900–1910. *Issues in Education, 4* (3), 216–218.

Shields, J. J. (1989). *Educational reform in Japan: Discontinuities in moral education and equality*. Paper presented at annual AERA conference, San Francisco, CA, April 1989.

Sim, W. K. (1990). Factors associated with job satisfaction and work centrality among Singaporean teachers. *Comparative Education, 26* (2–3), 259–276.

U.S. Bureau of the Census. (1950). Report P50. Washington, D.C.: Author.

Yip, J. (1982). Principalship in a decentralized system of education management. *Seminar proceedings*. Singapore, Ministry of Education.

3

The Quality of Teacher Work Life

Tsila Evers and Lya Kremer-Hayon

THE CONCEPT

In searching for the meaning of teaching across nine countries, this chapter will focus on how teachers perceive their quality of work life. The assumption that this quality has numerous ramifications for the teachers in the study is out.

The general concept of quality of work life does not have a clear definition according to Szalai and Andrews (1980). It is an umbrella term that loosely means a general affective orientation to life. This may include job satisfaction, family life, personal health, and more (Schmitt & Pulakos, 1985). The term work life is focused on work. Some of the social psychological literature on quality of work life examines the attributes that make the job more or less satisfactory. The assumption is that better quality of life on the job promotes greater satisfaction, which in turn creates better performance (Malen, Owaga, & Karnz, 1990; Rowan, 1990). Indeed, higher quality of the professional life of teachers may have an impact on their performance and, as a consequence, on student achievement (Good & Brophy, 1994). In light of the numerous problems facing teachers in many countries, it was timely and extremely important to find out how teachers perceive the quality of their professional lives.

International studies have reported rising dissatisfaction among teachers in many countries (Hargreaves, 1992; OECD, 1990; Neave, 1992; Poppleton, Gershunsky, & Pullin, 1994; Sauter, Hurrell, & Cooper, 1989) due to the stripping away of their autonomy and the resulting lack of professionalism. In addition, in many of the countries that participated in the study, teachers had to adapt to various levels of rapid change. At the same time, public opinion has relentlessly criticized the outcomes of educational changes. These developments are detrimental to the quality of the teachers' work life because they reduce morale and motivation. Therefore, we wished to probe the teachers' perceptions of a combination of work-related facets.

THE MODEL

In our study, the model of the quality of teacher work life consists of three distinct parts: (1) overall job satisfaction, (2) work centrality, and (3) job-related stress. Our model presupposed that overall job satisfaction, work centrality, and job-related stress would be critical quality of life dependent variables, influenced by a host of independent variables arising from work conditions, roles and responsibilities, and classroom practices, in addition to other life and work experiences.

Another important part of the model focused on the relationships between these three dependent variables. Detailed explanations and presentation of results is reported in later chapters. In this chapter, however, we introduce some highlights.

Work centrality and overall job satisfaction may be influenced by some of the same variables, but the magnitude of the relationship between them may be weaker than expected. According to Poppleton, who did a thorough analysis on the quality of work life in an earlier study, satisfaction is reward driven (i.e., it depends on benefits received) while work centrality is value driven (i.e., it is consistent with what one regards as important), as is stress (Menlo & Poppleton, 1990; Poppleton, 1989). The stress item was related negatively to satisfaction and positively to centrality. Similar results were reported by others (Evers, 1992; Fernandez, 1992; Sim, 1990).

The fact that the three dependent variables do not vary in the same direction adds complexity to the measurement of teachers' quality of work life. This is fitting since we know that this quality is influenced by a host of variables that can come from different facets of teachers' lives, including demographic characteristics. This chapter will shed light on the influence of demographics upon the teachers' quality of life. What follows is a description of the pertinent literature on job satisfaction, centrality, and stress, and how these factors were operationalized in this study.

Overall Job Satisfaction

It is important to study teacher job satisfaction because many of the problems—notably, the difficulty in attracting capable people to the profession and retaining them, and the prevalent teacher stress in many of the countries we studied—are closely related to job satisfaction, since teachers who enjoy their work are likely to teach better and encourage student achievement. In addition, several studies have established a link between overall job satisfaction and life satisfaction (Dubin & Champoux, 1977; Kalleberg, 1977; Pajak & Blase, 1989), and the influence may go in both directions. That fact makes understanding job satisfaction even more critical, because the insights gained may teach us about the relationship between a person's work and a person's general outlook.

Overall job satisfaction is an affective response to one's feeling about the job. It is a global outcome variable and may be influenced by a host of process and product variables. As a result, job satisfaction studies employ various correlative measures (Hoy & Miskel, 1987; Seashore & Taber, 1975) and they often involve debate over measurement methods. Job satisfaction, as a concept, has three main foci: (1) the worker's needs, values, and personal demographics, (2) the work conditions and climate variables of the workplace, and (3) the interaction between the worker and the workplace. The following will describe these foci and illustrate their application to educational research.

The Worker. In addition to attitudes related to personal demographics (e.g., gender, age, marital status), worker reactions to work situations are influenced by their needs and values.

Needs. Most need theories are based on Maslow's hierarchy (Maslow, 1954), which maps out the changes in the individual's needs over the course of human development. His "hierarchy of needs" was represented by a pyramid at the base of which were physical needs of food and shelter followed by those personal needs associated with security. Only when these needs are satisfied can the individual begin to be concerned about being accepted by the family and wider social relationships (acceptance needs) and, later, by being self-fulfilled (self-esteem and ego needs). Educators especially were urged to look to the fulfillment of "higher order" needs. People with higher order needs tend to seek out intrinsic rewards. They may have a sense of calling and want to feel that they make a difference. Most teachers feel frustrated in the fulfillment of higher order needs (Hoy & Miskel, 1987). The application of needs theories to education included the work of Anderson and Iwanicki (1984), Litt and Turk (1985), Pastor and Erlandson (1982), and Sweeney (1981), among others.

The application of Maslow's theory to job satisfaction has created some problems. Locke (1976) discussed them in his analysis of the nature and causes of job satisfaction. He claimed that different people could be motivated or frustrated by different needs; thus the universality of the hierarchy was brought into question. In addition, he found no empirical evidence to support Maslow's claim that once a need was satisfied the person was ready to move to the next one.

Regardless of such criticisms leveled against the hierarchical model, it has inspired many researchers and has served toward producing a great deal of knowledge about job satisfaction.

Values. Values are conceptually related to needs but are distinctly different. Needs theories tend to regard needs as innate, whereas their translation into specific values is mediated by the environment and socialization. According to job satisfaction theories based on values, what people desire and how much they desire it, would determine their level of satisfaction. Some of the prominent researchers in the area of value-driven satisfaction are Kalleberg (1977), Likert (1961), Locke (1976), and Wanous and Lawler (1972). Kalleberg, on whose theory this study is partially based, posits that the importance (read "values") that individuals attach to the rewards offered by the workplace determines their satisfaction. Kalleberg postulates that overall satisfaction is the sum of all the rewards obtained from each job facet in relation to the value that the individual places on that job facet.

Demographics. Age, gender, and marital status can play a vital role in workers' job satisfaction. A detailed analysis of demographics in relation to all quality of work life indexes appears later in this chapter.

The Workplace. The workplace has traditionally been the most widely researched area in job satisfaction studies. Most of the studies focusing on the workplace involve context theories, where factors were examined at the workplace in order to identify those which influenced job satisfaction.

One of the theories that has been most productive in terms of the research it has spawned was Herzberg's motivation–hygiene theory (Herzberg, Mausner, & Snyderman, 1959). Also called the two-factor theory, it claimed that job factors can be categorized into those which contribute to satisfaction and those which contribute to dissatisfaction, the first set comprising those which, when present, motivate the workers—hence they are "motivators." According to Herzberg, they include such factors as achievement, recognition, responsibility, advancement, the work itself, and growth opportunities. The second set comprises hygiene factors, because, when present, they act like preventive medicine. They are extrinsic factors like salary, job security, status, supervision, relations with coworkers, and resources. When they are present, they do not satisfy workers, but when they are absent they cause dissatisfaction. Herzberg posited that the two sets are mutually exclusive. Herzberg's theory was especially attractive to educational researchers because it harkened back to the idea of "higher order" innate needs based on Maslow's theory.

Herzberg's work opened up the way for employers to manipulate job motivation by introducing incentive and job enrichment schemes in order to enhance job satisfaction and, hence, productivity. The theory has been tested frequently in many types of occupations with varying results, and has attracted a great deal of criticism from those who tried to replicate his study. However, the present position is that the broad distinction between motivators and hygienes is a useful one because it helps to distinguish between those workers who see their work as central to their lives, and those for whom it is simply instrumental to other ends. It is difficult to have any study of job satisfaction without this dichotomy as at least a frame of reference.

Interactions between the Worker and the Job. The third aspect of job satisfaction theories focused on how the worker and the job interact. It implies that the teachers (their needs, values, and personal demographics) interact with their job factors (e.g., students, colleagues, administrators, climate, pay, and school demographics), and this interaction produces satisfaction or the lack thereof. The antecedents for satisfaction can be analyzed and interpreted in a number of ways, the most prominent ones being expectancy theory and equity theory.

Expectancy Theory. The expectancy theory proposed by Vroom (1964) postulates that an individual expects certain goals to be achieved as a result of one's efforts. Satisfaction then depends on the congruence or discrepancy between expected goals and effort. If discrepancy is minimal or nonexistent, the employee will be satisfied. If there is a big discrepancy, the employee will be dissatisfied (Wanous & Lawler, 1972).

Equity Theory. This theory is based on the idea of social exchange or social comparison theory. In its internal logic, equity theory is close to expectancy theory, but it focuses on the idea of fairness rather than on expectation. It posits that people are satisfied or dissatisfied if what they get as rewards in return for their efforts is equal to what a reference group might get for similar efforts. We used both theories in the interpretation of our results.

Work Centrality

Work centrality is the global evaluation people have of the importance of work in their lives. The idea of work as a central life interest emanates from the so-called Protestant work ethic. One of the pioneers in anchoring this idea within the theories and measurements of organizational psychology was Dubin (1956, 1958). Dubin posited that people who are work-oriented derive their major rewards from work, and that their life satisfaction or dissatisfaction in general depends to a great degree on how they feel about their work.

Dubin and Champoux (1977) reported that the general level of job satisfaction was found to be highest when the workers' lives were closely related to their job. The more they identified with the job, the more satisfied they reported themselves to be. In a related study, they found a strong correlation between central life interests of workers and their commitment to the organization.

Kalleberg and Loscocco (1983) found the same relationship between the salience of work and satisfaction. The more central the work was, the more satisfied people were. Miskel, DeFrain, and Wilcox (1980) found the same to be true for teachers. The more central teaching was in the life of educators, the more satisfaction they experienced. Rosenholtz (1987, 1989) found that when there was internal motivation, work was important. This resulted in commitment to stay on the job. Research on those who stay vis-à-vis those who leave the teaching profession indicates that the more committed teachers see their work as very important and central to their lives (Yee, 1990). This harkens back to Lortie's idea of teaching as a calling (Lortie, 1975).

Since Dubin's landmark study (Dubin, 1958), the idea of work as a central life interest evolved in various ways and, accordingly, different measurement scales were constructed. Lodhal and Kejner (1965) for example measured the degrees of job involvement with an emphasis on motivational aspects. They asserted that the more involved the person was with work, the more one's self esteem was involved. It followed logically that one's performance on the job and the feedback a person received on it could highly influence self-esteem. The idea was further researched by Lawler and Hall (1970) and Kanungo (1992). The Lawler and Hall study researched the degree of importance that work has in a worker's life. Lawler and Hall posited that a job may provide the satisfaction of personal needs. As a result, they hypothesized, the more involvement, the greater the job satisfaction. Kanungo was interested in the relation between involvement in a job and the level of identification with work. He suggested that the more needs are satisfied, the greater job involvement there would be.

In an important international study on the meaning of work (MOW, 1987) the conceptual orientation to work was quite similar to the one embedded in Dubin's study. In the MOW study, the researchers attributed two complementary meanings to the concept of work salience. The first is an ideological acceptance of the work ethic that gives work a central role in life (very close to the idea captured in Dubin's research). The second consists of a global affective response to the nature of work, leading one to devote time and concern to the job.

In the present study, we employed the work role centrality concept (Mannheim, 1975, 1983; Mannheim & Cohen, 1978). It is similar in orientation to both Dubin's emphasis on work as a central life interest and to the MOW concept. It differs, though, in its emphasis on the cognitive and ego-identity aspects of a worker, especially the deliberate investment of people in their work. It seemed especially appropriate for this study, given the deep involvement that most teachers have in their profession (Poppleton & Riseborough, 1990). It also allowed us to capture the preoccupation that many teachers experience with their work long after work hours are over, and their isolation vis-à-vis their need to be "in the know."

To summarize, teachers tend to take their work home with them. They are occupied with thoughts about lesson planning, discipline matters, and meeting their students' needs (Pajak & Blase, 1989; Lampert, 1984; Lightfoot, 1983; Rosenholtz, 1989; Yee, 1990). There may be a developmental trend in teachers' preoccupation with work. Younger teachers seem to be more preoccupied by lesson planning, grading, and teaching methods. The older ones focus more on their students' needs and problem students (Feiman-Nemser, 1983; Huberman, 1989; Pajak & Blase, 1989; Prick, 1989; Yee, 1990). The construction of a work centrality scale allowed us to ask teachers directly about how preoccupied they were and relate it later to the amount of stress that they perceived on the job.

Teachers are isolated in their classrooms for long hours, precluding the possibility of sharing their knowledge and experience (Darling-Hammond &

Goodwin, 1993). Extensive research indicates that teachers were eager for that kind of sharing. The professional interaction with peers is regarded by teachers as one of the most important contributors to satisfaction and to feeling empowered (Darling-Hammond, 1988; Darling-Hammond & Goodwin, 1993; Maeroff, 1988; Rosenholtz, 1989; Yee, 1990). Teachers can learn a great deal from each other (Ashton & Webb, 1986; Devaney & Sykes, 1988; Rosenholtz, 1989). Some teachers feel that they get more curriculum guidelines from other teachers than from their administrators (Kottkamp, Provenzo, & Cohn, 1986).

Teachers want to be involved in decision making in a meaningful way (Smylie, 1992). They want their voice to be heard and acted upon (Belasco & Alutto, 1972; Imber & Duke, 1984; Imber & Neidt, 1990). The work centrality scale enabled us to tap into the teachers' core sense of isolation and their need to communicate with other teachers and administrators about school matters. All the previously mentioned aspects (preoccupation with work, isolation in one's own classroom, the need to learn from each other, the need to be involved in decision making) could be tapped by using the work centrality scale.

Job-Related Stress

Stress does not have a single definition. Rather, it is an umbrella term for a psychological reaction. Kahn and colleagues (1964) described stress as a response to negative stimuli (stressor). Generally speaking, stress is dynamic—if a person copes with the environment, stress is relieved, but if that does not happen, stress will increase. It especially increases if the environment is perceived as a threatening one, or if the individual perceives herself as lacking in coping strategies.

Job stress can disrupt the individual both physically and emotionally. It can originate in the environment or in the individual and his or her fit to this environment. In the latter case, it is called "strain" (Aldwin, 1994). Any misfits between the person and the environment can lead to job dissatisfaction. In the long run, it may even result in burnout. Stress is a common theme in teaching, as in other helping professions. According to Cherniss (1980), who has written extensively on the psychological issues underlying the human services, stress is experienced because professionals in these fields rarely have a sense of accomplishment due to the fact that results are never clear or immediate.

Teachers experience three frequent contributors to stress: role conflict, role overload, and role ambiguity. These have been found to be key elements in causing stress (Jackson & Schuler, 1985; Kahn et al., 1964; Kahn & Byosiere, 1990). Teachers often complain about overload (too many things to do in too little time) or role conflict (developing rapport versus control), and about ambiguity (e.g., how to teach a certain topic, how to approach individual learning styles). Teachers worry on the job and, often, after work hours. This certainly contributes to stress. Role overload is negatively correlated with teacher job satisfaction (Kyriacou & Sutcliffe, 1978; Belasco & Alutto, 1972; Litt & Turk, 1985). Dunham (1980) found that teachers perceived their workload and conflicting demands as very stressful and a cause of dissatisfaction. Litt and Turk (1985) reported that teachers expressed confusion about their roles and that led to stress and dissatisfaction, which in turn had caused absenteeism, intentions to leave, and burnout.

The professional–bureaucrat conflict and its influence on stress was examined and discussed thoroughly by Blau and Scott (1962). They found that individuals with a more professional orientation were more likely to display critical behavior toward the "bureaucracy" in the organization and to disregard administrative requests. This dichotomy has great relevance in schools. Often, teachers are stressed because their professional ethics or insights may clash with the bureaucratic demands of the school. Corwin (1981) and Metz (1986) described how the classic professional–bureaucratic conflict manifests itself in the public school of North America. Teachers often embody this conflict. They complain a great deal about paperwork, which they regard as "busywork" that detracts from their important professional duties.

Teachers who do not perceive themselves as "reaching" their students and helping them toward achievement experience lack of efficacy, which results in stress. Unfortunately, teachers quite often experience a lack of self-efficacy. Cherniss (1980) points out that the helping professionals have a sense of responsibility for other people's lives and a sense of calling to better others. That makes self-efficacy so critical, and the perceived lack of it, so acute. The importance of a sense of self-efficacy has been recognized since the seminal work of Bandura (1977).

Teachers with a high sense of self-efficacy tend to have better managed classrooms (Kounin, 1970; Newmann, Rutter, & Smith, 1989). Their consistent and clear rules result in students' better performance, more teacher satisfaction, and less stress (Ashton & Webb, 1986). On the other hand, Lortie (1975) and Yee (1990) found that teachers who were not certain about their effectiveness were dissatisfied and stressed. There seems to be a consistent link between teachers sense of self-efficacy, stress, performance, and satisfaction. The question is about the direction and magnitude of this. Blase (1982, 1986) found, in his qualitative metaanalysis of linkages between teacher stress and performance, that the more stress teachers experience, the less able they are to perform well. This view may be oversimplistic. The following is an explanation of why the situation is more complex.

Although there is ample research suggesting that stress and teacher performance are inversely correlated, as are stress and satisfaction (Kyriacou & Sutcliffe, 1978; Reyes, 1990; Schwab & Iwanicki, 1982; Smilansky, 1984), the relationship is by no means clear-cut, and certainly does not seem to be a linear relationship. It may depend to a large degree on how people process stress cognitively and what their coping skills are, rather than the "objective" stress in their environment (Aldwin, 1994; Cohen & Wills, 1985; Lazarus & Folkman, 1984). More to the point, for our research, cultural contexts affect the appraisal of stress and the coping process. What is perceived in one culture as stressful may be seen as less so in another (Aldwin, 1994; Moore, 1990; Kashima & Triandis, 1986).

Not all stress is negative. Yee (1990) found that some of the highly motivated and involved teachers experienced stress but were obviously satisfied with their jobs. These teachers she called "good-fit stayers"; they were marked by a strong sense of efficacy and love of the subject matter. These teachers were also more committed.

Unfortunately, research as a whole indicates that, frequently, teachers' unrelieved stress can result in teacher burnout (Dworkin, 1987). Burnout has been recognized as an acute problem since the 1970s (Maslach & Pines, 1979). Burnout is the end result of long exposure to stress without relief, especially if there have been attempts to cope but they were unsuccessful (Farber, 1984, 1994; Maslach & Pines, 1978, 1979). In the case of teachers' burnout they become less committed, have much less sympathy for students, and blame students, parents, and administrators (Anderson & Iwanicki, 1984; Ashton & Webb, 1986; Farber & Miller, 1982; Yee, 1990). They become less creative, less caring, and do not pay attention to lesson plans (Farber & Miller, 1982). They experience emotional distance, psychosomatic ailments, and fatigue. This often leads to absenteeism, less commitment to school, and to a demoralizing effect on colleagues.

CONSTRUCTING THE QUALITY OF WORK LIFE ITEMS

The three quality of life indexes—overall job satisfaction, work centrality, and job-related stress—comprise our quality of work life. The assignment of items to each of the three indexes of quality of work life appears in the following section. What follows is a description of how these three concepts have been operationalized in the questionnaire.

Overall Job Satisfaction

Satisfaction can be measured directly by asking, How satisfied are you with your job? or indirectly by measuring how much one is satisfied with different specific facets. The first is called the "facet-free" or "overall" satisfaction (Holdaway, 1978). The following four facet-free items were thought to be most appropriate for this study.

1. In general, how much do you enjoy teaching as an occupation?
2. How much would you say that teaching measures up to what you wanted when you entered the profession?
3. Knowing what you know now, if you had to decide all over again whether to enter teaching, how likely is it that you would do so?
4. Considering all things, how satisfied would you say you are with your present job as a teacher?

Overall job satisfaction is a major dependent variable in this study. It consists of a set of four different measures of satisfaction, each dealing with a different aspect, and of a combined overall index of satisfaction obtained by averaging satisfaction scores on the four measures where one reflected the lowest satisfaction and four reflected a great deal of it.

Work Centrality

Work centrality in our study refers to the global evaluation of how important the work at school is in teachers' lives. Three facet specific items (five, six, and seven) measuring work role centrality were adopted from the work role centrality index (Mannheim, 1975, 1983; Mannheim & Cohen, 1978). Each of these used a four point scale, where one reflected the lowest centrality and four reflected a great deal of it.

The first question asks, To what extent is success at your work important to you? The intent of the question was to assess the absolute importance of work. The second item asks, To what extent do matters connected with your work occupy your thoughts outside working hours? The intent of this question was to assess how preoccupied teachers are with work. The last question inquires, To what extent do you want to know what is happening in school outside your own classroom? The intent of this question was to find out how much teachers wanted to be "in the know."

Job-Related Stress

The questionnaire measured the overall perception of stress as related to the teachers' present job by using the previously mentioned four-point scale for the following question: Overall, how much stress do you experience in your present job?

RESULTS

This section presents the analysis and results regarding the quality of work life (QWL) of teachers, consisting of overall job satisfaction, work centrality, and job-related stress. The results revolve around three questions.

1. How do teachers experience their working life in their own country?
2. How do teachers in different countries compare with respect to their work experiences?
3. What, if any, is the influence on these matters of the teachers' demographic characteristics: gender, age, and marital status?

The first question calls for within-country analyses, the second for between-country comparisons, and the third for both. We begin with an overall view of the highest and lowest rated items in each country before moving on to the grand mean scores of the QWL indexes and the question of how these might have been affected by gender, age, and marital status. For these purposes, comparable scales were achieved by the within-country transformation of ratings for each index into standardized scores having a mean of 50 and a standard deviation of 10. These are referred to as t-scores and allow us to compare the relative standing of items and indexes both within and across countries. As explained in Chapter 1, a difference of three points or more represents both statistical and effect size significance in comparing across countries or indexes. The mean t-scores of each country on the eight QWL items and three QWL indexes defined previously appear in Table 3.1. In the following sections, data from this table are analyzed with respect to each of the three questions listed.

Teachers' Experience of Work

The item scores displayed in the left section of Table 3.1 suggest that a major motivating factor for all teachers in every country was the experience of success at work, however it is personally defined. Of all countries, the Israeli teachers valued success most highly. Success is basically an intrinsic reward to be balanced against extrinsic factors in resolving the dilemmas of either remaining in the teaching profession or leaving it. Although the majority of teachers in every country said they were likely to enter teaching again if given the chance to decide all over again, a substantial minority in each country said they were unlikely to reenter teaching. These responses indicate a considerable degree of ambivalence about the state of teaching in the mid to late 1980s.

The relative positions of the QWL variables are shown in the bar charts in Figure 3.1, which is derived from the data in Table 3.1. Viewing the chart vertically for each country gives a profile of that country's teachers on each of the three variables and, since the countries are arranged in the same order (ascending order of job satisfaction), relative standing both within and across countries can be easily assessed. For example, Canadian teachers have the highest level of overall job satisfaction, are around average on work centrality, and are second lowest on stress. English teachers, on the other hand, have the lowest level of overall job satisfaction, the highest level (with Israel) of work centrality, and a slightly above average level of stress. Already we can see patterns emerging that will enable us to make sense of the differences both within and between countries.

Teachers' Quality of Work Life across Countries

The grand mean score in Table 3.1 provides a comparison of the relative emphasis on QWL indexes averaged over countries. Listed in descending

Table 3.1
Mean T-Scores by Country for Eight Items and Three Indexes in the Quality of Work Life Domain

Country	Mean T Scores on Eight Individual QWL Items								Mean T Scores on Three QWL Indexes		
	Item 1	Item 2	Item 3	Item 4	Item 5	Item 6	Item 7	Item 8	Job Sat.	Work Cen.	Job-Rel. Stress
US	52	48	45	48	57	50	51	48	48	53	48
England	51	46	42	46	56	53	55	51	45	56	51
Germany	51	46	53	48	52	47	53	50	49	51	50
Japan	50	43	46	45	55	54	54	53	46	54	53
Singapore	52	47	44	47	56	52	51	48	48	53	48
Canada	54	50	49	50	54	48	50	44	52	51	44
Poland	48	47	46	47	54	56	53	49	47	54	49
Israel	51	45	45	48	61	54	54	43	47	56	43
USSR	51	47	47	41	53	55	54	50	46	54	50
Grand Mean	51	46	46	46	55	53	53	49	47	54	49

Note: T-scores are computed within the quality of work life domain for each country and averaged to form indexes.

order of the magnitude, these are work centrality (54), stress (49), and overall job satisfaction (47). Averaged over countries, work centrality is significantly higher than either overall job satisfaction or job-related stress, but the latter two do not differ significantly. This pattern of differences among indexes was repeated in most countries. A major exception was in Canada where overall job satisfaction was significantly above the grand mean and tied with work centrality. Thus, the Canadian teachers may be said to be significantly more satisfied with their work than teachers in any other country. Israeli and English teachers share the highest score of 56 for work centrality, which differentiates them from colleagues in Singapore, the United States, Germany, and Canada. Japanese teachers recorded the highest levels of stress (53), and Israel the lowest (43).

Interestingly, the total mean score of work centrality was higher than those of the other two indexes in all nine countries. At first glance, this particular finding seems to be readily explicable. Since work centrality constitutes one facet of professionalism, its high score may be interpreted as a high level of professional orientation and identity, devotion and commitment. However, a high level of work centrality is not necessarily a desirable situation. There are cases in which this high level may be a result of the difficult problems encountered, to which teachers devote a great amount of time and preoccupa-

Figure 3.1
Mean T-Scores of Three Quality of Work Life Indexes by Country

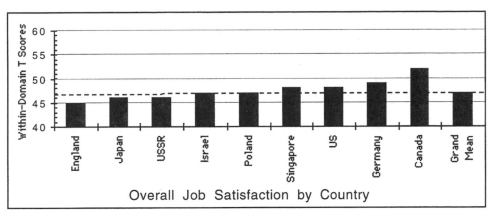

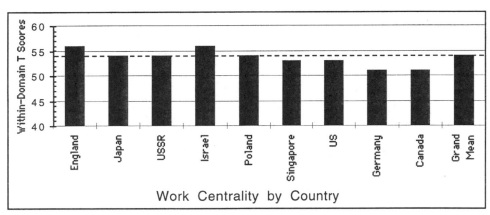

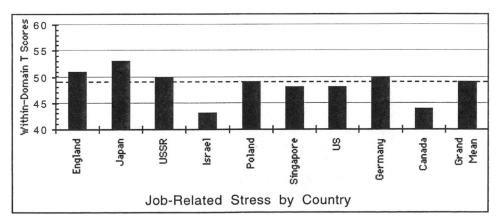

Note: This figure is derived from data in Table D-2 of the *Technical Supplement*.

tion—much more than is healthy. In extreme cases, such situations may result in burnout and frustration. One may also suspect that high scores on work centrality are an artifact of a "social desirability" tendency in responding to the questionnaire items, since we all like to see ourselves as hard workers. This is an issue that calls for further investigation.

Detailed results for each index are presented separately in subsequent sections.

Overall Job Satisfaction across Countries. Canadian teachers expressed the highest degree of satisfaction and the English teachers the lowest (52 and 45 respectively). A score difference of three points indicates a result that can be regarded as educationally (as well as statistically) significant, and this is enough to differentiate Canada from the mean scores of the remaining eight countries, and both Canada and Germany (49) from England (45), the Soviet Union (46), and Japan (46). U.S. teachers (48) also showed higher satisfaction than those in England and the Soviet Union.

An examination of the responses to the individual items comprising the satisfaction index reveals something of interest regarding the factors contributing to these results. Generally, enjoyment of teaching emerged as stronger than either the realization of their initial expectations, their satisfaction with the present post, or the likelihood of entering teaching all over again at this point in their careers, given the opportunity and all other things being equal. The German teachers seem to be a special case, since their greater likelihood of rechoosing teaching for their profession surpasses and seems independent of the other three considerations. This is especially marked in comparison with teachers in England and the United States, and suggests that conditions specific to Germany may be operating and that these may be illuminating for other countries where likely reentry is low.

Work Centrality across Countries. In contrast to the findings on overall job satisfaction, those for work centrality showed the highest scores for the English (56) and Israeli (56) teachers, who differed significantly from the Germans (51) and the Canadians (52). The work centrality score for teachers is clearly stronger, in most cases, than either their overall job satisfaction or job-related stress scores, Germany being an exception in that all the index scores for German teachers were about equal.

In sum, the results concerning work centrality point to the Israeli and English teachers as unique in their experiencing the highest degree of work centrality, and to the German and Canadian teachers as experiencing the lowest. This is almost certainly the result of the Israeli and English teachers' endorsements of the importance of achieving success at work. This item emerged as stronger than either the importance of being aware of what was happening outside the classroom or the extent to which work occupied the teacher's thoughts outside working hours (with the exception of teachers in Poland and Russia). What happens in classrooms has generally higher reward power than what happens in the broader context of the school. However, the need to plan, prepare, and know what is happening in the workplace as a whole contributes to a universally high level of involvement in work and work-related activities. Whether driven by internal or external forces, teachers are workaholics.

Job-Related Stress across Countries. In relation to other QWL items, job-related stress was highest for the Japanese (53), and it was lowest for the Israelis (43) and Canadians (44). The Japanese scored significantly higher and the Israelis and Canadians scored significantly lower than each of the other countries.

Index Relationships across Countries. Canadian teachers were unique among all countries in maintaining the highest satisfaction and lowest stress, and may have something positive to teach us all. At the same time, it is intriguing and seems reasonable to ask if joint conditions of highest satisfaction and lowest stress represent the ideal work setting, or whether they foster a setting with comparatively less energy and challenge. This latter possibility finds some support in the results of an earlier Consortium study (Menlo, 1991), which indicated that teachers' commitment to their work is not highest when all work conditions are at their best.

Perhaps the most interesting finding in this section relates to Israel, where the highest work centrality was combined with lowest stress, making Israeli teachers somewhat different from teachers in all of the other eight countries. While stress is lower than work centrality in all nine countries with the difference being educationally important in seven, the low stress in Israeli teachers is still surprising. Its difference from the accompanying work centrality (–13) is more than three times the average difference between stress and work centrality across the other eight countries (–4).

What is it, then, that promotes such a low level of occupational stress within these teachers, who not only have the ongoing expected stress-arousing experience of intranational strife and concerns of survival in international war, but also strongly reflect a characteristic (work centrality) which is more similar than different from the other eight countries? What is in operation here that might hold social science insights?

In order to pursue a deeper understanding of the forces behind this apparent uniqueness of the Israeli teachers, a group interview was arranged with twenty Israeli secondary teachers unassociated with this larger study. In these interviews, the low-stress finding was identified and then explored with reference to the interviewees' own work-life experiences. Two lines of response emerged as salient. One concerns the general high stress that transcends teaching because of the country's overall political and social unsteadiness. As one teacher put it, "We are having a bad time now in Israel in the political sense, and we are in a very bad mood, both collectively and individually. As for myself, I am very pessimistic. We live in a volcano which must erupt; we are not worried for ourselves, but for our children and grandchildren. What a cruel situation they are going to live in. These thoughts are with us twenty-four hours a day and make things look like a tunnel with no exit." The second line of response communicates a deep level of commitment to country and to actualizing this commitment through teaching. In a statement which seemed to summarize several other statements, one teacher said, "For me, teaching is a national mission. Our future depends on the next generation; so, although I work very hard, I don't feel stressed because I know I do something important for my country."

The first line of response seems to clearly identify the major item of thought for many teachers in Israel. This item is the fragile state of internal and external political affairs and the extent to which they and their future uncertainty undergird, surround, and surpass most other daily processes and events. The seemingly relentless stress of living in an unstable country would appear to reduce the power of potential stressors in other domains, such as occupational experience. In other words, occupational stress fades away in the face of larger problems in survival. As psychological field theory (Cartwright, 1951) has so clearly indicated, the effect of a given stimulus depends upon its place in the overall constellation of stimuli and upon the state of the particular persons at that time.

The second line of response may further explain the relatively low stress of Israeli teachers, as well as their relatively high work centrality. For some teachers, steadfastly using their professional abilities with students brings personal–social rewards of experiencing themselves as contributing significantly to the future of their country—especially where the difficulties are so complex that it seems impossible to be a source of constructive influence in any other way. This perception of the positive societal consequence of one's professional work would seem to have strong influence on the centrality of that work in the person's life.

In addition to the two just-described forces that appear as reducers of Israeli teachers' job-related stress, a likely third force arises from the study's data on school work conditions. According to Appendix Table D-1, the amount of support received by Israeli teachers from colleagues is indicated as being well beyond the average received by teachers in all nine countries (3.56 standard deviations above the nine-country mean). Social psychological research has been, and continues to be, replete with findings about the importance of supportiveness. For instance, various life stresses are less likely to lead to depressed moods or troubled mental states with persons who are with supportive rather than unsupportive associates (National Advisory Mental Health Council, 1995).

Thus, it seems very reasonable to explain, at least partially, the particularly low occupational stress in Israeli teachers' lives as being a function of potential occupational stress overshadowed and upstaged by greater national stress; experiencing one's occupation as a strong contributor to one's country; and being in the midst of a supportive occupational setting. In creative hands, there are interesting implications for the prevention and reduction of teacher stress.

Influence of Gender on Quality of Work Life

The information in Figure 3.2 is intended to show the relative QWL scores of male and female teachers in each country. Again, viewed vertically, we can see the relative position of each QWL variable within countries and viewed horizontally the position between countries. In the following sections, the information in Figure 3.2 is analyzed separately for each index.

Gender and Overall Job Satisfaction. In all countries except the Far Eastern countries of Japan and Singapore, women teachers expressed higher satisfaction with their work than men teachers did. It is of interest to note that the level of teacher job satisfaction within a country does not appear to predict which gender of teachers will be higher or lower than the other. This can be seen in Japan and England where, while having the lowest satisfaction levels among the nine countries, men are most satisfied in Japan and women are in England. Also, the home of the least satisfied women teachers is Japan (44) while the least satisfied men teachers were to be found in both England (44) and the Soviet Union (44). Another observation is that, while male teachers are more satisfied than female teachers in Japan and Singapore (thus breaking continuity with the opposite pattern set in the other seven countries), it is only in Japan that the difference is educationally significant. In these two countries, the roles of satisfaction for males and females are the reverse of the tendency over most countries for females to score higher. The Japanese male teachers emerged as a unique group by experiencing a significantly higher degree of overall job satisfaction than their female colleagues (47 and 44, respectively).

Of special interest is the lower degree of satisfaction expressed by male teachers found in seven countries. The reason may lie in the male teacher's aspiration for a prestigious career, for a high occupational status, and a relatively high income. Women are still not perceived as the ones who have to support their families economically; they are perceived as helping out, but not as main supporters. The reason for the different picture obtained for Japan and Singapore, where male teachers are more satisfied than their female colleagues, may well lie in the cultural ethos of the East, and especially in the status of women in the family and across occupations where they come to see themselves as second-class citizens.

In another context, both U.S. and English women teachers are generally more satisfied with their work than men, while these same men and women do not differ in the extent to which work is central to their lives or in the amount of stress they experience. This pattern does not exist in any of the other countries and suggests the operation of specific factors influencing job satisfaction such as differential promotion opportunities.

Gender and Work Centrality. Work centrality is not, on the whole, gender-differentiated, although significant differences between female and male teachers emerged in Canada (53 and 50), in Israel (58 and 54), and in the Soviet

Figure 3.2
Mean T-Scores for Quality of Work Life Indexes by Country and Teacher Gender

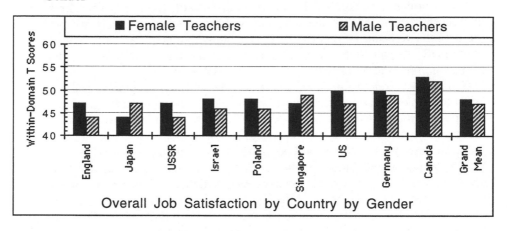

Overall Job Satisfaction by Country by Gender

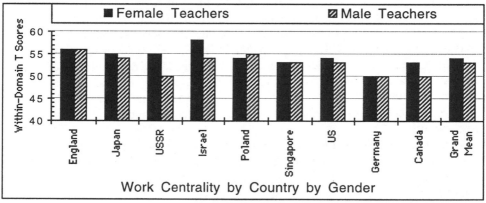

Work Centrality by Country by Gender

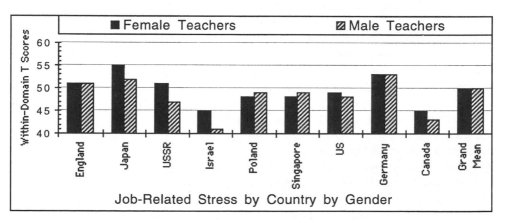

Job-Related Stress by Country by Gender

Note: This figure is derived from data in Table D-3 of the *Technical Supplement*.

Union (55 and 50). The overall tendency for work centrality to be high is very marked for both sexes. Germany, where it is exactly at the same level as job satisfaction, is an exception. Theoretically, work centrality varies also with the organization of the teaching day, patterns of responsibility, and extracurricular activities, but it also reflects the all-absorbing nature of the occupation that sets the tone for a common culture of teaching.

The tendency toward higher work centrality among female teachers, although generally not statistically different from that of male teachers, is rather surprising. One would expect the opposite to be true, since in general women still have responsibilities at home and in raising children. But perhaps this is where the explanation lies. Since women have to handle multiple responsibilities, they are almost forced to plan ahead and are continuously preoccupied with problems of both work and home. However, from a psychological angle we could ask, Is work centrality an affective-emotional rather than a cognitive element of the mind? If this is true, and if women are more emotionally oriented in their profession, we could very cautiously suggest an interpretation along this line of thought. Alternatively, looking through the glass of history and of the sociology of professions, we have been long witnessing a process of feminization of teaching. This process is probably a result of newly emerging occupations which seem more prestigious and attractive to men, and which in turn have resulted in lowering the sociological status of teaching. Such being the situation, it may be that male teachers are gradually becoming less likely to choose teaching as a career. This would not, however, explain why there are no significant gender differences in the remainder of the countries.

Gender and Job-Related Stress. Stress appears to have been gender related in three countries where significant differences were found favoring female over male teachers, respectively, for Japan (55 and 52), Israel (45 and 42), and the Soviet Union (51 and 47). Interestingly, Figure 3.2 shows much more variable patterns of job-related stress than in the case of either overall job satisfaction or work centrality. This argues for the influence of a large number of moderating factors present in the workplace, the nature of the work, and the match between teachers and the tasks of teaching.

Influence of Age on Quality of Work Life

The age distribution of the teachers was divided into three categories: up to age 34, age 35 to 49, and age 50 and up. These would roughly represent the early, middle, and late stages of the teaching career and the general tendencies within and across countries are similar to those already noted. The results for an age by country analyses of the three QWL indexes are summarized in Figure 3.3. Again, a discussion of findings is presented for each index separately.

Age and Overall Job Satisfaction. Significant differences in overall job satisfaction emerged between the youngest and oldest age groups in Japan

Figure 3.3
Mean T-Scores for Quality of Work Life Indexes by Country and Teacher Age

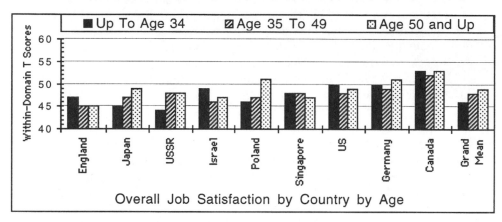

Overall Job Satisfaction by Country by Age

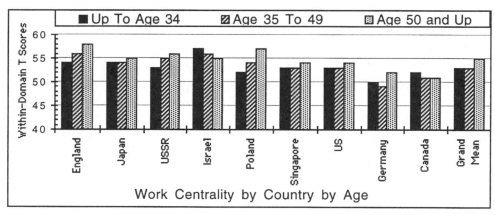

Work Centrality by Country by Age

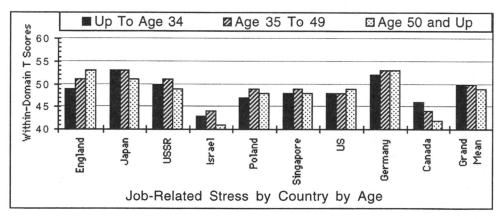

Job-Related Stress by Country by Age

Note: This figure is derived from data in Table D-4 of the *Technical Supplement*.

(45 and 49, respectively), Poland (46 and 51), and the Soviet Union (44 and 48). In the other six countries, age differences occurred at intermediate levels: from young to middle age groups in the Soviet Union, and from middle to older in Poland. The youngest group of English teachers reported the highest levels of overall job satisfaction, while the youngest teachers in Japan and the Soviet Union were the least satisfied. Linear increases from the youngest to the oldest groups can be seen in Japan and Poland, but there are no significant trends in the reverse direction in any country. Once more, the Canadian results did not discriminate between groupings.

It is highly likely that these differing results can be accounted for by cultural and structural factors that are country specific (e.g., unrest among teachers at structural changes affecting their hours of work and rates of pay; blocked promotion prospects; difficulties in moving to new jobs versus the excitement and energies of starting a new career). Some of these factors may emerge in other chapters dealing with working conditions and the teachers' roles and responsibilities.

Age and Overall Job Satisfaction. A slight tendency for higher work centrality in the older age levels as compared with the younger ones was noted. In Poland, England, and the Soviet Union, the experience of higher work centrality was more likely to be reported by older rather than younger teachers and between teachers of middle and upper age levels (54 and 57, respectively). Important differences also emerged in England and the Soviet Union between teachers of lower and upper age levels (54 and 58 in England, and 53 and 56 in the Soviet Union). In no country except Israel did work centrality decrease with age and, in the upper age level groups, the English teachers' score was the highest between countries. It differed significantly from the overall mean score (55) and, excluding Poland, from all the remaining countries.

There were no significant differences between teachers below 35 and those between 35 and 49 in any country suggesting that, within countries, the level of work centrality remains fairly stable until the age of 50. However, as noted, trends exist between the two extreme groups from younger to older in the case England, the Soviet Union, and Poland, and in the reverse direction in Israel.

Age Influence on Job-Related Stress. The age of the teacher significantly influences job-related stress in just three countries: England, Israel, and Canada, though in interestingly different ways. In England, where the overall level of stress was comparatively high, the younger teachers experienced significantly less stress than the older ones: the scores for the low and high age groups were 49 and 53 respectively. The reason was generally acknowledged to be the high rate of change associated with pending government reforms later embodied in the Education Reform Act of 1988. The young teachers did not experience these reforms as changes and so did not have to go through a difficult period of adjustment. In Canada, where overall stress was comparatively lower, it was the older teachers who were significantly less stressed than the middle group (42 and 46 respectively). In Israel, where overall stress was the lowest, the oldest group of teachers was the least stressed of all (41) and significantly lower than the middle group (44). In the remaining countries only very slight and negligible differences between age groups were noted. The highest degree of stress was reported by the Japanese teachers in the young and medium age teachers (53 and 53). Significant relationships between age and job-related stress appear once more to be the outcome of local, and possibly, temporary, factors.

Influence of Marital Status on Quality of Work Life

The influence of teachers' marital status on overall job satisfaction, work centrality, and job-related stress is graphically summarized in Figure 3.4, and will be discussed in the following sections on an index by index basis.

Marital Status and Overall Job Satisfaction. When each of the nine countries is considered separately, whether teachers are married or unmarried does not appear to have an educationally significant effect on the satisfaction they experience in their job. So, with the data at hand, one would not be encouraged to predict more or less job satisfaction from knowing a teacher's marital status. At the same time, however, there appear to be interesting comparisons across countries. In four countries, unmarried and married teachers do not differ at all in their extent of job satisfaction, but in five other countries there are small insignificant differences, and all of them favor the married teachers. It seems reasonable to speculate that, while the marital status of teachers in a school faculty does not allow one to predict levels of job satisfaction in any one country, being married may represent a slightly stronger positive influence on satisfaction with teaching than being unmarried. The researchability of such a speculation would certainly be complex and its applicability doubtful. It may be no more than a reflection of general life satisfaction; it has been found in prior studies that married persons tend to be happier in general than single persons and that life satisfaction and job satisfaction are positively related.

Marital Status and Work Centrality. In both England and Israel, those who were married were significantly more likely to experience higher levels of work centrality (56 and 53) than those who were unmarried, but there was no differentiation in any other country.

Marital Status and Job-Related Stress. Stress was experienced at a significantly higher level in England (52) by those who were married than by their unmarried colleagues (49). The same three-point difference exists in Germany (marrieds, 54 and unmarrieds, 51), but elsewhere the tendency was in the opposite direction.

Marital Status and Index Relations. Summarizing across the broadest landscape of interaction between marital status and the three dimensions of work life quality for all nine countries together, being married appeared to arouse greater work satisfaction, work centrality, and stress than not being married (Married = 13 highest scores, Unmarried = 6 highest and 8 equal scores). In

Figure 3.4
Mean T-Scores for Quality of Work Life Indexes by Country and Teacher Marital Status

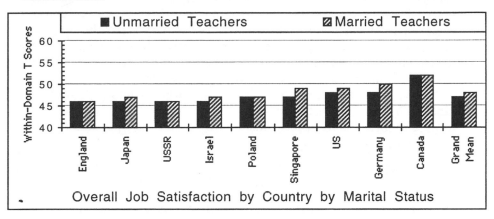

Overall Job Satisfaction by Country by Marital Status

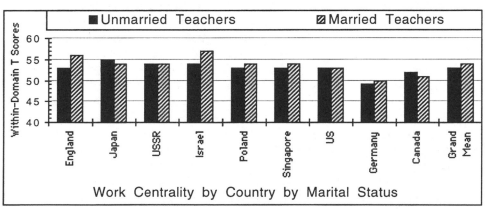

Work Centrality by Country by Marital Status

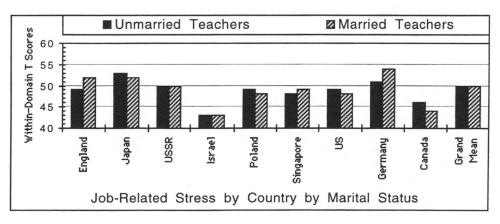

Job-Related Stress by Country by Marital Status

Note: This figure is derived from data in Table D-5 of the *Technical Supplement*.

addition, on the three occasions where marital status significantly affected a quality of work life dimension (two in England and one in Israel), it was always the married rather than the unmarried status that aroused the strongest impact. Thus, in school settings, satisfaction, centrality, and stress seemed to be experienced most by married teachers. The country where differences in marital status seemed to have the most significant effect was England, and the least the Soviet Union. In England, the tenure associated with a teaching post was rapidly disappearing and bringing new feelings of economic insecurity, which would be increased in the case of teachers with family responsibilities. One should also bear in mind that married teachers are likely to be older rather than younger and, at this stage of the analysis, the two influences cannot be separated out.

DISCUSSION

The analysis of the data yielded two distinct groups of countries. In one group, no specific tendencies or typicalities of significant importance emerged while, in the other group of countries, several did so. This part of our report includes only those country characteristics that emerged regularly as prominent in any respect relevant to this study. The countries in which such regularities were observed were Canada, England, and Israel. The mean score pattern for overall job satisfaction, work centrality, and job-related stress, respectively, for teachers in Canada can be summarized as high–low–low; in England it was low–high–low; and in Israel it was low–high–low.

Countries have been described as high or low on the basis of their relative positions in comparison with the overall across-country means, which were shown as dashed lines in Figure 3.1. A summary of the overall job satisfaction data points to the Canadian teachers as unique in the high degrees of satisfaction reported by both genders and at all three age levels, as well as by the married and unmarried groups of teachers. In addition, the Canadians appear to experience a low level of work centrality, and a low degree of job-related stress. This picture seems only natural and understandable as teachers who are satisfied are not likely to be stressed; in fact, negative correlations are found between overall job satisfaction and stress in every country except Singapore. The relationship between overall job satisfaction and work centrality is more problematic, however. If we see work centrality as desirable, it stands to reason that it will be positively associated with overall job satisfaction and inversely associated with job-related stress, but this does not happen in any of the three countries. Nor does such a picture emerge if one looks at the data as a whole.

The English teachers' scores reveal an entirely different picture. These teachers are not satisfied, they are high in work centrality, and they experience a high degree of stress. As previously mentioned, a high degree of work centrality may also be perceived as exhausting, time consuming, and undesirable, and consequently lead to stress and dissatisfaction. Such a preoccupation may well explain the inverse relation between work centrality and satisfaction. The contrasting results that emerged in the Canadian and English groups of teachers thus complement each other. Since our data analyses do not yield causalities, the relationships between QWL indexes did not tell us which one was a function of the other.

The Israelis, like the English teachers, appear to be a relatively less satisfied group of teachers, characterized by a high degree of work centrality but with a low degree of stress. They differ from the English teachers, as they do not experience a high degree of stress, resembling the Canadians in this respect. In fact, the stress scores of the Israeli teachers are the lowest in all instances. It has earlier been suggested that the reason for the low degree of stress lies in the overall high stress of the Israeli population beside which the stresses involved in teaching seem miniscule, but this is speculative and needs confirmation from other sources.

Finally, the results concerning the gender differences within countries are worthy of attention. They were the only ones that ran across countries, pointing to a clear tendency towards higher or equal scores of the female teachers as compared with those of the male teachers in work satisfaction, work centrality, and very slightly so in stress. Thus, gender differences appear to be more influential when compared to age levels and marital status. Are these gender differences embedded in cultural or structural characteristics? Poppleton and Riseborough (1990) note that one of the most striking sources of variation between the teaching professions of different countries is the balance of the sexes, which reflects both economic and sociocultural forces. On the assumption that the various teacher samples in this study were reasonably representative, the profession appears to have been male-dominated in Japan and Germany; over half were male in England and the United States; and in Singapore and the Soviet Union, two-thirds were female. These proportions do not remain stable over time, and there is evidence of the steady feminization of teaching in most Western industrialized societies. The important point is that the gender composition of the survey samples may influence the results. Consequently, as the proportion of women teachers rises, analyses such as the ones reported here will increasingly represent the woman's viewpoint, especially in countries where there is no equal opportunities policy. We may conclude that, for whatever reason, female teachers from most countries in the late 1980s were generally more likely than their male colleagues to be satisfied with their work and to experience high work centrality, particularly in Western countries. The position was reversed in Japan and Singapore. As regards age, the position varied more according to country, and the effect of marital status appeared small and specific.

CONCLUSIONS

In complex survey data, it is often difficult to see the forest for the trees, but we have attempted to extract the main trends from the quality of work life data.

Our first conclusion is that there are far more similarities than differences among teachers from these nine countries in regard to quality of work life. Most of these similarities occur with work centrality, second-most with overall job satisfaction, and third-most with job-related stress. This would seem to support the existence of a strong, uniform culture of teaching that transcends national boundaries and arises mainly from the imperative of the tasks. At the same time, however, there is sufficient variability within countries to argue that teachers are not as homogeneous a group of people as many of the studies quoted in the first part of this chapter appear to suggest.

In order to maintain teaching at a high standard of professionalism in conditions of variability, teachers' individual needs require attention and, in order to maximize the quality of the working life for teachers, we should identify and enhance those things that increase the enjoyment of teaching as well as those that increase the opportunities for success. These may seem like simple, common-sense solutions to complex problems, but we are still a long way from knowing how, in different circumstances, to enhance job satisfaction and reduce stress.

Nor have we been able to answer the question of how important the demographic characteristics are when compared with a whole range of other environmental influences—physical, psychological, and social. These themes will be explored in following chapters.

REFERENCES

Aldwin, C. M. (1994). *Stress, coping, and development.* New York: Guilford Press.

Aldwin, C. M.; and Stokols, D. (1988). The effects of environmental change on individuals and groups: Some neglected issues in stress research. *Journal of Environmental Psychology, 8* (1), 57–75.

Anderson, M.; and Iwanicki, E. (1984). Teacher motivation and its relationship to burnout. *Educational Administration Quarterly, 20* (2), 109–132.

Ashton, P. W.; and Webb, R. B. (1986). *Making a difference: Teachers' sense of efficacy and student achievement.* New York: Longman.

Bandura, A. (1977). Self-efficacy: Toward a unifying theory of behavioral change. *Psychological Review, 84* (2), 191–215.

Belasco, J. A.; and Alutto, J. A. (1972). Decisional participation and teacher satisfaction. *Educational Administration Quarterly, 8* (1), 44–58.

Blase, J. J. (1982). A social psychological grounded theory of teacher stress and burnout. *Educational Administration Quarterly, 18* (4), 93–113.

Blase, J. J. (1986). A qualitative analysis of sources of teacher stress: Consequences for performance. *American Educational Research Journal, 23* (1), 13–40.

Blau, P. M.; and Scott, R. W. (1962). *Formal organizations: A comparative approach.* San Francisco: Chandler.

Cartwright, D. (Ed.). (1951). *Field theory in social science: Selected papers by Kurt Lewin.* New York: Harper and Row.

Cherniss, C. (1980). *Staff burnout: Job stress in the human services.* Beverly Hills, CA: Sage.

Cohen, S.; and Wills, T. A. (1985). Stress, social support and the buffering hypothesis. *Psychological Bulletin, 98* (2), 310–357.

Corwin, R. B. (1981). Patterns of organizational control and teacher militancy: Theoretical continuities in the idea of "loose coupling." In A. C. Kerckhoff (Ed.), *Research in the sociology of education and socialization: Vol. 2.* Greenwich, CT: JAI Press.

Darling-Hammond, L. (1988). Policy and professionalism. In Ann Lieberman (Ed.), *Building a professional culture in schools.* New York: Teachers College Press.

Darling-Hammond, L.; and Goodwin, A. (1993). Progress toward professionalism in teaching. In ASCD Yearbook 19–52, *Challenges and Achievements of American Education.* Alexandria, VA: American Association for Supervision and Curriculum Development.

Devaney, K.; and Sykes, G. (1988). Making the case for professionalism. In Ann Lieberman (Ed.), *Building a professional culture in schools.* New York: Teachers College Press.

Dubin, R. (1956). Industrial workers' worlds: A study for the central life interest of industrial workers. *Social Problems, 3*, 131–142.

Dubin, R. (1958). *The world of work.* Englewood Cliffs, NJ: Prentice Hall.

Dubin, R.; and Champoux, J. E. (1977). Central life interests and job satisfaction. *Organizational Behavior and Human Performance, 18* (2), 366–377.

Dunham, J. (1980). An exploratory comprehensive study of staff stress in comprehensive schools. *Educational Review, 52* (1), 44–47.

Dworkin, A. G. (1987). *Teacher burnout in the public schools: Structural causes and consequences for children.* Albany: State University of New York.

Evers, T. (1992). *Factors affecting job satisfaction in secondary school teachers in Michigan.* Unpublished Ph.D. diss., University of Michigan, Ann Arbor.

Farber, B. A. (1984). Stress and burnout of suburban teachers. *Journal of Educational Research, 77* (6), 325–331.

Farber, B. A. (1994). Teacher burnout: Assumptions, myths and issues. *Teachers College Record, 84–86* (2), 235–243.

Farber, B. A.; and Miller, J. (1982). Teacher burnout: A psychoeducational perspective. *Educational Digest, 83* (2), 235–243.

Feiman-Nemser, S. (1983). Learning to teach. In L. S. Shulman and G. Sykes (Eds.), *Handbook of teaching and policy.* New York: Longman.

Fernandez, R. (1992). *Work attitudes among secondary school teachers in Japan and Michigan.* Unpublished Ph.D. diss., University of Michigan, Ann Arbor.

Good, T.; and Brophy, J. (1994). *Looking in classrooms.* New York: HarperCollins College Publications.

Hargreaves, A. (1992). *Changing teachers, changing times: Teachers' work and culture in the postmodern age.* London: Cassell.

Herzberg, F.; Mausner, B.; and Snyderman, B. (1959). *The motivation to work.* New York: John Wiley & Sons.

Holdaway, E. A. (1978). Facet and overall satisfiers of teachers. *Education Administration Quarterly, 14* (1), 30–47.

Hoy, W. K.; and Miskel, C. G. (1987). *Educational administration: Theory, research, and practice* (3d ed.). New York: Random House.

Huberman, M. (1989). The professional life cycle of teachers. *Teachers College Record, 91* (1), 31–57.

Imber, M.; and Duke, D. L. (1984). Teacher participation in school decision-making: A framework for research. *Journal of Educational Administration, 22* (1), 24–34.

Imber, M.; and Neidt, W. A. (1990). Teacher participation in school decision making. In P. Reyes (Ed.), *Teachers and their workplace: Commitment performance and productivity.* Newbury Park, CA: Sage.

Jackson, S. E.; and Schuler, R. S. (1985). A meta analysis and conceptual critique of research on role ambiguity and work conflict in work settings. *Organizational Behavior and Human Decision Processes, 36* (1), 16–78.

Kahn, R. L.; and Byosiere, R. (1990). Stress in organizations. In M. Dunnette and L. M. Hough (Eds.), *Handbook of industrial and organizational psychology: Vol. 3.* Palo Alto, CA: Consulting Psychologists Press.

Kahn, R. L.; Wolfe, D. M.; Quinn, R. P.; Snoek, D. J.; and Rosenthal, R. A. (1964). *Organizational stress: Studies in role conflict and ambiguity.* New York: John Wiley & Sons.

Kalleberg, A. L. (1977). Work values and job rewards: A theory of job satisfaction. *American Sociological Review, 42,* 124–143.

Kalleberg, A. L.; and Loscocco, K. A. (1983). Aging, values, and rewards: Explaining age differences in job satisfaction. *American Sociological Review, 48* (1), 78–90.

Kanungo, R. N. (1992). Measurement of job and work involvement. *Journal of Applied Psychology, 17* (3), 341–349.

Kashima, Y.; and Triandis, H. C. (1986). The self-serving bias in attributions as a coping strategy: A cross-cultural study. *Journal of Cross-Cultural Psychology, 17* (1), 83–97.

Kottkamp, R. F.; Provenzo, E. F.; and Cohn, M. M. (1986). Stability and change in a profession: Two decades of teacher attitudes, 1964–1984. *Phi Delta Kappan, 67,* 559–567.

Kounin, J. (1970). *Discipline and group management in classrooms.* New York: Holt, Rinehart and Winston.

Kyriacou, C.; and Sutcliffe, J. (1978). Teacher stress: Prevalence, sources and symptoms. *British Journal of Educational Psychology, 48* (2), 159–167.

Lampert, M. (1984). Teaching about thinking and thinking about teaching. *Journal of Curriculum Studies, 16* (1), 1–18.

Lawler, E. E.; and Hall, D. T. (1970). Relationship of job characteristics to job involvement, satisfaction, and intrinsic motivation. *Journal of Applied Psychology, 54* (4), 305–312.

Lazarus, R. S.; and Folkman, S. (1984). *Stress appraisal and coping.* New York: Singer.

Lightfoot, S. L. (1983). The lives of teachers. In Lee S. Shulman and G. Sykes (Eds.), *Handbook of teaching and policy.* New York: Longman.

Likert, R. (1961). *New patterns of management.* New York: McGraw-Hill.

Litt, M. D.; and Turk, D. C. (1985). Sources of stress and dissatisfaction in experienced high school teachers. *Journal of Educational Research, 78* (3), 178–185.

Locke, E. (1976). The nature and causes of job satisfaction. In M. Dunnette (Ed.), *Handbook of industrial and organizational psychology.* Chicago: Rand McNally College Publications.

Lodhal, T.; and Kejner, M. (1965). The definition and measurement of job involvement. *Journal of Applied Psychology, 49,* 24–33.

Lortie, D. (1975). *Schoolteacher: A sociological study.* Chicago: University of Chicago Press.

Maeroff, G. I. (1988). A blueprint for empowering teachers. *Phi Delta Kappan, 69* (7), 472–477.

Malen, B.; Owaga, R. T.; and Karnz, J. (1990). What do we know about school-based management? A case study of the literature—a call for research. In W. H. Clune and J. F. Witte (Eds.), *Choice and control in American education: Vol. 2. The practice of choice, decentralization, and school restructuring.* New York: Falmer.

Mannheim, B. (1975). A comparative study of work centrality, job rewards, and satisfaction. *Sociology of Work and Occupations, 2,* 79–101.

Mannheim, B. (1983). Male and female industrial workers: Job satisfaction work-role centrality, and workplace preference. *Work and Occupation, 10* (4), 314–436.

Mannheim, B.; and Cohen, A. (1978). Multivariate analysis of factors affecting work centrality of occupational categories. *Human Relations, 31,* 525–553.

Maslach, C.; and Pines, A. (1978). The burnout syndrome in the day-care setting. *Child Care Quarterly, 16* (2), 100–113.

Maslach, C.; and Pines, A. (1979). Burnout: The loss of human caring. In A. Pines and C. Maslach (Eds.), *Experiencing social psychology.* New York: Knopf.

Maslow, A. (1954). *Motivation and personality.* New York: Harper and Row.

Menlo, A. (1991). The centrality of work in teachers' lives in the United States. In A. Przlysz (Ed.), *Teachers' job satisfaction* (Bulletin 49 of series on Sociological Research on Educational Problems). Warsaw: University of Warsaw.

Menlo, A.; and Poppleton, P. (1990). A five country study of work perceptions of secondary school teachers in England, United States, Japan, Singapore, and West Germany. *Comparative Education, 26* (2–3), 173–182.

Metz, M. (1986). *Different by design: The context and character of three magnet schools.* London: Routledge and Kegan Paul.

Miskel, C. G.; Defrain, J. R.; and Wilcox, K. (1980). A test of expectancy motivation theory in education organizations. *Educational Administration Quarterly, 16* (1), 70–92.

Moore, R. (1990). Ethnographic assessment of pain coping perceptions. *Psychosomatic Medicine, 52* (2), 171–181.

MOW International Research Team. (1987). *The meaning of working.* Orlando, FL: Academic Press.

National Advisory Mental Health Council. (1995). *Basic behavioral science research for mental health: A national investment.* Washington, D.C.: U.S. Department of Health and Human Services.

Neave, G. (1992). *The teaching nation: Prospects for teachers in the European community.* Oxford: Pergamon Press.

Newmann, F. M.; Rutter, R. A.; and Smith, M. (1989). Organizational factors that affect schools' sense of efficacy, community and expectations. *Sociology of Education, 62* (4), 221–238.

Nias, J. (1981). Teacher satisfaction and dissatisfaction: Herzberg's two-factor hypothesis revisited. *British Journal of Sociology of Education, 2* (3), 235–246.

Organization for Economic Cooperation and Development (OECD). (1990). *The teacher today: Tasks, conditions, policies.* Paris: OECD.

Pajak, E.; and Blase, J. J. (1989). The impact of teachers' personal lives on professional role enactment: A qualitative analysis. *American Educational Research Journal, 26* (2), 283–291.

Pastor, M. C.; and Erlandson, D. A. (1982). A study of higher order need strength in secondary public school teachers. *Journal of Educational Administration, 20* (2), 172–183.

Poppleton, P. (1989). Rewards and values in secondary teachers' perceptions of their job satisfaction. *Research Papers in Education, 95* (4), 71–94.

Poppleton, P.; Gershunsky, B.; and Pullin, R. (1994). Changes in administrative control and teacher satisfaction in England and the U.S.S.R. *Comparative Education Review, 38* (3), 323–346.

Poppleton, P.; and Riseborough, G. F. (1990). Teaching in the mid-1980s: The centrality of work in secondary teachers' lives. *British Educational Research Journal, 16* (2), 105–124.

Prick, L. G. (1989). Satisfaction and stress among teachers. *International Journal of Educational Research, 13* (4), 363–377.

Reyes, P. (1990). *Teachers and their workplace: Commitment performance and productivity.* Newbury Park, CA: Sage.

Rosenholtz, S. J. (1987). Educational reform strategies: Will they increase teacher commitment? *American Journal of Education, 95* (4), 534–562.

Rosenholtz, S. J. (1989). *Teacher's workplace: The social organization of schools.* New York: Longman.

Rowan, B. (1990). Commitment and control: Alternative strategies for the organizational design of schools. In B. Cazden (Ed.), *Review of research in education: Vol. 16.* Washington, D.C.: American Educational Research Association.

Sauter, S.; Hurrell, J. J.; and Cooper, C. L. (1989). *Job control and worker health.* New York: John Wiley & Sons.

Schmitt, N.; and Pulakos, E. D. (1985). Predicting job satisfaction from life satisfaction: Is there a general satisfaction factor? *International Journal of Psychology, 20* (2), 155–167.

Schwab, R. L.; and Iwanicki, E. F. (1982). Perceived role conflict: Role ambiguity and teacher burnout. *Educational Administration Quarterly, 18* (1), 60–74.

Seashore, S. E.; and Taber, T. D. (1975). Job satisfaction indicators and their correlates. *American Behavioral Scientist, 18* (3), 333–368.

Sim, W. K. (1990). Factors associated with job satisfaction and work centrality among Singapore teachers. *Comparative Education, 26* (2–3), 259–276.

Smilansky, J. (1984). External and internal correlates of teachers' satisfaction and willingness to report stress. *British Journal of Educational Psychology, 54* (1), 84–92.

Smylie, M. A. (1992). Teachers participation in school decision making: Assessing willingness to participate. *Educational Evaluation and Policy Analysis, 14* (1), 53–67.

Sweeney, J. (1981). Professional discretion and teacher satisfaction. *High School Journal, 65* (1), 1–6.

Szalai, A.; and Andrews, F. M. (Eds.). (1980). *The quality of life: Comparative studies.* Beverly Hills, CA: Sage.

Vroom, V. H. (1964). *Work and motivation.* New York: John Wiley & Sons.

Wanous, J.; and Lawler, E. E. (1972) Measurement and meaning of job satisfaction. *Journal of Applied Psychology, 56* (2), 95–105.

Yee, S. M. (1990). *Careers in the classroom.* New York: Teachers College Press.

4

The Teacher's Roles and Responsibilities

Pam Poppleton

Secondary school teachers differ in the roles they occupy and the responsibilities they are asked to shoulder in addition to their work in the classroom. These activities are often distinguished by teachers from the "real" work of teaching, in the accounts they have given to researchers of the Consortium for Cross-Cultural Research in Education. The teachers involved in the study reside in the United States (Michigan), the United Kingdom (Northern England), Germany (Hesse), Japan, Singapore, the former Soviet Union, Poland, Israel, and Canada (Ontario). The eighteen items selected for this section are mainly concerned with activities carried on *outside* the classroom, those having to do with community and professional relationships, activities related to the teacher's own professional development, administrative responsibilities, the general welfare and academic progress of students, and the supervision and training of new entrants. These activities were selected in order to explore the degree to which they were regarded as legitimate aspects of teachers' work.

In the process of searching for the meaning of teaching, this chapter asks, How have the activities of teaching contributed to job satisfaction or to what extent have they produced stress; to what degree are they seen as central to the quality of their working lives and what difference does it make to be a man or a woman, married or single, young or old? How do the teachers mark out the teaching career and relate to the quality of teaching itself?

This chapter will first establish concepts and meanings relating to the *range of roles* that teachers occupy, the *extent of the responsibilities* they undertake, and the extent of *specialization* in the schools of the nine countries involved.

These will later serve as a contextual framework for the analysis of the data and discussion of the results. Second, comparisons are reported, both within and between countries, of teachers' ratings—these ratings measure the extent of their involvement in each of the eighteen activities and its importance to their job satisfaction. Measures of *overall role involvement* show the extent of differences between countries, and additional measures based on the *five role indexes* derived from the raw data are also compared. The contributions of the three demographic indicators—gender, age, and marital status—are examined with respect to country of origin. Third, the results of multiple regressions carried out for each country are reported, using all of these measures as independent variables to predict *overall job satisfaction, work centrality,* and *job-related stress.* Finally, the results are summarized and discussed in the context of the conceptual framework introduced earlier. The phenomena of *responsibility enlargement, extended versus restricted professionality,* and the *specialization* of the teachers' work are considered in an international context. Some tentative conclusions are drawn about the implications for the roles and responsibilities of teachers and schools in today's changing society.

CONCEPTS AND MEANINGS

The concept of *role* enjoyed great popularity during the 1950s and 1960s on the grounds that it offered "an effective means by which teacher behavior can be described, particularly as it interacts with context" (Rosencrantz & Biddle, 1963). However, neglect of context was one reason why many role studies failed to carry conviction and why interest switched to exploring the effects of contexts themselves—in classrooms, schools, communities, and states. One of the important components of context is the degree of differentiation that a system provides in delegating responsibilities in relation to the teacher's adaptability and exercise of choice. This section will consider how teachers' responsibilities are allocated between the administrative, relationship, and professional functions, in addition to the instructional one, to define the roles that they undertake in the schools of each country.

In recent years, demands on teachers have changed in accordance with the appearance of new technologies for communication and instructional purposes. These, together with the impact of social changes on the schools, have affected the balance between the role elements. The effects have been described as *responsibility enlargement* by Neave (1992)—a process of acquisition, either by intention or stealth, of new responsibilities that may occur in the curricular domain (e.g., developments in instructional technology or prevocational courses); the administrative domain (e.g., timetabling, record keeping, supervision of new teachers); or the psychosocial domain (e.g., provision of counseling and guidance or fostering links with parents and the community).

It is the last area in which Neave (1992) drew particular attention to responsibility enlargement as a phenomenon in which "schools or other institutions take over functions that were formerly the responsibility of the 'at risk' family." Thus "the rise of remedial specialists, guidance counselors, careers advisers, reflect the fact that, at a time of the rapid restructuring of society, the knowledge possessed by the preceding generation is not adequate, or even relevant to, the circumstances faced by its children." By referring to the "at risk" family, however, Neave indicates that the additional responsibilities are not confined to remedying knowledge deficit but also, in some measure, to supplementing the parental role, and that in the absence of specialists, teachers may be required to take on tasks for which they have not been adequately trained or for which they may not possess the interest or aptitude. Each enlargement would normally be added onto the teacher's ordinary work and finally come to be incorporated into the professional role.

The teacher's response to such opportunities is not always predictable. While some are content (indeed anxious) to limit their work to classroom instruction, others are eager to look outside the classroom to extend their contacts with parents and the school community as well as their contacts with colleagues in other schools and the profession in general. These two aspects of the individual teacher's general orientation towards work has been described by Hoyle (1980) in terms of *restricted* or *extended* professionality. Hoyle presented his typology as an empirically untested, heuristic device based on various educational and sociological sources, and described it as follows.

Restricted professionality is "intuitive, classroom-focused, and based on experience rather than theory. The good restricted professional is sensitive to the development of individual pupils, an inventive teacher and a skillful class manager. He is unencumbered with theory, is not given to comparing his work with that of others, tends not to perceive classroom activities in a broader context, and values his classroom autonomy."

Extended professionality produces a teacher who is "concerned with locating his classroom teaching in a broader educational context, comparing his work with that of other teachers, evaluating his own work systematically, and collaborating with other teachers. . . . He reads educational books and journals, becomes involved in various professional activities and is concerned to further his own professional development through in-service work. He sees teaching as a rational activity amenable to improvement on the basis of research and development."

Hoyle goes on to ask if restricted and extended professionality are fundamentally different perspectives, and, in view of the deprofessionalization debate, whether any policy of extending teacher professionality could lead to a loss of job satisfaction and perhaps of teaching skill? Insofar as we can identify restricted and extended perspectives either within or between countries, we should be able to say something about what each means for teachers in terms of their job satisfaction, work centrality, and job-related stress.

Role restriction tendencies are relevant to the extent of *specialization in a school* and can have a number of origins. Secondary and High school teachers are prone to think of themselves as "subject matter specialists and that their social ties are primarily to their departments rather than to the school as a whole environment" (Bryk & Frank, 1989). In principle at least, "This specialization serves to enhance the work of teachers by fostering professional interactions around subject matter and related pedagogic considerations" (e.g., administrative responsibilities to do with such matters as the organization of the curriculum, record keeping, new teacher training, and the supervision of student teachers among others). They add that state-run comprehensive schools, which are the subject of the present study, often offer opportunities for specialization via a wide internal course market and a high degree of freedom of choice, but we should remember that, equally often, freedom of choice does not extend to the teacher.

For teachers, life in secondary schools is the outcome of "jockeying for position within the informal hierarchy of each department as well as vying for the rewards that accrue to those who make their way up the career ladder in the formal hierarchy of the school" (Liebermann & Miller, 1992). These two hierarchies represent respectively, the teacher's general orientation toward work and the responsibilities attached to positions in the organizational system. Between them lie "positions that are not quite administrative and not quite teaching in nature," including, in the American high school, "guidance counselors, nurses, social workers, student activities directors, consultants, security guards and custodians." It is in this no-man's land that the elements of the teacher's role are often negotiated in circumstances where resource provision is inadequate to provide for specialist services.

The differences between the nine countries included in the study are unlikely to be clear-cut, and they may be arise from either system or cultural–historical factors. Different contexts may give rise to variations in job satisfaction and job-related stress. The teachers may also vary in their degree of work commitment and work centrality (see Chapter 3). Analyzing these factors in an international context will help to identify the relevant factors that are most likely to respond to policy initiatives and those that are most deeply embedded in the cultures of schooling.

RESEARCH QUESTIONS

The questions to be asked were

1. How do teachers in each of the nine countries differ in the breadth or narrowness of their roles and responsibilities overall?
2. Are there any specific areas of work in which teachers in each of nine countries show similarities and differences in the nature of the work done and in its importance to job satisfaction?
3. What is the nature and significance of the extent and direction of the gap between a teacher's involvement in a work activity and its importance to overall job satisfaction?

4. How large is the contribution of the demographic variables of gender, age, and marital status to these findings?

5. How do the findings relate to the theoretical concepts of responsibility enlargement, professionality, and specialization in determining the nature and management of the teacher's work?

6. To what extent do the findings advance our understanding of the teacher's role in an international context?

METHODOLOGY

The general methodology of the study is described in Chapter 1. The main research instrument used was a structured self-completion questionnaire devised by the American and English research teams and thoroughly piloted in each participating country. We pay special attention here to the problems of measurement relevant to the study of roles and responsibilities.

Items and Indexes

Figure 4.1 shows the eighteen items in the questionnaire representing the roles performed and responsibilities held. These roles and responsibilities were grouped into five indexes formed on the basis of consensus between researchers about which items belonged together. Teachers in each of the nine countries endorsed each item by rating it according to the extent they actually performed the activity represented (amount) and the extent to which they considered it to be important for their job satisfaction (importance). Ratings were made on a three-point scale representing for amount (3) a lot; (2) to some extent; and (1) little. For importance, subjects rated items as (3) very important; (2) to some extent; and (1) of little importance. Averaging items gave a score for each of the indexes and a total score indicating a teacher's total role involvement. In each case, a high degree of emphasis was assigned the score of 3. Arithmetic means for each subset of items were calculated and transformed into standardized t-scores on the same scale (mean = 50, standard deviation = 10), so that within- and between-country comparisons could be made on all items and indexes.

Issues

A word should be said about the *incongruity* between the extent to which people are engaged in an activity and the extent to which they value it. An incongruity index was constructed from the size of the gap between the ratings of a variable's importance to job satisfaction and the degree to which teachers perceived it to be present. Where the former exceeds the latter, it indicates that performance does not, and probably never will, rise to the level of the value attached to it, and so workload and effort will be under constant

Figure 4.1
Conceptual Schema for the Roles and Responsibilities Section of the Overall Study

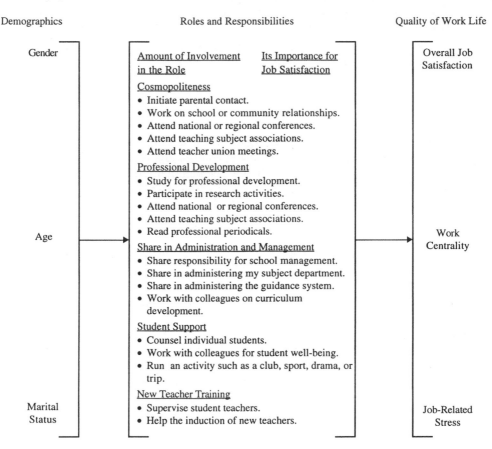

Demographics   Roles and Responsibilities   Quality of Work Life

Gender

Amount of Involvement   Its Importance for
in the Role   Job Satisfaction

Cosmopoliteness
• Initiate parental contact.
• Work on school or community relationships.
• Attend national or regional conferences.
• Attend teaching subject associations.
• Attend teacher union meetings.

Professional Development
• Study for professional development.
• Participate in research activities.
• Attend national or regional conferences.
• Attend teaching subject associations.
• Read professional periodicals.

Share in Administration and Management
• Share responsibility for school management.
• Share in administering my subject department.
• Share in administering the guidance system.
• Work with colleagues on curriculum development.

Student Support
• Counsel individual students.
• Work with colleagues for student well-being.
• Run an activity such as a club, sport, drama, or trip.

New Teacher Training
• Supervise student teachers.
• Help the induction of new teachers.

Age

Marital Status

Overall Job Satisfaction

Work Centrality

Job-Related Stress

pressure to increase so as to narrow the gap (Wall & Payne, 1973). This is often referred to as the "deprivation effect." When the level of performance exceeds the level of importance, however, it is referred to as the "satiation effect," and one must look for extrinsic factors that are usually outside the individual's control. Although teachers will normally choose to direct the extra effort into those things which matter most to them (professional, administrative, or affective), the tendency to collect a "ragbag" of responsibilities is one element of the *intensification* of teaching (Apple, 1986).

The incongruity index is a variant of the deficiency score in investigating the relationship between job satisfaction, the facet variables that may be influenced by the way in which questions are phrased (Wanous & Lawlor, 1972), and the tendency for all respondents to rate every facet of a job of equal importance (Evans, 1969). The importance measure may also suffer from restriction of range or be contained within the satisfaction ratings (Kalleberg, 1977). These are not theoretical questions, since the success of job enrichment programs depends on the meanings that people attribute to the work situation. Kalleberg offered a model of job satisfaction in which the central factor was the "fit" between work values and job rewards, which was applied to a prior analysis of the data from five of the countries (Poppleton, 1989).

Linguistic and Conceptual Equivalence

The items presented to each sample of teachers were identical in each country, as far as could be achieved by careful translation and back translation, but linguistic equivalence does not necessarily imply conceptual equivalence (Broadfoot & Osborn, 1992), and, in spite of extensive pilot testing, there was no way of eliminating ambiguity of response to the questionnaire items that referred to counseling, guidance, or pupil welfare. For example, there is evidence that some Soviet and Japanese teachers interpreted giving individual counseling and guidance as "giving coaching." Others may have checked any item that involved them in one-to-one relationships with students. Similar ambiguities arose over the item "participate in research activities," since research activities could vary from working on an independent research project to a relatively small dissertation. However, all are role-enlargement tendencies that broaden job scope and, almost inevitably, increase workloads. All have implications for the provision of specialist training. It may be added that differences of interpretation between countries provided additional insights, and having the Consortium members as a source of help was invaluable.

Biased Ratings and Response Sets

Adams's (1970) technique of estimating bias consists of placing the mean scores for each item in rank order within each country to indicate the possible presence of a persistent country tendency. We were fortunate to have the raw data from the earlier analysis, which enabled this procedure to be used for six out of the nine countries (Poppleton, 1990). In addition, the same data had been standardized to produce a common scale and a more even distribution of responses within countries. Comparisons between the two sets of raw and transformed data could then be used to indicate whether any evidence of a persistent country bias had been eradicated by the standardization process.

The dimensions of extent of role involvement and its importance to job satisfaction were treated separately. Identifying the highest ranking country for each item in the amount dimension gave, for the 1990 data, a total of 8 items rated highest by teachers in the United States; 3 by Japanese teachers; and 7 by those in the Soviet Union (out of a total of 18). In the importance dimension, Japan rated 11, and the Soviet Union, 7. These are quite impres-

sive indications of some kind of country-determined response sets, whether
or not they are cultural in origin. They may now be compared with the more
recent standardized mean scores for the same items. From these scores, which
have been standardized to a mean of 50 and a standard deviation of 10 within
each country, it is again possible to pick out the country with the highest
mean on each item. In the amount dimension, Japan has 4 and England has 4,
while Canada, Poland, and Israel have 3 each, the United States and Singapore
have 1 each, and the Soviet Union has none. High scores in the importance
dimension are similarly distributed across countries, so that the net effect of
the standardization process has been to greatly reduce the effect of response
"set" from whatever cause and to encourage greater confidence that any differences revealed between countries will be meaningful. Unfortunately, it may
also have removed some of the most important cultural influences, which
make comparative study so interesting and important. For example, Japan's
overwhelming dominance of the original importance ratings may be referred
to the well-known importance of "busyness" in the Japanese culture. Kudomi
(1992) quotes surveys of teachers' work in Japan, which indicate the extreme
busyness of teachers while Ninomiya and Okato (1990) observe that "in Japan we have a culture wherein we exchange in our daily lives a conversation
like this: 'How are you? Are you busy?' 'Yes, fortunately, very busy.' 'That's
good. Take care!'"

It will be clear that there is no absolute measure of breadth of role and that
it can only have meaning in the context of an international study by comparing the mean ratings of amount in each case. It is assumed that, if respondents
said that they undertook each activity "a lot," then their total scores in each of
the amount and importance dimensions would vary accordingly.

Comparisons between countries could, therefore, be made in two ways: (1)
by comparing the relative standing of the indexes within countries, and (2) by
analysis of variance between the total scores of all the countries. Also, on the
basis of correlations between variables, it was possible to use multiple regression techniques to examine the relative contributions made to the teacher's
work satisfaction, work centrality, and job-related stress, by the role indexes
together with the demographic factors of gender, age, and marital status. The
regression procedures are described in Chapter 7.

Interviews

It has to be admitted that, while a large scale survey yields some interesting
comparative data, it is not able to probe the meaning of teaching to those
individuals employed in it. One way of correcting possible biases and deep-
ening our understanding of the teacher's working life is to elicit first-hand
accounts from a representative sample of the teachers with whom we are
concerned. This requires conducting in-depth interviews with a much smaller
number of teachers, which will complement the survey data. Such interviews

were undertaken by research teams in the United States, the United Kingdom, Poland, Singapore, and Germany. A separate study showed them to have construct validity in representing teacher groups (or types) that were included in the surveys. Extracts from the interviews will be given, where appropriate, from those available to the author.

RESULTS

Between-Country Comparisons in Overall Role Involvement

Figure 4.2 shows the overall role involvement and role importance by country, above or below the nine-country means for each dimension, transformed into t-deviations around a mean of zero with a standard deviation of ten.

The first point to note is the considerable variation in the amount dimension (breadth of role) between countries, which appear to fall into three groups: (1) those that were above average and differed significantly from all others (Soviet Union and Poland); (2) those that did not differ significantly from the overall mean but differed from each other (Canada, United States, and Israel differed significantly from England and Japan); and (3) those (Germany and Singapore) that were significantly below average and differed from all the rest. If amount done equates with degree of overall role involvement, then the

Figure 4.2
T Deviations of Country Raw-Score Means for Role Amount and Importance from the Corresponding Nine-Country Means

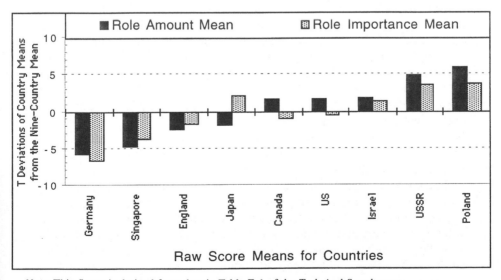

Note: This figure is derived from data in Table E-1 of the *Technical Supplement*.

Polish and the Soviet teachers would appear to have the greatest comparative role involvement, and German and Singaporean teachers, the least.

The importance dimension follows a similar pattern, the amount of role involvement tending to exceed the importance of the satisfaction derived from it. Only the Japanese teachers (being busy) perceived the importance of the total role involvement significantly to exceed role occupancy.

Finally, remembering that these are comparative rather than absolute measures, most of the differences between overall amount and importance are small and superficial. The general tendency for the extent of role involvement to exceed the value placed upon it is a satiation condition, which implies that a considerable part of the role set may be accounted for by roles and responsibilities acquired through delegation rather than desire. This was the case in all countries except Japan, where roles and responsibilities were regarded as significantly more important than opportunities seemed to allow—a deprivation condition, suggesting the influence of strong cultural values. Are these relationships repeated by relative standings on the indexes?

Within-Country Profiles

Figures 4.3 and 4.4 show the within-country profiles that will be presented under the headings of the five indexes by the mean scores derived, on this occasion, from within-country standardization procedures. In this analysis, the items were grouped subjectively into the five indexes shown in Figure 4.1 and described (from left to right) as *involvement in teacher training, cosmopoliteness, professional development, sharing in management,* and *giving student support.* The bar charts should be read vertically to show the relative standing of the indexes in each country and horizontally to make visual comparisons between country profiles. As before, score differences in either direction must be three or more in order to be regarded as statistically significant.

Both visual inspection and statistical test show that in Germany, the United States, and Canada, teachers were significantly more involved in student support activities than in those represented by the remaining indexes. Shared management activities were accorded the highest status by teachers in England on both dimensions, while in other countries they generally take second place. In Israel and Poland, professional development has a more prominent place. The activities included in each index will be described and discussed in the order of priority shown from right to left in the figures.

Student Support. Involvement in student support activities and perceptions of their importance stand above the dimension means in all countries. The contributory items to do with counseling individuals, working on the well-being of students, and running extracurricular activities may be associated with the student's academic work, career development, or personal–pastoral guidance. Teachers could, therefore, obtain a similar score for different reasons. Canadian teachers were outstanding in this area, while in Japan teach-

Figure 4.3
Profiles of Role Amount Index Means for Each Country

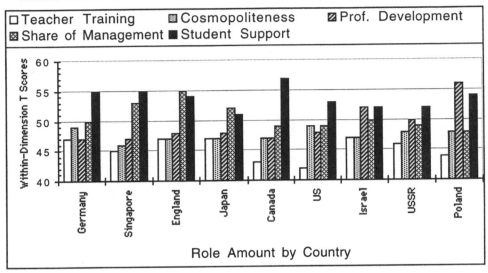

Note: This figure is derived from data in Table E-2 of the *Technical Supplement*.

Figure 4.4
Profiles of Role Importance Index Means for Each Country

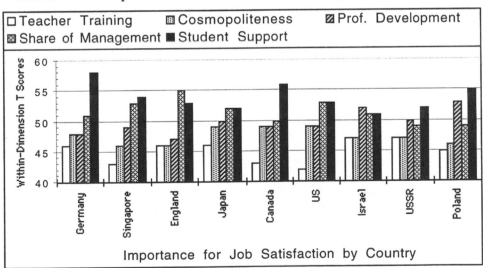

Note: This figure is derived from data in Table E-3 of the *Technical Supplement*.

ers allocated low ratings to some aspects of student support relative to other activities (though not significantly so).

Inspection of the individual items shows that teachers in Israel and the Soviet Union undertook few extracurricular activities—these tended to be conducted by agencies outside the schools. Japanese teachers paid little attention to counseling or fostering the well-being of students. The Canadian teachers had the highest t-score means of any country in all three areas. They were significantly more involved in out-of-school activities, promoting the well-being of students and evaluating their progress than others, while in Germany emphasis was on counseling in the sense of vocational counseling, and in England and Singapore, working with colleagues on the well-being of students took precedence. Poland had a number of item endorsements at or slightly above the country mean.

A great deal depends on whether the activities involved are rewarded or not. This could take the form of extra pay or a promotion, or may simply be regarded as part and parcel of the teacher's professional commitment which carries its own reward. There are no indications in the questionnaire data about this, though all were regarded as being important to job satisfaction, and it is known that the presence and type of reward varies from country to country. Undertaking other activities of an extracurricular nature is a case in point. In England, it has been regarded as part and parcel of the teacher's professional commitment, undertaken largely for career reasons. At the time of the survey, this was a key issue in a certain industrial dispute, and many teachers were refusing to cooperate in this area—regarding it as a case of unwelcome responsibility enlargement and confirming the sensitivity of the index. In the United States and the Soviet Union, teachers could choose to run extracurricular activities and were able to do so as a means of supplementing their salaries. There was also evidence of the broadening of the teacher's social role from the endorsement of the pastoral, guidance, and counseling items. An English teacher's point of view was vividly expressed in the following interview, illustrating what responsibility enlargement means to the average English teacher:

I think that the role that we're expected to play is increasing and it concerns me sometimes that we are taking the parent's role . . . not by choice. Not only do we provide the teaching but there's all this huge social role as well. The family as a unit is just disintegrating . . . and because it is disintegrating our roles have widened considerably, otherwise you wouldn't need pastoral year heads and so on. Parents are just not being responsible for their kids in the same way as they were 20 years ago.

An American teacher said, "We cannot be responsible for moral and ethical values. They should be learned at home." Teachers in both England and the United States emphasized in interviews how the public expected teachers to solve all the additional expectations placed on them and how this was leading to frustration and stress.

Sharing in Management. This index brings together four items to do with responsibility for administration at school level, department level, in the guidance system, and in curriculum development. Similar translation problems occurred in choosing terms that accurately described what appeared to be the same processes (e.g., counseling, consultation, guidance, pastoral care, or pupil welfare). The nature of each function was indicated by representing it in terms that would convey the same meaning as closely as possible in another language.

Figures 4.3 and 4.4 show that this group of activities is strongly related to the previous index through administrative roles that strengthen and administer student support and that vary between countries in a similar manner. English teachers gave such activities equal importance in regards to both the amount done and its importance to job satisfaction, and the highest priority, scoring significantly above the country mean in each dimension on involvement in school and subject department management as well as curriculum development. They were significantly more involved than their American colleagues, for whom the importance mean score was significantly higher than that for the amount done. Singaporeans also saw administration mainly in terms of the subject department, so the evidence shows a high emphasis on the subject-related concerns that they engaged in to a greater extent than teachers in any other country. Teachers in Germany, the United States, Canada, and Poland did not have such a strong administrative role since there is a separate class of administrators, but higher emphasis was shown by the Japanese teachers who were mainly involved in giving academic guidance and in school management.[1] Generally, across countries, the data supports the view expressed earlier that "high school teachers perceive themselves as subject matter specialists and that their social ties are primarily to their departments" (Bryk & Frank, 1989). Here is one type of "career" teacher, but there are others: "There's various routes on my career map—I don't know which one I'll follow. There's the obvious one to a Head of Department. . . . I also like the thought of moving away . . . into the advisory service, into the Education Offices—that's another avenue which is over there in the distance."

Clearly, some form of administrative activity is present in the career map of some teachers, even though it may be accepted by the majority as a chore to be completed as quickly as possible and an unwanted diversion from the "real" job of teaching. It is necessary to distinguish between management activities and routine administrative tasks. Marich and Swift (1987) found that administrative responsibilities were a strong source of discouragement to teachers in the United States, England, and Germany. An American teacher commented, "We are always filling out forms and collecting data, but we never see meaningful results." But the Michigan research team found also that the roles in which their teachers were most involved and from which they gained greatest satisfaction were curriculum development, the evaluation of students' progress, and fostering the well-being of students.

Professional Development. Professional development activities are normally central to career development. One would expect a great deal of attendance at in-service courses, conferences, and subject-association meetings to be undertaken in connection with study and research for professional development. Were such courses promoted more highly in some countries than in others?

Attendance at in-service courses was compulsory at different points in the Polish teacher's career, reflected in the high-priority ratings, higher than any other country. It might be expected that countries which find themselves in the throes of technological or social change will offer their teachers greater incentives to adopt new methods and techniques; similarly, the teachers will be more highly motivated to engage in them. A significantly higher proportion of Polish, Israeli, and Soviet teachers also claimed to read professional periodicals and attend national or regional conferences. Japanese and Singaporean teachers were below average in these respects, but the Japanese claimed to participate in research activities more than others. It was not always clear what teachers meant by "research activities," but, whatever form it took, it was not a popular activity in any country; a finding which has important practical implications in relation to the efforts of academics who would wish to see every teacher becoming a teacher–researcher.

There was a tendency for all teachers to rate professional development significantly more important for their job satisfaction than for their actual involvement especially in Canada and Singapore, but ratings on this area of activity were uniformly low, for whatever reason. This cluster of activities is related more to "extended" than "restricted" professionality, an example being the following.

It's difficult to keep up with how your subject's changing. I take one or two journals which I read and pick up ideas from . . . and different ways of putting over ideas, different types of equipment. I'd go on any course I thought was going to be interesting, not necessarily useful, but if I thought I could gain something. . . . *We're a learning profession aren't we?* . . . I would certainly like to go on a more specialized teaching course.

The low level of interest shown in aspects of professional development reflects what Lortie (1975) called the "presentism" of the teaching profession. Generally, however, it is interesting to note that professional development appears to be a less highly valued activity in Western countries than in countries which have been slower to develop economically and have a different political culture.

Cosmopoliteness. The cosmopoliteness index represents the extent to which the teachers are sensitive to external influences through their ratings of the extent of their involvement in initiating parental contacts, the supervision of student teaching, and attendance at conferences, subject association meetings, and teacher union meetings. This index has some overlap with professional development in sharing the "attendance" items. It is not surprising therefore, that there is a high correlation between them and a strong similarity of profile.

Figure 4.3 shows that the general level of involvement was low. Teachers in the United States, Germany, and Japan were rather more likely to be aware of the world outside the classroom than their colleagues elsewhere, particularly in Canada. American teachers claimed the making of parental contacts to be part of their job. Attendance at conferences and meetings generally was claimed as important by Polish teachers, but these activities were generally regarded with apathy in countries at the other end of the scale. Sim (1990) pointed out that Singaporean teachers hardly attended such meetings. German teachers were also reluctant to attend professional meetings and were little involved in community contacts and activities in a system where they needed to be in school only when they were teaching. In regard to union meetings, however, Lissmann and Gigerich (1990) commented that "to attend teacher union meetings is more important for German colleagues than to engage in research activities or attend conferences for cultural enrichment." In England, making parental contacts would generally be tasks that belong to the area of responsibility enlargement and would normally be restricted to the more senior members of staff. There are a number of factors that contribute to this index and vary between countries.

The truly "cosmopolite" teacher would be an extended professional. One such English teacher commented, "I didn't come into teaching just to teach; to me it's everything to do with the school and I want to be involved with pupils not only in lessons, but outside . . . I like the social aspects, the pastoral aspects and find myself in a dilemma. I think they should be part of my role but that I should be sufficiently recompensed for doing them (Poppleton & Riseborough, 1990).[2]

It seems that this is an aspect of the teacher's work life that is generally judged in terms of its incentive power as much as for personal satisfaction— the "hedonism of the future" rather than the "hedonism of the past" (Wanous & Lawlor, 1972).

New Teacher Training. The items making up this index represent part of what has been thought to be the hallmark of professionalism—the training of new teachers. They are items five and six: "Am involved in the supervision of student teachers" and "Am involved in the induction of new teachers." They are the lowest rated activities of all, particularly in Canada and the United States. Teachers reported few responsibilities in this area and either regarded it with general apathy or did not have any opportunity for participating in training activities.

Generally the ratings of importance on this index exceed those of presence only in the Soviet Union and Poland. In other words, most teachers in these countries play their part in this aspect of professional responsibility up to the extent required but do not see it as particularly important to their job satisfaction. An English assistant head teacher commented, "When we know we are getting a student, basically, we know we are fulfilling a professional obligation to give people the opportunity to learn the trade in the classroom. But I wouldn't say we devote a lot of time to considering how to develop them on-site because, to be honest, there's not enough in it for us."

The training of future generations of skilled workers has been regarded as one of the hallmarks of professionalism, but the sad reality is that few teachers regard it as a rewarding activity except in terms of promotion for a few. Yet "quality teaching" has been a major theme of the late 1980s and early 1990s, with an emphasis on exploring new ways of coordinating the work of the schools and the training institutions in more effective ways. Though some countries have invested comparatively greater resources in teacher training at all levels, there is still a long way to go. Since the survey, new teacher training in England and Wales has undergone some radical changes, with a higher proportion of training taking place in the schools and a much more organized system in place, in which teachers work in partnership with training institutions.

Profiles Based on the Rank Order of Indexes

Table 4.1 shows that, when the indexes are placed in rank order of their t-scores within countries, there is remarkable unanimity across countries as to where the priorities lie both in the nature of role involvement and its importance to job satisfaction. Profiles for the United States, England, Germany, Singapore, and Canada on the two indexes, shared management and student support, are practically identical. In fact, involvement in the activities contributing to student support are given the highest priority in seven out of the nine countries, the pattern being broken only by Japan (which places shared management first) and Poland (which gives highest priority to professional development). At the bottom end, involvement in teacher training is ranked lowest of the indexes by all countries with the exception of Canada.

The relative standing of countries on cosmopoliteness and professional development was generally shared between third and fourth positions. If we are looking for universal characteristics of the teacher culture, this profile similarity should be a candidate. But it is worth remembering that, because of the ipsative nature of the scales produced by the standardization technique, a compensation factor is operating, which ensures that some indexes will be ranked above the overall mean and others below to an equal, but opposite, amount. However, the data suggest that if there is any broadening of the role set, it occurs in two areas and is based on the activities of management and student support. These two areas offer plenty of scope for responsibility enlargement through a variety of roles and are most evident in Germany, England, the United States, Canada, and Singapore.

In summary, between-country comparisons identified two countries that appear below the nine-country mean on almost all the indexes (Singapore and Germany), with the high end fluctuating between Poland, Israel, and the Soviet Union. These are significant differences both statistically and educationally. The group in the middle shifts about somewhat more; it included the

Table 4.1
Rank Order of Role Amount and Role Importance Indexes within Countries

COUNTRY	Student Support	Share of Management	Professional Development	Cosmopoliteness	Teacher Training
US	1 (1)	2 (2)	4 (3)	3 (4)	5 (5)
England	1 (2)	2 (1)	3 (3)	4 (4)	5 (5)
Germany	1 (1)	2 (2)	3 (4)	4 (3)	5 (5)
Japan	2 (2)	1 (1)	4 (3)	3 (4)	5 (5)
Singapore	1 (2)	2 (2)	4 (3)	3 (4)	5 (5)
Canada	1 (1)	2 (2)	5 (3)	3 (4)	4 (5)
Poland	2 (2)	4 (3)	1 (1)	3 (4)	5 (5)
Israel	1 (2)	3 (3)	2 (2)	4 (5)	5 (5)
USSR	1 (1)	3 (3)	2 (4)	4 (5)	5 (5)

Note: This table is derived from Table E-2 of the *Technical Supplement*. Cell entries are in this order: amount (importance).

United States, England, Japan, and Canada. But within-country analyses show some remarkable examples of consensus between teachers on the strength and attractions of department administrative responsibilities that have to do with student support in countries influenced by Western thought and practices, and of professional development priorities in those countries open to Eastern European influences. Consensus is also observable on the lack of importance attached to involvement in professional training, undertaking research (whatever that may mean), or in getting involved in the "outside" world.

Overall Role Involvement and the Quality of the Working Life

It is instructive to compare the relative positions of the teachers in their total role involvement between countries with their relative positions on the quality of work life variables described in Chapter 3 (see Table 4.2). Where t-scores were practically the same, two countries are shown. Comparisons show that the countries at either extreme above and below the nine-country mean (Canada and England) reverse their positions on the job satisfaction and work centrality–stress measures. These two countries do not appear at the extremes on role involvement, being replaced by Poland and the Soviet Union at the high end and Germany and Singapore at the low. Thus, the correlation between overall role involvement and the quality of working life represented by the three criterion measures is low or around zero. We may note also that there appears to be a negative correlation between job satisfaction on the one hand, and both work centrality and job stress on the other.

Table 4.2
The Relative Positions of Countries in Two Domains: Quality of Work Life and
Overall Role Involvement

INDEX	High T Scores	Low T Scores
Overall Job Satisfaction	Canada	England and Japan (tie)
Work Centrality	England and Israel (tie)	Canada and Germany (tie)
Job-Related Stress	Japan and England (tie)	Israel and Canada (tie)
Overall Role Involvement	Poland and USSR (tie)	Germany and Singapore (tie)

The Influence of Demographic Characteristics

Would these relationships hold if the teachers' demographic characteristics
were taken into account? The three demographic indicators selected for this study
were gender, age, and marital status. We now examine the part that these variables may have played in producing within- and between-country differences.

Gender. Although each of the national samples was shown to be representative of the respective populations, Marlin and Biddle (1970) noted that raw
national results tend to be affected by any imbalance in the sex ratio between
countries. To take a hypothetical example, suppose that the teaching profession in a country is 100-percent male or 100-percent female; there would be
little point in looking for gender differences in response. Generally, the greater
the imbalance, the more the responses will tend to reflect the composition of
the teaching force. In our case, 82 and 75 percent of teachers in the Soviet
Union and Poland, respectively, were female, so gender comparisons have
little meaning for these countries. The female proportions in the remaining
countries varied between 23 (Japan) and 68 (Singapore) percent. Only in the
United States and England did the proportions approach the 50-percent level.

That said, statistically significant gender differences in roles and responsibilities were hard to find. Out of a total of 90 comparisons in both the amount
and importance dimensions, only 10 were located, and of these, 5 involved
single countries. The most striking finding occurred in the area of shared
management, where 4 out of the 9 countries showed male teachers to have
been more involved in administrative functions than their female colleagues
at levels of statistical significance. The Soviet Union was a striking exception, reflecting the gender composition noted.

Table 4.3 sheds further light on the significance of gender differences by breaking
down the index into its three components: involvement in school, subject department, and guidance system administration. An analysis of the relative proportions of men and women exercising these functions compared with their relative
proportions in each country's total sample was carried out in a prior analysis of
the data from six countries (Poppleton, 1992). The results of the countries, for
which the data was available at that time, are shown in Table 4.3.

Table 4.3
Percentage of Men and Women Teachers "Very Involved" in Sharing Responsibility for Administration, by Country

Country	N	%Female	Whole School		Guidance System		Subject Department	
			M	F	M	F	M	F
US	888	43	10	9	8	13	47	49
England	686	45	18	6**	23	22	54	35**
Germany	694	36	15	4***	14	10*	38	25**
Japan	1308	23	16	8***	23	20	15	11
Singapore	930	68	11	4***	16	22	36	31
USSR	1208	82	13	24***	18	44***	24	28

Key: *Significance level (Chi-Square) equal to or less than 0.050; **Significance level (Chi-Square) equal to or less than 0.010; ***Significance level (Chi-Square) equal to or less than 0.001.

The first and second columns show the total sample numbers and the percentage of women teachers in each country. Subsequent columns show the percentages of men and women respectively whose responses indicated that they were "very involved" in each of the three areas. These two sets of figures were compared using the chi-squared test for categorized data on the hypothesis that the proportions of the two sexes claiming they were very involved would not differ significantly from those in the total sample. It can be seen that

• There was general underrepresentation of women in subject-department management especially in Germany and England.
• Moving to the guidance system, there was less gender discrimination, except for the Soviet Union where 82 percent of the sample were female anyway.
• Moving to whole school management, the proportion of women involved falls steadily, and highly significant gender differences favoring men are found, with the exception of the United States, where it is a function of administrators, teachers generally having little role.

Responsibilities in the latter two areas tend to reflect the teachers' ages and years of teaching experience, so that the progression described may be a function of seniority and career development as much as gender. Nevertheless, taking into account all these factors, it is difficult to avoid the conclusion that secondary school management and administration in the late 1980s was seen predominantly as a male job and valued by males as integral to the career ladder. On the other hand, guidance roles tend to be seen as female territory, stereotypically identified with "caring." Ball (1987) has pointed out that "what is being indicated is that women can only achieve senior positions when a specially reserved role is carved out for them." This does not appear to have been the case in the United States, however.

Age. Confirming the previous findings on gender, the data show the trends and significant differences of roles by age categories. In particular, the data show that student support activities tended to be a function of relative youth, being highest in the below-35 age range in the United States, England, and Canada, three countries in which career building starts early. The older and more experienced one becomes, the greater the responsibilities acquired, and so shared management activities tends to increase steadily with age in England, Japan, Singapore, Poland, and the Soviet Union. The same upward trends with age are to be observed in the case of all the other indexes. Involvement in professional development work also increases markedly with age in Japan, Poland, Israel, and the Soviet Union, as do teacher training responsibilities across all countries. Cosmopoliteness also favors the older teacher. Ratings of importance are more diffuse with the younger teachers seeking the more extended professionality through awareness of school–community relationships, parental relationships, and contacts with other teachers.

Overall, the mean t-scores for the amount dimension are significantly higher for those over the age of 35 than for those below in six out of the nine countries, Canada, Israel, and the United States being the exceptions. In the importance dimension, Poland is the only country where this occurs. It must be borne in mind, however that, while age as a variable has validity for within-country comparisons, it is less valid between countries, since the age of entry into teaching varies so much in different countries.

Marital Status. The analysis of role indexes by country and marital status are not included here because there are few significant effects, but the information can be obtained from the available *Technical Supplement* described in the appendix. The most striking feature of these data is that in England and Japan those teachers who were married scored sigificantly above their single colleagues on the three indexes of cosmopoliteness, professional development, and shared management in amount, but there were no significant differences between these countries on the importance dimension. This seems to indicate that married teachers were more strongly into career development than their single colleagues. The same tendency was evident in the case of the United States but not at a statistically significant level. The table data confirm the existence of a similar picture over all five role indexes, suggesting also that role breadth was greater for married than unmarried teachers.

Predicting the Quality of the Working Life

We are now in a position to examine the contribution that all the role indexes (including the incongruity indexes) make to the quality of a teacher's working life represented by job satisfaction, work centrality, and job-related stress as well as the demographic variables. First, for each country separately, the combined set of role indexes with demographics as control variables were entered as independent variables into multiple regression equations with each QWL measure as the dependent variable. The resulting values of r-squared showed that they accounted for between 4.9 percent (Singapore) and 11 percent (United States) of the variance of overall job satisfaction, between 9.3 percent (Singapore) and 22.2 percent (Poland) of the variance of work centrality, and from 2.2 percent (United States) to 9.9 percent (Singapore) of the variance of job-related stress. This means that measures of work centrality showed the greatest country-to-country disparity of the three QWL variables in the amount of variance accounted for by role indexes. Except for stress in Canada and Israel, the increments in r-squared attributable to roles are all strongly significant statistically, but, in general, only a small proportion of the variance in each case was contributed by the role indexes incorporated in this questionnaire, in comparison with the proportions that might be accounted for by working conditions, classroom practices, or other work and life experiences that were not included.

It should be noted that the analyses reported in Chapter 7 appear to yield different results. This is because *all* of the indexes in *all* of the domains were included in an "optimum" set of thirty-five predictor variables in the Chapter 7 analyses, whereas the present analysis deals with the roles domain only.

Predicting Overall Job Satisfaction. It would generally be acknowledged that high job satisfaction would play a substantial part in having a good quality working life, but amount of role involvement appears to play a minor role. When job satisfaction was regressed on the five role indexes, the three demographic variables, and the incongruity index, it was found that only 5 to 13 percent of the variance was extracted in the United States, England, Poland, and the Soviet Union. Confirming earlier findings, values of the regression coefficient (beta) showed the greatest contributions to have been made in these countries by the two categories of student support and shared management (mainly in the subject department). In Germany and Canada, only student support emerged as significant predictors, in Singapore only shared management, and student support was linked with professional development in the case of Japanese teachers. The incongruity index did not enter the prediction equation for job satisfaction except in the Soviet Union. However, it correlated negatively with job satisfaction in all countries when the effects of gender, age, and marital status were controlled; that is, the smaller the gap between the importance of an activity and the extent to which it is done, the greater the job satisfaction. This may be an example of what Nias (1981) called a "negative satisfier," since the removal or amelioration of such a condition by coming to see it as less important could lead to higher levels of job satisfaction irrespective of other factors. On the basis of this analysis, the satisfied teacher in every country would likely be active in some form of student support activity, would share in subject department management except in Canada and Germany, and would be younger than average in Singapore and the Soviet Union.

Predicting Work Centrality. In England, Poland, and Israel, around 20 percent of the variance of work centrality was predicted by roles indexes. The picture is similar to that for job satisfaction, where student support appeared as a significant predictor in every country, being paired with shared management in five cases and with professional development in others. Although countries differed in the amount of variance extracted, an outstanding feature in the prediction of work centrality was the significant contribution of the incongruity index in every country except Canada, where it was nearly significant (p = 0.07). The concept of *role satiation* implies that the activities of teaching will sometimes outstrip the worker's desires being interpreted as enhanced workloads. This offers an alternative interpretation of negative satisfiers, as there was evidence from our interviews that teachers would endure extra workloads as long as they could see that the effort would support the interests of the students. Clearly, however, there will be a threshold to such commitment beyond which they will not, or cannot, go. Japan was the only country in which a significant level of role deprivation existed.

As far as the nature of the work is concerned, we may say that the workaholic teacher (whether by preference or design) would strive to achieve objectives and would most likely have management–administrative responsibilities in the area of student support activities, combined with a professional development program. Such a teacher would most likely be single and female in Canada, the Soviet Union, and Israel, with age making no difference.

Predicting Job-Related Stress. The stressed teacher has very few identifiable role characteristics in this analysis. The major predictor was, once more, the incongruity index. It also contributed positively and significantly to the prediction of stress in the United States, Germany, Japan, the Soviet Union, and England, where it combined with shared management, student support, and professional development. In Singapore, shared management was the major contributor to stress associated with student support, while the demands of professional development predominated in Japan and Israel. Student support was a particularly strong predictor of stress among Polish teachers. Only a few of the factors contributing to job stress in teaching can be identified from the variables included here, but the single item measure of stress, being less reliable than multiitem indexes, has less potentially predictable variance in the first place.

Summary of Results

The procedures described in the previous section have identified some distinctive patterns in the relationships between the indexes and job satisfaction, work centrality, and job-related stress that may be summarized as follows.

Similarities

1. There were almost identical rankings of the role indexes over countries for both amount and importance. The most highly ranked index was student support, with shared management second, and professional development in third place. The lowest ranked activity in every case was teacher training.

2. On one or both of the indexes, student support and shared management made generally positive contributions to both job satisfaction and work centrality, giving rise to images of happy workaholics as well as unhappy workhorses. Subject department allegiances were strong in both of these areas.

3. The share of the variance produced by the role indexes (plus the demographic variables) to each of the three quality of work life domains was greatest in the case of work centrality and least in the case of job-related stress.

4. As a predictor variable, the incongruity index between importance and amount ratings played a significant role in the prediction of work centrality and job-related stress where the condition was one of satiation. However, it made no significant difference to the prediction of job satisfaction in any country except the Soviet Union.

5. The very low levels of the involvement of teachers in training and supervision was common to all countries.

6. For those who believe that the classroom door should not mark the boundary between school and the wider community, the lack of response to cosmopoliteness will be an affirmation of the inward-looking nature of the teacher's world at a time when awareness of other countries and of other aspects of the adult world should be permeating the schools.

Differences

1. Ratings of overall role involvement and its importance to job satisfaction define three groups of countries in which the Soviet Union and Poland stood above average and are significantly different from all others. Germany and Singapore were significantly below average, and a middle group in which Canada, the United States, and Israel differed from England and Japan, but not from the nine-country mean.

2. Japan is unique in that the importance of overall role involvement to job satisfaction exceeded actual role occupancy to a statistically significant amount and appears to be the product of cultural forces, such as the culture of obligation and hard work.

3. Polish teachers gave professional development higher priority than any other country. Together with Soviet teachers, they claimed to read professional literature more than others, while Japanese and Singaporean teachers were below average in these respects.

4. English teachers gave particularly high emphasis to shared management in conjunction with student support.

5. Involvement in professional development and teacher training contributed to the existence of differences between specific countries.

DISCUSSION AND IMPLICATIONS

What do these similarities and differences imply in the search for a world-wide culture of teaching? Kohn (1989) suggested that the existence of cross-national similarities normally indicates the presence of social–structural similarities (however they may have come into being), while cross-national differences need to be explained in terms of the differences in "culture and political and economic systems that support the structures." The fact that this study is primarily concerned with teachers' perceptions of their work should not blind us to the reality that lies beneath any interpretation of the findings. We should consider, therefore, the structure of the various education systems examined as well as deeper, underlying cultural factors that may be responsible, while bearing in mind that any attempted explanation must, to some extent, be speculative.

Discussion of the findings will aim to synthesize the main findings and draw them to a conclusion in an international context. It will move from considerations of role diversity versus specialization to questions of national profiles and priorities, and will then consider the relationships between roles and the quality of the teachers' work lives, taking account of the contribution of the teacher's demographic characteristics. Some theoretical issues concerning the incongruity index will be discussed. The conclusion will consider the implications of the role study for schools and teachers and present some questions to be asked and answered by all the contributing countries.

Role Diversity versus Specialization

It is undoubtedly an oversimplification to separate any consideration of roles and responsibilities outside the classroom from those inside, for the classroom is the focal arena for every teacher. All additional activities are undertaken for a number of reasons—adding variety and challenge to the job, a conviction that teaching is enriched and classroom control made easier by greater knowledge of the pupils, or the more mundane considerations of career advancement and higher salaries. These motivations and incentives are often combined in the development of alternative career routes to senior status. But, lacking such incentives, classroom teachers who have to take on additional duties within the school frequently complain of crippling workloads arising from them. As represented in Figure 4.2, breadth of role is taken to imply an enlargement of responsibility beyond the instructional function. It was more prevalent in some countries than in others; it is not an absolute but relative to other circumstances and other places. Wherever it occurs, however, it might legitimately be defined as part and parcel of "teaching."

Two pairs of countries at the extremes of the continuum were defined as being alike but significantly different from all the others in their overall involvement in teachers' roles and responsibilities. German and Singaporean teachers had significantly lower levels of involvement than teachers in any of the other countries, while in Poland and the Soviet Union, they were significantly higher. Each pair produced some strongly similar patterns in the perceptions of their teachers, and yet Germany and Singapore appear, on the surface, to be very different. What can a small island republic and a large, major European power have in common? The schools from which the teacher samples were drawn in each case were state comprehensive schools that coexisted with other selective secondary schools; both had a centralized administration delivered locally, and teachers had little say in decision making.

The two countries had another important aspect in common—the length of the working day. In Germany, teachers work in the secondary school for an average of twenty-one hours a week (or 26 lessons) spent entirely in instructional activities (Neave, 1992), while, in Singapore, the average is around twenty-two. Under such circumstances there was no apparent allowance in either system for role or professional responsibility development of the kind common in England and Wales, for example, where teachers are required to be in school for thirty-two hours per week, ten of these being spent on the premises in noninstructional activities. It is interesting to note that in Singapore, since 1992, a comprehensive program of pastoral care for students was introduced. In German schools also, counseling and guidance was delivered through a system in which every teacher had tutorial responsibility for the children in his or her teaching group and was likely to be concerned primarily with the academic and vocational education programs. It should also be noted that, whereas the teachers in Singapore were predominantly young and female and those in Germany predominantly male and older, neither gender nor age appeared to have any cross-national implications. However, while the factors producing these similarities were undoubtedly embedded in different historical and cultural origins, they were associated with similar administrative structures.

What can be said about teachers in the former USSR and Poland, both of whose overall role involvements were significantly higher than in other countries? The enlarged responsibilities of teachers in the former communist states has been noted as reflecting the function of schools in society. Leszczynska and Olek (1997) note that, before the overthrow of communism in Central and Eastern European States, teachers in these countries were perceived as "servants of the state" and as "educational bureaucrats whose role was to conform politically and to faithfully carry out a detailed and ideologically correct school program." In fact, they did not see themselves as powerless victims of the state so much as wielding power *through* the state. In this sense it is easy to see how they felt that they had an enlarged role. Thus, in this case we have a combination of similar administrative structures combined with an all-embracing ideology, which was culturally and historically different from that in any of our other countries.

Profiles and Priorities

The varied programs of secondary comprehensive schools would seem to be the ideal vehicle to encourage role diversity, but when each country's indexes were placed together (Figures 4.3 and 4.4), things done and things valued were shown to yield strikingly similar country profiles. The opportunities both provided and valued most highly were neither narrow nor technical, but those to do with the fostering of different kinds of teacher–student relationships from those normally encountered in the classroom. These can be expressed in a number of ways allowing individual teachers to choose their preferred ways of knowing and supporting their students. As Neave (1992) indicates, some supplement the parental role in the form of counselors, remedial specialists, and career advisors, while others encourage the development of special abilities through activities developed outside the normal school curriculum. All were embodied in the student support index. Shared management was the second most preferred role with teachers in England, the United States, and Singapore being outstanding in this respect. Officially encouraged in-service courses in Japan and Singapore provided career incentives, while a management role in the subject department or in the pastoral system was a career step for English teachers. Professional development was ranked third or fourth by most teachers, alternating with cosmopoliteness. A large measure of similarity was also shown by the low ranking of involvement in teacher training by teachers in practically every country, who clearly regard this as an "add-on" activity and a chore rather than a priority. When the indexes were placed in rank order (Table 4.1), the results would seem to support the existence of a common culture of teaching which allocated priorities to the same activities in the same (or similar) order. This suggests that institutional norms were operating in the allocation of responsibilities as well as in individual orientations to a preferred professionality.

Between-country differences are more complicated to interpret because some results apply only to single countries which, in the profusion of possible comparisons, may yield statistical artifacts. However, there is little doubt that Japan is a special case, illuminating the role played by cultural forces in accounting for differences. The incongruity index for Japanese teachers shows significantly higher rating of importance over amount of overall role involvement—the importance of "busyness" in the Japanese culture has already been mentioned. Kudomi (1992) mentions how surveys have shown the extreme busyness of teachers, in which female teachers feel more busy than males, classroom teachers than others, and those with between five and twenty-nine years experience more than the younger or older. Because of the intense competitiveness of Japanese education, there is enormous pressure on the teachers to achieve good results; consequently, their overall role incongruity is significantly higher than that of their overseas colleagues. However, this role set is also narrow in scope and set in "the web of reciprocal obligations in which the social order is enmeshed" (Shields, 1989). This extends over a myriad of areas such as work, collegial relationships, marriage, and topics of conversation.

It may be recalled that the Japanese data was strongly suggestive of the existence of cultural bias in the original ratings made by teachers and that standardization techniques were applied for the purpose of rendering between country data sets comparable. In doing so, there was a danger that the cultural factors might also remove meaning. The comparative researcher using sophisticated statistical techniques alone risks overkill. In fact, Japan is a good case to illustrate the importance of the cultural background in interpreting cross-national differences. Taken alone, the figures reveal little about the meanings of teaching and require supplementing from interviews and other sources.

Role Relationships and the Quality of Work Life

Moving now to the relationship between the roles domain and the quality of work life variables and considering overall job satisfaction, Cohn (1992) reported a marked decline in teacher satisfaction over a twenty-year period between Lortie's (1975) Florida study of teachers and her own replication, and pointed to changed attitudes towards accountability by parents and administrators, which has led to a narrower and more technical conception of teaching. Cohn's findings support the supposition that restricting professionality can be seen as a form of deskilling, a loss of professionalism, and a loss of job satisfaction (Apple, 1986). Equally, however, we have already seen that a policy of extending teacher professionality could lower it. The relative position of countries in this study does not show a clear relationship between job satisfaction and breadth of role involvement, but it remains to be established that there may be a threshold of role breadth, below which job satisfaction increases, and above which job satisfaction may decline.

The combined role domain and demographic indexes contributed considerably more to the variance of work centrality than to either overall job satisfaction or job-related stress, being particularly high in the case of the English teachers. This is an area where common sense and research meet, for there must, for each individual, be optimal levels of work centrality beyond which the level of stress increases regardless of the level of job satisfaction. There is a fine balance to be struck between these two opposing tendencies. It was not the case at the time when the survey was conducted, when the English teaching profession was in a state of turmoil. Since a restricted measure of stress was employed, it is not possible to say what the optimal level would be—this would require a separate investigation.

Teachers in the Soviet Union and Poland were significantly more involved overall in their personal and social roles (Figure 4.3). "It is vital to understand that in the Soviet school, the ethical and moral aims of education are taken seriously by the teachers, are not an optional extra and are not seen as something divorced from the academic aims of education" (Muckle, 1990). Thus, the teacher's role was to incorporate these aims not only in the academic teaching, but also in every aspect of school life, with the added responsibility of maintaining the machinery to support this via the various youth movements, labor education, extracurricular activities, and parents' councils in the schools. Since the 1990 revolution and the abolition of the Communist Party as the sole political influence, this picture has changed, though the schools are having to cope with the socialization vacuum that was created (Gershunsky, 1993), and it is unlikely that the teachers' load has substantially decreased. This is confirmed by Leszczynska and Olek (1997), who found that Polish teachers insist on their political independence and politically neutral values and do not see any need for change. Poland is also the country in which teachers take study for professional development most seriously.

The most outstanding consensus overall is the salience for teachers of giving students support in their work and as developing human beings—provided that it is a rewarded activity. Its central position in relation to their work centrality indicates high levels of commitment to the work of teaching. The structures that support such commitment are not identical nor are they always seen as adequate by the teachers in every country, but they are there—by necessity—in the structures of the comprehensive schools that accept children of all abilities and social backgrounds. Keeping to the strict definition of the takeover by schools of family responsibilities (which is best represented by the student support index), apart from political considerations, the nature of the systems themselves does not appear to be an important factor. It is apparent that responsibility enlargement occurs in both centralized and decentralized systems, though its form differs in different countries. It is significantly higher than average in both Poland (centralized) and Canada (decentralized), and significantly lower in Japan—an example of a centralized system in which the municipal authorities administer standardized programs. In the United States and Germany, it has been accompanied by greater specialization, in which a large part of the extra work is sidelined into separate administrative functions—which can also be frustrating for the teacher who then has no role in the decision-making process. The critical factor in this process is the way in which responsibility enlargement consumes time; one important structural factor being the length and organization of the teaching day and week. The working day cannot absorb change and increased activity indefinitely, and soon reaches the point where intensification of the work is counterproductive. "Heightened expectations, broader demands, increased accountability, more 'social work' responsibilities, multiple innovations, increased amounts of administration and meetings—all are testimony to the problems of chronic work overload" (Hargreaves, 1994).

The relationships between job satisfaction, work centrality, and job-related stress are complex. Poppleton and Riseborough (1990) found that high job satisfaction combined with high work centrality and low stress was a characteristic of extended professionality, whereas low job satisfaction combined with high work centrality and high stress was associated with restricted professionality. No country in Table 4.2 corresponds to the extended professionality profile, though Canada comes close. English teachers as a whole show the characteristics of restricted professionality. It is noticeable, however, that the Japanese teachers, who report the lowest levels of activity related to student support, also experience the lowest level of job satisfaction of any country (Canada being the highest). This at least suggests that an extended professionality plays a part in greater job satisfaction. It means that education managers must be clear about what this means, and must involve both teachers and schools in their decision making in order to maximize job satisfaction and minimize stress.

The Contribution of the Demographic Variables

Sexism and ageism are embedded in occupational cultures that have developed well-defined career structures within which gender and age responsibility patterns become established. Marital status can also be an issue in the workplace, but did not emerge as a separate source of influence and was generally diffused throughout other considerations.

In the analysis of the roles data, few instances have emerged of perceived teacher role characteristics linked to gender and age, except insofar as they reflected the makeup of the teaching force. They did emerge in the interviews, however, when teachers reflected upon the balance of counseling, guidance, or pastoral tutoring that they were required to do, seeing it as an aspect of the "caring" role deemed particularly suitable for women and sometimes in conflict with the instructional role, if not inferior to it.

The perceived influence of age was generally seen to be strongly related to changes in economic systems and conditions of employment, though culturally determined attitudes toward age were also important. Age carried most influence in the data through (1) the age of admission to the profession, which tended to be younger than average in Singapore; (2) the association of senior, and therefore, older people who held administrative and management responsibilities in England as well as the length of teaching experience generally deemed necessary to occupy such positions.

Role Incongruities

How, therefore, to explain situations in which the amount done is greater than its perceived importance (role satiation)? The role incongruity index in the area of roles and responsibilities plays a much larger part in the experience of work centrality in most countries, than in either job satisfaction or stress. Thinking about work outside working hours and striving for success are central components of work centrality well known to those who accept managerial responsibilities. One explanation might be that, as Hargreaves (1994) points out, the rewards outweigh the drawbacks for many teachers, especially if they arise from intrinsic sources such as commitment to worthy ends or to enhancing the self-image of being a professional. On the other hand, it is likely that the importance of such activities is equally related to the extrinsic rewards of career development and higher pay. In either case, responsibility enlargement over and above the demands of routine classroom teaching is regarded as a mixed blessing by most teachers.

Where role deprivation is concerned, and perceptions of role importance (to job satisfaction) exceed those of extent of involvement, the existence of a gap might be regarded as a strong motivational force in encouraging efforts to close the gap; also, work centrality would be high. If, however, the gap is so large that closure is unlikely to be achieved, the net effect will be frustration, and eventually, dropout unless the activity comes to be less valued (the negative satisfier effect). Thus, if a job attribute is highly valued but absent, job satisfaction will be low and stress high; if it is both valued and present, both job satisfaction and work centrality will be high and stress low. If an attribute is not valued, then its presence or absence will make no difference to the level of job satisfaction, work centrality, or stress. In other words, first of all we need to know whether the attribute is valued and to what degree.

CONCLUSION

In the occupational culture of secondary school teaching, there exists a slow, osmotic process whereby teachers are, somewhat reluctantly, drawn outwards from their classrooms, to engage in what Lieberman and Miller (1992) called "another structure of influences that intrudes on the lives of teachers in the complex organization of the secondary school." These arise from activities such as extending community links, recognizing accountability to parents, engaging in the development of prevocational studies for their students and giving high priority to supporting them in their school lives. Although the process itself is practically universal, the nature of the activities vary over time and place, sometimes reflecting the school's role in society, sometimes dominated by political ideologies, and always determined by the level of available resources, both financial and human. It is the combination of social expectations of the school with the work ethic of the teachers that produces the responsibility enlargement, which contributes to high work centrality and to stress in some cases.

Neave (1992) sees responsibility enlargement as a long-term secular trend that is a reflection of the changing role of the teacher in society. In times of change, educational policy makers have a choice between asking teachers to take on extra responsibilities or making a clear split between teaching and administration; between role enlargement and specialization. What usually happens, however, is a series of adjustments to unforeseen developments of a socioeconomic or political nature that result in confusion and uncertainty. The phenomenon of work intensification places a low ceiling on the possibilities of role enlargement, and whichever system is adopted will have consequences for the pupils, since specialized teachers mean specialized pupils as well.

Teachers may prefer a restricted or extended professionality, a specialized or enlarged role, but motivated teachers also need the capability for occupational self-direction. As teaching grows more complex, schools should consider carefully the range of skills that they require of their teachers, ensure that they should have greater access to means for better professional development, and be prepared to employ professionally qualified specialists. This entails the provision of training for the exacting tasks that are often involved.

The expectations that people have of educational institutions have steadily been rising, to the point that they are often at a higher level than can rationally be met by teachers and schools. It may, therefore, be appropriate to ask what responsibilities they *should* accept, bearing in mind their working conditions, both material and psychological, the support services with which they are provided, and the competence of administrators. When one or all of these are not adequate for the tasks, the result is a breakdown in public confidence and a collapse in teacher morale such as has been recently seen in Britain.

One question that emerges from this analysis is a very old one: Who should be responsible for the socialization process—the family, the school, or the state? The process was handled in different ways by the countries in this study, but the problems were recognized. Whatever the solution, this question impinged on the teacher's work. In Germany and Singapore, the answer was the *family*; in Poland and the Soviet Union, it was the *state*; in Canada, England, and the United States, the *school*. Greater ambiguity marked the solutions in other countries. Today's comprehensive schools do not have universal solutions.

Yet the consensus demonstrated in this study about the priorities accorded to different aspects of the teaching role indicates the existence of a strong, worldwide culture of the teaching profession. Where countries differ, it is in how the cultural values are expressed in each case. These findings are important for would-be "borrowers" of other countries' practices. They are also important for the schools and teachers: "Teachers are at the core of any improvement effort. We must pay particular attention to their needs, their longings, their personal and professional concerns, and the ways in which they function as a separate culture in the high school" (Lieberman & Miller, 1992).

What we may claim to have done is to show how teachers in different countries have interpreted teachers' roles and responsibilities and something of what it has meant for them. If, in the process we have learned more about our own country's educational problems and the possible solutions, the search will have been worthwhile.

NOTES

1. At certain times of the year, all members of staff in Japanese schools meet together to discuss problems relating to school management. In this way, involvement may be shared without being actively pursued (Y. Kudomi, personal communication, June 1996).

2. The quotes from English teachers are taken from the open-ended question at the end of the questionnaire where teachers were asked to comment freely on any aspect of the survey which seemed relevant to them. The quoted contributions came from the "modal" teachers in groups defined by cluster analysis of all the scores of the English sample on the three major variables of job satisfaction, work centrality, and stress. As a result, it was possible to identify two of the clusters as representing restricted and extended professionals.

REFERENCES

Adams, R. S. (1970). Perceived teaching styles. *Comparative Education Review, 14* (1), 50–59.

Apple, M. W. (1986). *Teachers and texts*. New York: Routledge and Kegan Paul.

Ball, S. J. (1987). *The micro-politics of the school: Towards a theory of school organization*. London: Methuen.

Broadfoot, P.; and Osborn, M. J. (1992). French lessons: Comparative perspectives on what it means to be a teacher. In D. Phillips (Ed.), *Oxford studies in comparative education: Vol. 1. Lessons of cross-national comparison in education* (69–88). Wallingford, England: Triangle Books.

Bryk, A. S.; and Frank, K. (1989). The specialization of teachers' work: An initial exploration. Paper presented to the ESRC International Conference on Multilevel Methods, University of Edinburgh, August.

Cohn, M. M. (1992). How teachers perceive teaching: Change over the decades, 1964–84. In A. Lieberman (Ed.), *The changing concepts of teaching* (110–137). Chicago: University of Chicago Press.

Evans, M. G. (1969). Conceptual and operational problems in the measurement of various aspects of job satisfaction. *Journal of Applied Psychology, 53* (2), 93–101.

Gershunsky, B. S. (1993). *Russia in darkness*. San Francisco, CA: Caddo Press.

Hargreaves, A. (1994). *Changing teachers, changing times: Teachers' work and culture in the postmodern age*. London: Cassell.

Hoyle, E. (1980). Professionalisation and deprofessionalisation in education. In E. Hoyle and J. Megarry (Eds.), *World yearbook of education, 1980: Professional development of teachers* (42–54). London: Kogan.

Kalleberg, A. L. (1977). Work values and job rewards: A theory of job satisfaction. *American Sociological Review, 42* (1), 124–143.

Kohn, M. L. (1989). Cross-national research as an analytic strategy. In M. L. Kohn (Ed.), *Cross-national research in sociology*. Newbury Park, CA: Sage.

Kudomi, Y. (1992). Teachers' culture in Japan: Narrowness of teachers' field. *Hitotsubashi Journal of Social Studies, 24* (1), 1–12.

Leszczynska, E.; and Olek, H. (1997). Polish teachers: Still faithful servants of the state? Paper presented at the European Conference on Educational Research. Frankfurt-am-Main, Germany, September 24–27.

Liebermann, A.; and Miller, L. (1992). *Teachers—Their world and their work: Implications for school improvement*. New York: Teachers College Press.

Lissmann, H. J.; and Gigerich, R. (1990). A changed school and educational culture: Job orientation and teacher satisfaction at the Gesamtschulen in the state of Hessen, West Germany—Some international comparisons. *Comparative Education, 26* (2–3), 277–284.

Lortie, D. C. (1975). *Schoolteacher: A sociological study*. Chicago: University of Chicago Press.

Marich, M.; and Swift, K. (1987). *Teachers in England, West Germany and the United States speak about professional enthusiasm and discouragement*. Paper presented at the Annual Meeting of the American Educational Research Association, Washington D.C., March 27–31.

Marlin, M.; and Biddle, B. J. (1970). Analysis procedures for Phase 11. *Comparative Education Review, 14* (1), 14–19.

Muckle, J. (1990). *Portrait of a school under Glasnost*. London: Macmillan.

Neave, G. (1992). *The teaching nation: Prospects for teachers in the European community*. Oxford: Pergamon Press.

Nias, J. (1981). Teacher satisfaction and dissatisfaction: Herzberg's "two factor" hypothesis revisited. *British Journal of Sociology of Education, 3*, 235–246.

Ninomiya, A.; and Okato, T. (1990). A critical analysis of job-satisfied teachers in Japan. *Comparative Education, 26* (2–3), 249–258.

Poppleton, P. (1989). Rewards and values in secondary teachers' perceptions of their job satisfaction. *Research Papers in Education, 4–3*, 71–94.

Poppleton, P. (1990). The survey data. *Comparative Education, 26* (2), 183–210.

Poppleton, P. (1992). *Gender differences in the work perceptions of a sample of English secondary school teachers in international context*. Paper presented at the Annual Meeting of the American Educational Research Association, San Francisco, CA, April.

Poppleton, P.; and Riseborough, G. (1990). Teaching in the mid-1980s: The centrality of work in secondary teachers' lives. *British Educational Research Journal, 16* (2), 105–124.

Rosencrantz, H. A.; and Biddle, B. J. (1963). The role approach to teacher competence. In B. J. Biddle and W. J. Ellena (Eds.), *Contemporary research on teacher effectiveness* (232–264). New York: Holt, Rinehart and Winston.

Shields, J. J., Jr. (1989). Educational reform in Japan: Discontinuities in moral education and educational equality. Paper presented at the annual meeting of the American Educational Research Association, San Francisco, CA, March 27.

Sim, W. K. (1990). Factors associated with job satisfaction and work centrality among Singapore teachers. *Comparative Education, 26* (2–3), 259–275.

Wall, T. D.; and Payne, R. (1973). Are deficiency scores deficient? *Journal of Applied Psychology, 58* (3), 322–326.

Wanous, J. P.; and Lawler, E. E. (1972). Measurement and meaning of job satisfaction. *Journal of Applied Psychology, 56* (2), 95–105.

5

Working Conditions

Linda Weller-Ferris

Working conditions are an integral aspect of teachers' work lives, and to a large extent, they shape the context of teachers' daily experiences. It is important to examine teachers' views of their working conditions and to understand the impact they have on how teachers go about their work, and how they relate to job-related stress and overall job satisfaction. As countries move forward in educational reform efforts, it is important that we take time to explore the meaning and importance of working conditions to teachers. We know that teachers want to teach (Lortie, 1975). However, in order for them to do that successfully, they not only require personal skills and knowledge, but also need appropriate physical assets, social networks, and personal motivators. A cross-cultural exploration of *teachers' work context* provides a deeper understanding of the complex ways in which teachers' working conditions contribute to job satisfaction, job-related stress, and work centrality.

This chapter reports on teachers' perceptions of a wide variety of work conditions based on responses to twenty-one questions used to evaluate seven central aspects of working conditions, including teacher support, autonomy, professional support, workload, esprit de corps, physical resources, and economic incentives. First, the chapter examines the similarities and differences in teachers' ratings of work conditions in schools across nine countries. The importance of these specific work conditions for job satisfaction also are discussed. The extent of incongruity between the presence of work conditions versus the importance for teachers' job satisfaction addresses an important question: "*Are teachers getting what they want in their work environments?*" Since a rank ordering of indexes gives added insight into working conditions comparatively, the chapter further examines the pattern of evaluations of work conditions within each country; this analysis also presented the importance ratings on the seven aspects of work conditions.

Second, the chapter explores the influence of gender, marital status, and age on perceptions of working conditions, as well as the importance attached to them by teachers in nine countries. Third, it compares similarities and differences in the contribution of work conditions to overall ratings of overall job satisfaction, work centrality, and job-related stress for this sample of teachers. The conceptual schema of the chapter as outlined and a list of the work conditions are summarized in Figure 5.1.

In closing the chapter, there is reflection on the universal principles and country-specific insights gained about teachers' working conditions. How work conditions universally improve or detract from the work lives of teachers in diverse cultures is discussed in relation to job satisfaction theory, school improvement efforts, and policy formation.

THE CONCEPT OF WORKING CONDITIONS

Schools are workplaces. While human resources are the most central aspect to the operation of schools, there is a growing realization that good teaching environments and the resources afforded to teachers are central to teachers' effectiveness and productivity in classrooms. As a profession, teachers around the world are facing increasingly rigid educational requirements and stricter certification procedures. At the same time, many countries have growing economic and demographic pressures on the profession. These factors force the profession to address a new reality—that the teaching profession must work actively to attract and retain talented individuals. Just what aspects of work contribute positively to teaching environments, and what resources are important personal motivators to teachers? What work conditions are associated with greater satisfaction, lower stress, and greater work centrality? The answers to these questions will be explored in this chapter.

The conditions of work reported here are based on teachers' ratings of the amount present and the extent to which a condition contributes directly to job satisfaction. This is referred to as *importance* in the following discussions. The questions posed to teachers address major constructs associated with work conditions in quality-of-work-life literature. The seven indexes explored in depth are based on twenty-one questions and include (1) *teacher support* from colleagues, parents, and community; (2) *professional autonomy*; (3) *professional support*, referring to intellectual guidance and problem solving from support staff, colleagues, and supervisor; (4) *workload*, encompassing class size, planning time, and after-school and administrative work; (5) esprit de corps or school leadership and school climate; (6) *physical resources*, including materials, equipment, and clerical support; and (7) *economic incentives* of the profession, including pay, benefits, and promotion opportunities.

Figure 5.1
Conceptual Schema for the Work Conditions Section of the Overall Study

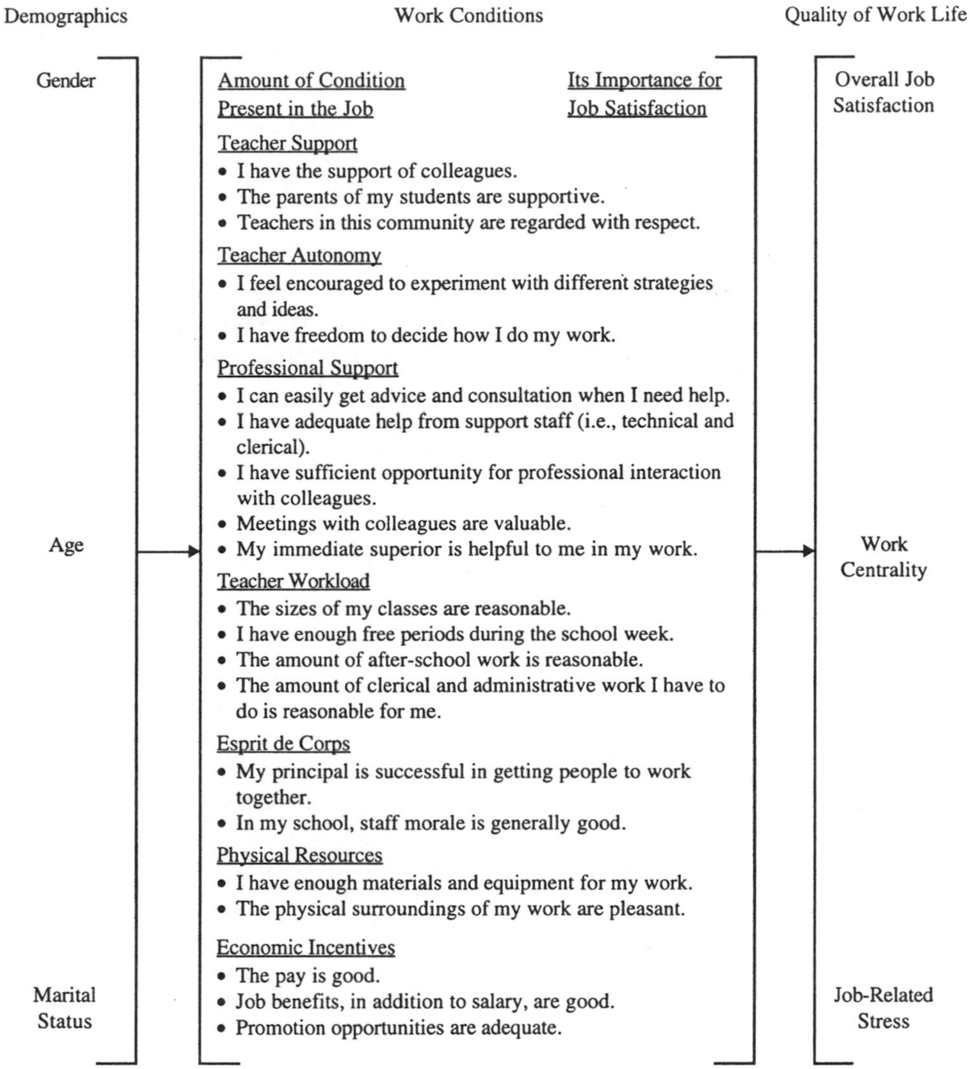

Demographics   Work Conditions   Quality of Work Life

| Gender | Amount of Condition Present in the Job | Its Importance for Job Satisfaction | Overall Job Satisfaction |

Teacher Support
- I have the support of colleagues.
- The parents of my students are supportive.
- Teachers in this community are regarded with respect.

Teacher Autonomy
- I feel encouraged to experiment with different strategies and ideas.
- I have freedom to decide how I do my work.

Professional Support
- I can easily get advice and consultation when I need help.
- I have adequate help from support staff (i.e., technical and clerical).
- I have sufficient opportunity for professional interaction with colleagues.
- Meetings with colleagues are valuable.

Age — My immediate superior is helpful to me in my work. — Work Centrality

Teacher Workload
- The sizes of my classes are reasonable.
- I have enough free periods during the school week.
- The amount of after-school work is reasonable.
- The amount of clerical and administrative work I have to do is reasonable for me.

Esprit de Corps
- My principal is successful in getting people to work together.
- In my school, staff morale is generally good.

Physical Resources
- I have enough materials and equipment for my work.
- The physical surroundings of my work are pleasant.

Economic Incentives
- The pay is good.

Marital Status
- Job benefits, in addition to salary, are good.   Job-Related Stress
- Promotion opportunities are adequate.

RESEARCH QUESTIONS REGARDING
WORK CONDITIONS

The study of teachers' work conditions was directed by six research questions:

1. How do teachers across nine countries compare regarding their evaluations of working conditions?

2. How do teachers across nine countries compare regarding the importance they assign to each work condition for their job satisfaction?

3. What incongruities do teachers across nine countries have regarding their ratings of work condition versus the value they assign to them? What implications, if any, might these incongruities have for teachers' overall job satisfaction, work centrality, and stress?

4. How do teachers across nine countries compare regarding associations of gender, age, and marital status with perceptions of work conditions, as well as the importance they attach to work conditions for job satisfaction?

5. Considering all other facets of teachers' daily work, what contributions do work conditions make to teachers' overall job satisfaction, job-related stress, and work centrality?

6. Given the findings, what implications do they have generally when making efforts to improve teachers' work life or establishing policies related to work conditions within diverse cultures?

EVALUATING WORKING CONDITIONS
CROSS-CULTURALLY

Overall Working Conditions in Nine Countries

Dramatic differences are seen in the ways that teachers in nine countries both critique and value their working conditions. Figure 5.2 provides an initial clue to how teachers evaluate their work conditions. The figure summarizes the t-deviations scores from the grand means of all countries together on the thirty-three questions regarding work conditions. Again, these scores report both the presence and importance of work conditions of teachers in nine countries, and allow for visible comparisons across countries.

Canadian teachers have a far more positive outlook on their work conditions than do teachers in eight other countries; Canadian scores depart dramatically from the scores of all other teachers studied. U.S., Israeli, and to a lesser extent, German teachers give high marks overall to the state of their working conditions. On the contrary, Japanese teachers offer the lowest rating of the quality of their working conditions overall, followed closely by Poland. Teachers in the Soviet Union and England are only slightly less critical of the shortcomings of their work conditions than are Polish teachers. Singapore teachers give moderate ratings to their working conditions overall.

Overall Importance Assigned to Work Conditions. While work conditions vary across countries overall, an appropriate question to ask is, "So what?" In order to begin to tease out an answer to this question, one must again refer to the overall T deviations from the nine-country mean score in Figure 5.2. Teachers differ to a great extent in that they view working conditions as important for their job satisfaction. Teachers in England generally attach the greatest importance overall to the quality of working conditions for their job satisfac-

Figure 5.2
T Deviations of Country Raw-Score Means for Condition Amount and Importance
from the Corresponding Nine-Country Means

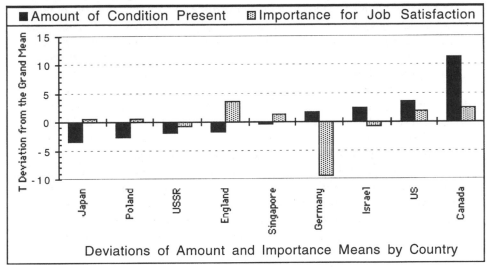

Note: This figure is derived from data in Table F-1 of the *Technical Supplement*.

tion than teachers in other countries. Teachers in Canada and the United States also place moderately high value on work conditions for job satisfaction, in comparison to others. Teachers in Singapore, Poland, Israel, the Soviet Union, and Japan generally view working conditions as moderately important for job satisfaction. German teachers stand alone in their perspective; their extremely low rating overall of the importance of working conditions for their job satisfaction departs dramatically from the views of all other teachers studied here. The roots of this difference will be explored shortly.

The overall scores of each country do not tell the complete story. Teachers across the nine countries rate varying aspects of work conditions positively and negatively, creating unique configurations of strengths and weaknesses within countries. Another way to explore this issue is to compare specifically the mean t-scores for the seven aspects of work (indexes). The seven index scores of all countries were translated into standard scores; this transformation allows us to easily compare measures within a country, as well as to make between-country comparison. *It is important to remember that actual scores are not being compared.* We are examining the standing of a score among a number of scores within a given country. For our purposes, a three-point difference between scores is considered to be both educationally important and statistically significant ($p = 0.05$ or less).

Turning our attention to the seven specific aspects of work, how do teachers in this study evaluate specific work conditions and relate them to their job satisfaction?

Teacher Support: Amount and Importance. Three questions were posed to teachers having to do with the support they receive from colleagues, parents, and the community. This kind of surrounding social support from others significant to one's self and social image emerges as a central construct in quality-of-work-life literature, the presence of which has been linked to increased job satisfaction, lowered stress, and increased work centrality (Herzberg, Mausner, & Snyderman, 1959; Kahn & Boulding, 1964; Sergiovanni, 1967; Maslow, 1970; Lawler & Hall, 1970; Lawler, 1973; Holdaway, 1978; Hackman & Oldham, 1980; Nias, 1981; Pastor & Erlandson, 1982; MOW, 1987). Figure 5.3 summarizes the average scores that teachers in nine countries assign to the amount and importance of support for their teaching. *There is universal agreement among teachers that they generally receive support for their work*, although not always as much as they wish to have. Polish teachers enjoy the greatest amount of support in their work, and substantially more than teachers in all other countries. Teachers in the Soviet Union, Germany, and Canada rank the lowest, respectively, among countries.

Examining specific sources of support, it appears that English teachers enjoy significantly more collegial support than teachers in any other country.

Figure 5.3
Relative Amount and Importance of Teacher Support from Parents and Colleagues, by Country

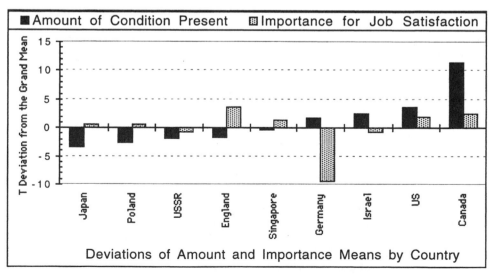

Note: This figure is derived from data in Table F-2 of the *Technical Supplement*.

This ranking fits with the success that British teachers have with professional development, pastoral care, and the sharing of department management (Riseborough & Poppleton, 1991).

Israeli teachers rank in top position for the extent of parental support that they receive, while Polish teachers experience substantially greater respect from their communities than teachers in other countries.

Interestingly, *teachers almost universally attach moderate importance to adult interpersonal support*, with strong exception taken by Polish teachers. They attach significantly less importance to various sources of support than do teachers in all other countries, and yet enjoy substantially more of it than teachers elsewhere. It would seem that in situations of intense saturation, where one's needs are being met, it becomes easier to lower one's assessment of importance of that dimension. Teachers in Germany and Singapore rank in the top two positions in their desire for collegial support for job satisfaction. U.S. teachers rank highest in the importance they attach to support generally, and desire significantly more support from parents and respect from the community than teachers in all other countries.

Teacher Autonomy: Amount and Importance. Two questions were posed to teachers regarding the extent and importance they attribute to autonomy on the job. The questions defined autonomy as the freedom to experiment with different teaching strategies and ideas and to decide how to teach. Figure 5.4

Figure 5.4
Relative Amount and Importance of Teacher Autonomy, by Country

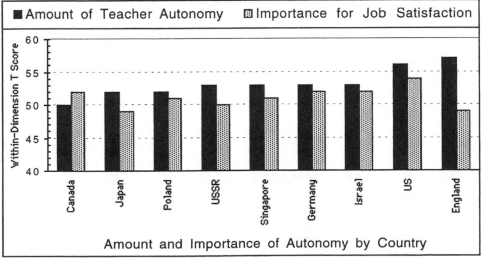

Note: This figure is derived from data in Table F-2 of the *Technical Supplement*.

summarizes the mean scores regarding the amount and importance teachers associate with their work autonomy. *Scores on this index are consistently high across all countries.* U.S. and English teachers enjoy substantially more freedom and autonomy in their work, far outranking their counterparts' ratings. However, counter to stereotypic views, teachers in Canada, Japan, Poland, the Soviet Union, Singapore, Germany, and Israel actually offer moderate to moderately high ratings of autonomy.

Readers may predict that the responses of teachers would vary rather dramatically, depending on the extent of control and centralization of ministries or departments of education within a country (Postlethwaite, 1988). However, these results challenge stereotypic notions of autonomy in teaching as a direct reflection of political systems. Despite centralized control of curriculum and standardized testing by ministries of education in many countries, teachers in this study report the joy of work autonomy. Apparently, they are relatively successful in finding ways to experiment with different teaching strategies and to make decisions about *how* to teach. Canadian, Japanese, and Polish teachers enjoy the least freedom and autonomy in their work, but only significantly less than teachers in the United States and England.

Regarding the importance of work autonomy for job satisfaction, teachers in all countries, with the exception of Canada, experience conditions of autonomy that exceed the importance they attach to it for job satisfaction. U.S. teachers attach the greatest importance to autonomy, followed closely by Canadian, German, Israeli, and Polish teachers. In contrast, English and Japanese teachers have the lowest regard for autonomy in association with their job satisfaction, and yet get significantly freer reign in their work than is viewed as important for their job satisfaction.

Professional Support: Amount and Importance. Five questions evaluated the extent and importance of professional support. The questions address the ability of teachers to secure advice and consultation when needed, to gain adequate help from support staff, to benefit from professional interaction with colleagues, to take part in meetings that are valuable with colleagues, and to experience a helpful immediate superior. Figure 5.5 presents the contrasting ratings of amount and importance of professional support teachers experience in these nine countries.

Teachers in England, Japan, and Singapore take the top three rankings, experiencing greater professional support in their work than teachers in other countries. Teachers in England reap the benefits of programs to enhance professional skills, pedagogy, and aspects of pastoral care of students (Poppleton & Riseborough, 1988; Poppleton, 1990). British teachers report considerable success in securing advice, consult, and help from their immediate superior, as well as from the support staff. British teachers also benefit from productive meetings with their colleagues.

Meanwhile, teachers in Poland and Canada have lower than average ratings of professional support, and have a more difficult time in securing pro-

Figure 5.5
Relative Amount and Importance of Professional Support, by Country

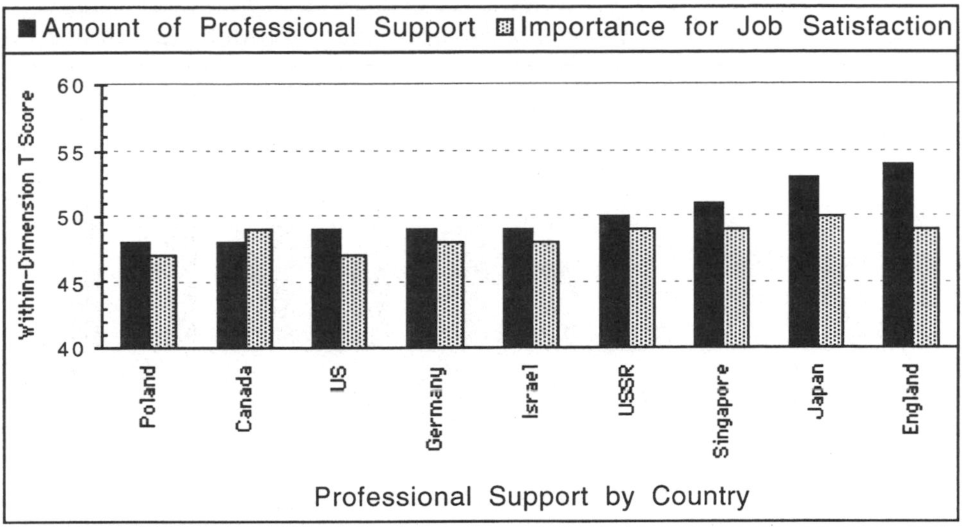

Note: This figure is derived from data in Table F-2 of the *Technical Supplement*.

fessional support than do teachers in other countries. Here teachers get the least amount of consultation and advice when they need them. U.S., German, and Soviet teachers also rate the extent of their overall professional support as low. German teachers specifically rate their ability to secure advice and consultation as extremely compromised, and also offer the lowest ratings in comparison to other countries of the abilities of their immediate superiors to be helpful. Soviet teachers have the most difficulty in getting help from support staff, including technical and clerical, in comparison to teachers in other countries.

How important is professional support to the job satisfaction of teachers? *Teachers universally do not attach much importance to professional support in order to feel satisfied with their work.* As illustrated in Figure 5.5, teachers in eight countries are getting more professional support than they rate as necessary for their job satisfaction, with the exception of Canadian teachers. Comparing the nine countries, teachers in England, Japan, Canada, Singapore, and the Soviet Union do not associate professional support with their job satisfaction. While Polish teachers suffer the greatest deprivation in the amount of professional support they receive, they give it the lowest ranking in the importance they attach to it.

Teacher Workload: Amount and Importance. Four questions comprise the index that evaluates teacher workload. The questions assess class size, adequacy of free periods, amount of after-school work, and amount of clerical and administrative work. Examining Figure 5.6, teachers across countries

Figure 5.6
Relative Amount and Importance of Teacher Workload, by Country

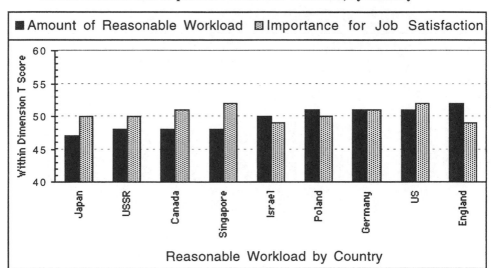

Note: This figure is derived from data in Table F-2 of the *Technical Supplement*.

have highly variable perceptions of workload. In about half the countries studied, including England, the United States, Germany, Poland, and Israel, teachers generally evaluate workload as reasonable. In the remaining countries, including Japan, the Soviet Union, Canada, and Singapore, teachers evaluate the quantity of work as overloaded, unreasonable, and burdensome.

Japanese teachers take issue with large class sizes, lack of free periods to plan work, and an excessive amount of work after school hours. Soviet teachers perceive particular deprivation in the amount of free periods during school hours. Canadian teachers take issue with the amount of administrative work and after-school work.

What value do teachers attach to ratings of their workload? Teachers in Singapore, the United States, Canada, and Germany attach the greatest and almost equal amounts of importance to workload for job satisfaction in comparison to teachers in other countries. On the other hand, British and Israeli teachers view workload as less importance for job satisfaction than teachers in all other countries.

Teachers in the United States attach particular importance to reasonable class size for job satisfaction. Interestingly, in comparison to other countries, German teachers place the highest value on reasonable class size and the lowest value on the amount of administrative work in relation to their job satisfaction.

To what extent is there agreement between the workload experienced and that desired? *Teachers in all countries except Germany cannot seem to get what they want in this regard.* In England, where teachers have the best evaluation of workload overall, teachers attach significantly less importance to reasonable workload for job satisfaction. *Again, getting what one desires is associated with a lower value.* In five countries, including the United States, Singapore, Canada, the Soviet Union, and Japan, conditions of deprivation are apparent, whereby importance ratings for workload outrank current conditions. Only German teachers have a workload that meets their desires.

Esprit de Corps: Amount and Importance. Two questions make up the index labeled esprit de corps. These questions examine the success of a school principal in getting people to work together and the extent of positive staff morale. Conceptually, these questions assess school climate issues, which have been linked to both teacher job satisfaction and positive student learning outcomes (Katz & Kahn, 1978; Erlandson & Pastor, 1981; Johnson, 1987). Figure 5.7 summarizes the finding that generally, teachers in Eastern countries experience significantly higher ratings of esprit de corps. They focus on team work and one's contribution to the good of the whole. Topping the rankings are Japan, Poland, and Singapore. Canada stands alone with a significantly lower rating of school climate (amount of esprit de corps) than all other countries.

Looking at the importance of this index for job satisfaction, Figure 5.7 shows that teachers in all countries rate esprit de corps as moderately important for their job satisfaction. Teachers around the world associate job satis-

Figure 5.7
Relative Amount and Importance of Esprit de Corps, by Country

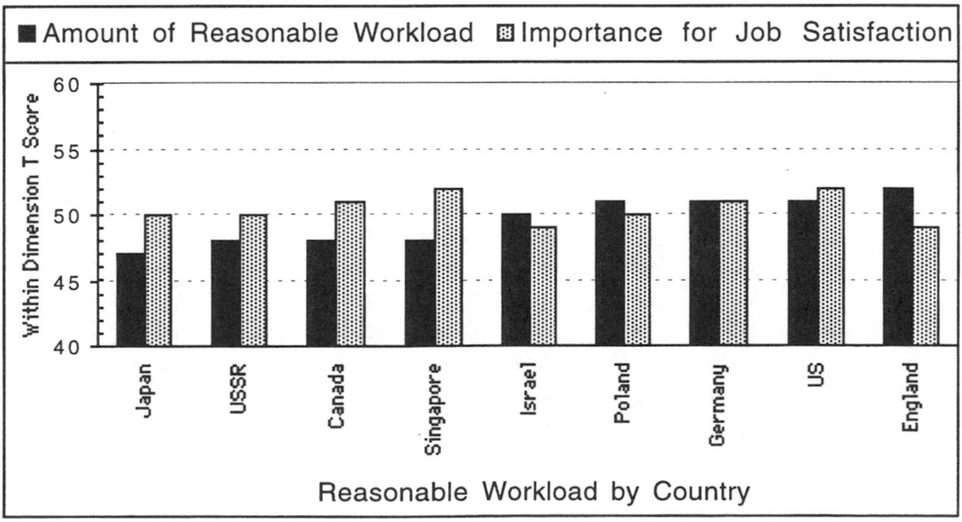

Note: This figure is derived from data in Table F-2 of the *Technical Supplement*.

faction with positive staff morale and the success of principals in getting teachers to work together.

Physical Resources: Amount and Importance. It is imperative that employees in any profession have adequate physical resources to successfully complete their work. The quality of physical resources on the job has long been recognized as a necessary and vital component of job satisfaction. Three questions were posed to teachers about their physical resources. Teachers were asked about the adequacy of materials and equipment, physical surroundings, and extent of help from support staff, including technical and clerical. As illustrated in Figure 5.8, Singapore, Israel, the United States, and England take the top four spots when compared to other countries. The physical resources of teachers in these countries are significantly better than that of teachers in Canada, the Soviet Union, and Poland. Teachers in the Soviet Union had the lowest rating of questions relating to the extent of help from support staff and having enough material and equipment.

Just how important are physical resources to teachers' job satisfaction? Polish teachers place significantly more value on the quality of their physical resources than teachers in all other countries. Teachers in the other eight countries did not vary in their evaluation of the importance of physical resources; they all attached moderate importance to physical resources for job satisfaction. Clearly, Polish teachers struggle the most with regard to physical resources, since they have the greatest and significant disparity in the high value

Figure 5.8
Relative Amount and Importance of Physical Resources, by Country

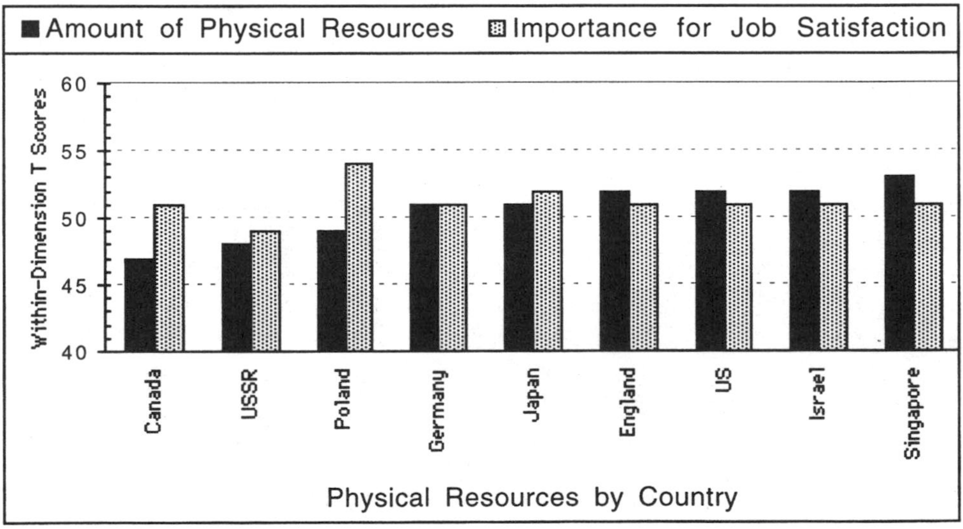

Note: This figure is derived from data in Table F-2 of the *Technical Supplement*.

they assign to physical resources for job satisfaction versus limited physical resources. Canadian teachers also experience a disparity between lower rating of extent of physical resources versus the importance they attach to them.

Economic Incentives: Amount and Importance. Economic incentives, such as pay, benefits, and promotion opportunities, have long been associated with employee job satisfaction. Three questions were posed to teachers with regard to economics. They assessed perceptions of pay, job benefits, and opportunities for promotion. With the exceptions of Canada and Germany, teachers in all countries assigned the lowest scores to the amount of economic incentives they have on the job. *This is consistently the weakest and most problematic area of work conditions for teachers.*

Figure 5.9 shows that there is generally great disparity in the current evaluation of economic condition of teachers across the nine countries. Teachers in Canada, Germany, and the United States enjoy top ranking in economic incentives. Canadian teachers give high marks to pay and benefits, but lower marks to their promotional opportunities. Japanese, Israeli, Polish, and English teachers suffer the most and almost equally with regard to their lack of economic incentives. Comparatively, Polish teachers had the lowest rating of pay, while Japanese and Israeli teachers had the lowest evaluations of benefits. While German teachers overall give high marks to pay and benefits, they have the lowest evaluation of promotional opportunities than teachers in other countries.

Figure 5.9
Relative Amount and Importance of Economic Incentives, by Country

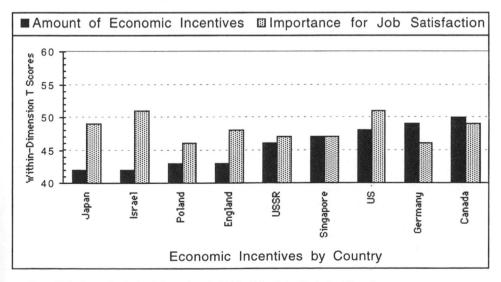

Note: This figure is derived from data in Table F-2 of the *Technical Supplement*.

There is great variability in the importance teachers across countries attach to economics. Generally speaking, teacher associate economics to job satisfaction to a moderate extent. Comparatively speaking, Israeli, U.S., Japanese, Canadian, and British teachers attach the greatest importance to economic incentives for job satisfaction than teachers in other countries, but these are moderate ratings. Teachers in Germany, Poland, Singapore, and the Soviet Union attach less value to economics for job satisfaction.

Generally, teachers in all countries place greater importance on pay and benefits than to promotional opportunities. Teachers appear quite satisfied to teach, and not advance into administrative positions of authority. U.S. teachers have the highest mean scores in importance of pay and benefits than teachers in any other country. Israeli teachers, on the other hand, rank the highest of teachers in all other countries in the importance of promotional opportunities; they are unique in this regard.

It is interesting to note that in five countries, teachers are not getting what they want with regard to the economics of the profession. Teachers in Israel, Japan, England, Poland, and the United States experience extreme or moderate deprivation in the amount of economic incentives present versus the amount desired for job satisfaction. Teachers in the Soviet Union, Singapore, and Canada have economic incentives that match their level of desire in order for them to be satisfied. Only in Germany do the economic incentives of teaching exceed the importance attached to them.

Evaluating Working Conditions within Countries

Assessing Overall Work Conditions. While the previous discussions focused on the similarities and differences between countries, it is intriguing to assess the patterns of responses within countries. Each country has variability in its ratings across indexes. By arranging the indexes in rank order within a country, one may capture a snapshot of how within-country profiles of work conditions sort out. Table 5.1 arranges the indexes in rank order within countries so that one may assess the amount and importance of the seven work conditions. A ranking of 1 is highest and 7 lowest with regard to evaluations of extent present and importance for job satisfaction.

The results in Table 5.1 show similarities and differences across countries. The profile of ratings across indexes of current work conditions is most similar for teachers in the United States, England, and Israel. Teachers in Japan and Singapore also share a similar pattern of their rank order of work conditions. Teachers in six of nine countries give extent of autonomy their top rating. Teachers in seven countries of nine rate the amount of economic incentives as the work condition least present.

Analysis of the pattern of rankings within countries of the importance of work conditions is not as telling as the extent ratings, since there is significantly less variability in mean scores of importance ratings across indexes.

Table 5.1
Within-Country Rank Order of Condition Index Means for Amount and Importance for Job Satisfaction

Country	Teacher Autonomy	Physical Resources	Teacher Support	Teacher Workload	Professional Support	Esprit de Corps	Economic Incentives
US	1 (1)	2 (5)	3 (2)	4 (3)	5 (7)	6 (4)	7 (6)
England	1 (6)	3 (3)	5 (2)	4 (4)	2 (5)	6 (1)	7 (7)
Germany	1 (1)	2 (3)	6 (4)	3 (2)	5 (6)	7 (5)	4 (7)
Japan	3 (7)	5 (2)	4 (3)	6 (4)	2 (5)	1 (1)	7 (6)
Singapore	2 (4)	1 (3)	5 (5)	6 (2)	4 (6)	3 (1)	7 (7)
Canada	1 (1)	6 (2)	3 (4)	4 (5)	5 (7)	7 (3)	2 (6)
Poland	3 (3)	5 (1)	1 (5)	4 (4)	6 (6)	2 (2)	7 (7)
Israel	1 (1)	2 (3)	3 (5)	5 (6)	6 (7)	4 (2)	7 (4)
USSR	1 (4)	4 (5)	6 (2)	5 (3)	3 (6)	2 (1)	7 (7)

Note: Condition amount and condition importance ranks in each cell are entered in this order: amount (importance).

Using the rankings to evaluate within-country similarities or differences in the importance of work conditions to job satisfaction is misleading, since actual mean scores are, in fact, quite close. Teachers in all nine countries share consistently moderate to moderately high ratings with regard to the importance they give to work conditions for job satisfaction. Germany and Canada follow almost identical patterns of ratings of indexes. It should be noted that all the ratings of importance by Polish teachers form the most unique pattern of results. Again, economic incentives have a consistently low ranking across countries, as does professional support when considering job satisfaction. The importance attached to autonomy and esprit de corps varies significantly more, capturing top and bottom rankings in some countries.

Incongruities: Are Teachers Getting the Work Conditions They Desire? Having evaluated the extent of presence of work conditions, as well as the importance for job satisfaction that teachers attach to work conditions, one may ask if teachers in these countries are experiencing the kinds of working conditions they desire for job satisfaction. Teachers may be coping with situations of *deprivation*, where their work conditions are not present to the extent that they desire or value for their job satisfaction. On the other hand, teachers may find themselves in situations of *saturation*, where the quality of working conditions exceed the extent to which they associate them with job satisfaction.

Incongruities in working conditions, therefore, are construed as the difference between ratings of extent of presence versus the importance attached to a working condition for job satisfaction. These data provide another clue in understanding the complex way in which work conditions impact the psyche of teachers. Many long-standing theories of job satisfaction relate to the notion that individuals want consistency between their values and perceptions of reality (Hoppock, 1935; Schaffer, 1955; Festinger, 1957, 1964; Adams, 1963; Weick, 1966; Kalleberg, 1977). Understanding incongruities lend valuable information on how to reduce intrapersonal stressors, resulting in greater work centrality and more productive workplaces for teachers.

Based on the T deviation scores from the nine-country mean, Table 5.2 allows us to quickly assess the extent of congruency between the assessments of working conditions versus the importance attached to them. Teachers in six of nine countries experience significant differences in the quality of their work conditions overall versus the importance they give to them. Teachers in five of the nine countries, including the Soviet Union, Singapore, Poland, Japan, and England, have general situations of deprivation. On the other hand, teachers in four countries, including Canada, the United States, Israel, and

Table 5.2
Cross-Cultural Comparison of Overall Means for Condition Amount and Importance for Job Satisfaction: Are Teachers Getting What They Want?

Country	Overall Mean: All 33 Condition Amount Items	Overall Mean: All 33 Condition Importance Items	State of Deprivation or Saturation	Extent of Incongruity
USSR	-1.84	-0.74	Deprived	+1.10
Singapore	-0.07	1.33	Deprived	+1.40
US	3.55	1.93	Saturated	-1.62
Israel	2.53	-0.69	Saturated	-3.22
Poland	-2.69	0.64	Deprived	+3.33
Japan	-3.36	0.57	Deprived	+3.93
England	-1.64	3.87	Deprived	+5.51
Canada	11.49	2.54	Saturated	-8.95
Germany	1.73	-9.48	Saturated	-11.21

Note: The numbers in the second and third columns are the deviation in t-score units of each country's raw-score amount and importance mean from the corresponding means for all nine countries. This table is derived from data in Table F-1 of the *Technical Supplement*.

Germany, generally rate the qualities of their working conditions as saturated, and in the cases of Canada and Germany, as extremely saturated. Teachers in the Soviet Union, Singapore, and the United States are getting closest to what they want, meaning that the current state of working conditions more closely matches the extent of importance they attach to them for their job satisfaction overall.

Table 5.3 looks at the seven categories of work conditions, and indicates the number of the countries where teachers rate work conditions equivalent to the value they assign them, and where teachers find themselves in conditions of deprivation or saturation. Forty-three of the sixty-three (68%) ratings of the work conditions are equivalent to the amount of importance teachers attach to them for job satisfaction. In those circumstances, teachers are getting close to what they want. In 16 percent of the ratings, specifically with regard to economic incentives, workload, physical resources, and esprit de corps, teachers find themselves deprived. In the remaining 16 percent of the ratings and dispersed across all categories except physical resources, teachers report saturation. The implications of the link between saturation and devaluation of aspects of work will be explored at the end of the chapter.

Considering Gender, Age, and Marital Status

Perceptions of Working Conditions Given Gender. Do males and females in these nine countries evaluate their working conditions differently? *For the most part, males and females across cultures share* great agreement *on their*

Table 5.3
Are Teachers Getting What They Want? Comparing Within-Country Amount and Importance of T-Scores for Seven Work Condition Indexes

INDEX	Number of Countries Where Amount and Importance Are Not Significantly Different	Number of Countries Where Amount Is Significantly Less Than Importance (Deprived)	Number of Countries Where Amount Is Significantly More Than Importance (Saturated)
Teacher Support	8	0	1
Teacher Autonomy	6	0	3
Professional Support	7	0	2
Teacher Workload	5	3	1
Esprit de Corps	7	1	1
Physical Resources	7	2	0
Economic Incentives	3	4	2
TOTAL	43	10	10

Note: The numbers in this table are derived from data in Table F-2 of the *Technical Supplement*.

evaluations of their working conditions. There were only eight differences in ratings of working conditions by males and females in nine countries. Four gender differences were observed in Israel where Israeli females offer higher ratings of teacher support, professional support, and esprit de corps than their male counterparts; however, male teachers in Israel rated the amount of workload as significantly more reasonable than Israeli females.

Workload is the one index where males and females across countries differ the most when evaluating extent and importance (Guttentag & Secord, 1983; Hess & Ferree, 1987; Swanson-Kauffman, 1987; Hearn, Sheppard, Tancred-Sheriff, and Burrell, 1989). Male teachers in Singapore and the United States, in addition to Israel, rated the amount of workload as more reasonable than their female counterparts. Polish males rated the economic incentives of teaching in that country more positively than did females, while German males had more positive ratings of physical resources than German female teachers.

Do males and females differ in the importance they attach specifically to the various work conditions evaluated in this survey? *Male and female teachers share equal value judgments of the importance of specific working conditions for job satisfaction,* with the exception of teachers in the Soviet Union, Israel, and to a lesser extent, Singapore. There were a total of eleven gender differences on the importance ratings. Males and females in the Soviet Union diverge more frequently than do the genders in other countries with regard to how much value they attach to working conditions for job satisfaction. For job satisfaction, Soviet females value community support, professional support, economic incentives, physical resources, reasonable workload, and esprit de corps more than do their male colleagues.

Meanwhile, females in Israel attach more importance to professional support, community support, and autonomy than their male colleagues. Female teachers in Singapore give greater importance to support and a reasonable workload for job satisfaction than do male teachers in that country. In all countries where differences in ratings of importance of work conditions arise, it is females who place greater value on a work condition than do their male colleagues. In general, it is only in the Soviet Union, Israel, and Singapore where male and female teachers differ in the value placed on certain working conditions for job satisfaction. Male and female teachers in the United States, England, Germany, Japan, Canada, and Poland do not differ in any regard around the importance they associate with working conditions for job satisfaction.

Perceptions of Working Conditions Given Marital Status. Do married and unmarried teachers in these nine countries perceive their work conditions differently? This question addresses the notion that teachers' familial context to a large extent shape their work-related experiences, needs, desires, stresses, and expectations. *An analysis of differences in the rating of work conditions between married and unmarried teachers reveals relatively few differences.* In total there are only six differences noted in the ratings of married versus unmarried teachers across seven indexes in nine countries. There are no differences in the ratings of married versus unmarried teachers in England, Canada, Poland, and the Soviet Union.

Differences in ratings of married versus unmarried teachers also center around highly specific issues. Only in ratings of economic incentives, workload, and esprit de corps are there differences in the ratings of presence of work conditions. Married and unmarried teachers evaluate the economic incentives of their profession quite differently. Unmarried teachers in Japan evaluate their economic incentives more positively than do married teachers, and understandably so, since they are likely to be free of the financial burdens of family. On the other hand, unmarried teachers in Singapore and Israel have lower ratings of the economic incentives of the teaching profession than do married teachers in those countries. Following the same notion, unmarried teachers in the United States and Germany assess the workload demands less favorably than do married teachers. This may be attributed to the differences in lifestyle of married and unmarried teachers, and of the amount of after-school work demands teachers experience. Again in the United States, unmarried teachers offer significantly lower ratings of esprit de corps than do their married cohorts, leading one to question if being "unattached" impairs collegial interactions, and ultimately results in lower ratings of school climate.

Do married and unmarried teachers differ in the importance they attach specifically to the various work conditions evaluated in this survey? Married and unmarried teachers share almost full agreement on the work conditions they value for job satisfaction; there are only two differences in this regard. Only unmarried teachers in Israel place greater value on autonomy than do married teachers in that country, while married teachers in England associate greater job satisfaction with economic incentives than do their unmarried colleagues. Interestingly, no differences emerge in the importance attached to community support, professional support, physical resources, workload, and esprit de corps in relation to marital status. *This finding indicates that, for the most part across cultures, marital status does not impact job satisfaction in relation to specific working conditions.*

Perceptions of Working Conditions Given Age. The final question surrounding demographic variables involves age. Do young, middle-aged, or older teachers in these nine countries perceive work conditions differently? *Age, more so than gender or marital status, is a variable that is associated with a large number differences when evaluating work conditions, and to a minor extent, the importance of specific work conditions to job satisfaction.* Teachers' evaluations of the seven work-condition indexes were analyzed across three categories of age: Young includes those 35 years old and younger, middle-age includes 35 to 49-year-olds, and older teachers were considered 50 years old and older.

Regarding ratings of the presence of work conditions, there are a total of 38 age-related differences in rating across 9 countries and 7 indexes—a total of sixty-three responses. In all countries with the exception of the United States and

Israel, teachers who are older offer significantly higher ratings of physical resources than do younger teachers. In Israel, young teachers evaluate the amount of physical resources significantly more positive than do middle-aged teachers.

Ratings of extent of professional support differed across age groups in seven of nine countries, to the exclusion of Canada and Poland. Older teachers in the Soviet Union, Singapore, Japan, Germany, and England experience more support than younger teachers, while older teachers in the United States and Israel report less support than younger teachers. Generally, older teachers in England, Germany, Singapore, Canada, Poland, and the Soviet Union offer higher ratings of the economic incentives than do younger teachers, while teachers across ages in the United States, Japan, and Israel share equal judgments of economic incentives.

Teachers' perceptions of workload also change over time. As teachers age in England, Germany, Singapore, Poland, and Israel, they view their workload as increasingly more reasonable, and their school climate more positively. The more positive ratings of workload with age may be associated with teachers' learning, increased skill in teaching, and an accumulation of teaching resources. Teachers in England, Germany, Japan, Singapore, and the Soviet Union also offer higher ratings of esprit de corps as they age. This is in keeping with the fact that older teachers in England, Germany, and the Soviet Union give higher evaluations of the support they receive from parents, community, and colleagues. Only in Israel do older teachers perceive less support than middle-aged and younger teachers. The area of work conditions with the least age-related differences in ratings is autonomy. Only in Japan, Poland, and the Soviet Union do teachers perceive significantly greater autonomy as they age.

All in all, teachers in England, Germany, and the Soviet Union have the most age-related differences—in six of seven indexes of work conditions. Singapore teachers tally five of seven; Japan, Poland, and Israel total age-related differences in four of seven areas of work conditions. Canada and the United States have the least age-related differences, two and one respectively. Thirty-four out of thirty-eight differences in evaluations of the work conditions are increasingly positive as the age of teacher increases. In Israel, three work conditions—support, professional support, and physical resources—are perceived to decrease with age. In the United States, ratings of amount of professional support decrease with increasing age of the teacher.

These differences lead one to speculate that perceptions truly change with time, and that with age, teachers may become either desensitized or less critical of their work conditions. They may also have more diverse life experiences and a larger knowledge base on which to critique working conditions.

What can be said of changes or differences in the value attached to work conditions as teachers age? Overall, there are significantly fewer differences in the importance of specific work conditions across the age of teacher. There are only eleven differences in ratings of importance when analyzed across age groups. The importance of work autonomy increases with age for teachers in the United States and the Soviet Union, but decreases for teachers in

Israel. The importance of professional support again decreases with age for teachers in Israel and Germany, as does the importance of community support in Israel and Canada. The importance of economic incentives also decreases with age of a teacher in England, and drops in importance for middle-aged teachers in Singapore. The importance of workload decreases with age for Canadian teachers, while the importance of esprit de corps increases with age for teachers in Poland.

With regard to importance of work conditions and teacher age, we see mixed trends, and no universal patterns emerge. Increased importance of certain work conditions occur for teachers in the United States, Singapore, Poland, and the Soviet Union, while importance decreased for certain work conditions for teachers in England, Germany, Canada, and Israel. Only in Japan is aging not associated with a change in the values attached to working conditions for job satisfaction.

THE CONTRIBUTION OF WORK CONDITIONS TO QUALITY OF TEACHER LIFE

Observing that teachers teach in extremely variable work conditions and attach varying degrees of importance to specific work conditions, it is important to explore the contribution that working conditions make to overall quality of work life. The survey asked teachers from all countries to rate overall job satisfaction, work centrality, and job-related stress. It is important that all relationships among work conditions, controlling for demographic variables, and quality of work life be understood before making any recommendations for policy changes. Multiple regression analysis is an effective way of assessing the influence of conditions variables on quality of work life. The results from separate regressions of overall job satisfaction, work centrality, and job-related stress on the relevant indexes of work conditions are not included here because of space limitations, but are included as Tables F-10, F-11, and F-12, respectively, in the available *Technical Supplement* described in the appendix. Because demographic distributions are radically different from country to country, the three demographic indexes (gender, age, and marital status) were included in each regression. The influences discussed in the following sections are based on the regression weights attached to separate condition indexes and the change in multiple R-squared attributable to the total effect of all conditions, with the effects of demographics controlled statistically. Because of space limitations, only the overall regression weights are presented in chapter tables.

Work Conditions and Overall Job Satisfaction

Teachers in this study gave ratings of their overall job satisfaction, including extent of enjoyment of teaching as an occupation, extent to which teaching measures up to expectations, the likelihood of entering teaching again, and overall satisfaction with one's present job as a teacher. To what extent do work conditions, in combination with demographic variables, account for overall job satisfaction ratings? Table 5.4 summarizes in rank order the over-all results of the multiple regression, with the unique contribution and signifi-cance level of work conditions appearing in the last two columns. The combined work condition indexes plus demographics account for a signifi-cant proportion of overall job satisfaction variance in all nine countries, with percentages ranging from a high of 27.3 percent in England to a low of 12.1 percent in the Soviet Union. *Working conditions universally impact teachers' overall job satisfaction.*

What indexes account for most of the variance? Support from parents, com-munity, and colleagues contributes significantly to overall job satisfaction for teachers in all nine countries, followed by work autonomy, which also con-tributes positively to teachers' job satisfaction in all countries, with the ex-ception of Canada. Esprit de corps also proves to be a predictor of overall job satisfaction in all countries but the United States. Workload is significantly predictive of overall job satisfaction in only five of nine countries, including the United States, Germany, Singapore, Canada, and Poland, as are economic incentives in the United States, England, Japan, Singapore, and Poland. Physi-cal resources and professional support do not contribute to the prediction of overall job satisfaction in eight of nine countries; only in Germany (physical resources) and England (professional support) do these indexes have a sig-nificant impact on overall job satisfaction. Contrary to expectation, incongru-

Table 5.4
The Contribution of Work Conditions and Demographics to Overall Job Satisfaction

COUNTRY	Overall R^2	Overall R^2 Significance	R^2 Attributed to Conditions Indexes	Significance of R^2 for Conditions Indexes
England	.305	.000	.273	.000
Poland	.278	.000	.267	.000
Israel	.286	.000	.262	.000
US	.272	.000	.255	.000
Canada	.242	.000	.236	.000
Germany	.230	.000	.221	.000
Japan	.194	.000	.162	.000
Singapore	.192	.000	.176	.000
USSR	.158	.000	.121	.000

Note: The numbers in this table are derived from data in Table F-10 of the *Technical Supplement*.

ities between ratings of the importance and extent of presence of work conditions are significant negative predictors of overall job satisfaction in only two countries: Germany and Israel.

Work Conditions and Job-Related Stress

To what extent do work conditions contribute to job-related stress? Teachers were asked how much stress overall they experienced in their present jobs. Table 5.5 provides a summary of the results of the multiple regression analysis of job-related stress, with the unique contribution and significance level of work conditions again presented in the last two columns. The combined condition indexes account for a significant proportion of job-related stress variance in all nine countries, with percentages ranging from a high of 18.1 percent in Israel to a low of 4.2 percent in Poland.

Incongruence between the importance and amount of presence of work conditions is a strong and very significant positive predictor of increased job-related stress in all countries but Singapore, where it is an insignificant positive predictor. Workload is another strong predictor of reduced stress for teachers in six of nine countries, including the United States, England, Germany, Japan, Canada, and Israel. Professional support contributes to the prediction of reduced stress in four countries: Germany, Japan, Singapore, and the Soviet Union. Economic incentives significantly predicts reduced stress only for teachers in England and Canada, while support of colleagues predicts reduced stress for teachers in England and Israel. Autonomy and esprit

Table 5.5
The Contribution of Work Conditions and Demographics to Job-Related Stress

COUNTRY	Overall R^2	Overall R^2 Significance	R^2 Attributed To Conditions Indexes	Significance of R^2 for Conditions Indexes
Israel	.195	.000	.181	.000
Germany	.156	.000	.143	.000
Canada	.162	.000	.137	.000
England	.158	.000	.134	.000
US	.118	.000	.115	.000
Japan	.127	.000	.113	.000
Singapore	.070	.000	.063	.000
USSR	.070	.000	.046	.000
Poland	.048	.002	.042	.010

Note: The numbers in this table are derived from data in Table F-12 of the *Technical Supplement*.

de corps are associated with reduced stress only for teachers in Singapore. For U.S. teachers, a lack of physical resources is a significant predictor of increased stress.

Work Conditions and Work Centrality

To what extent do work conditions contribute to work centrality, controlling for demographic variables? Teachers were asked several questions to capture the extent of work centrality, including the importance they associate with success at work, the amount of preoccupation with work outside of working hours, and the extent of engagement with activities associated with school-wide issues, including school policy development, student discipline and curriculum. Table 5.6 summarizes in rank order the results of the multiple regression analysis of work centrality, with the unique contribution and significance level of work conditions again appearing in the last two columns. The combined condition indexes account for a significant proportion of work centrality variance in all nine countries, with percentages ranging from a high of 18.2 percent in Israel to a low of 5.4 percent in Germany. This range is similar to the results seen in the analysis of job-related stress.

Increased incongruence significantly predicts reduced work centrality in all countries but Japan, where it inexplicably predicts a significant increase. Increases in workload, autonomy, and esprit de corps, on the other hand, are predictive of increased work centrality in most countries. In fact, increased autonomy significantly predicts increased work centrality in six of nine countries, including the United States, England, Germany, Singapore, Poland, and

Table 5.6

The Contribution of Work Conditions and Demographics to Work Centrality

Country	Overall R^2	Overall R^2 Significance	R^2 Attributed To Conditions Indexes	Significance of R^2 for Conditions Indexes
Israel	.222	.000	.182	.000
USSR	.164	.000	.104	.000
Poland	.120	.000	.100	.000
Japan	.089	.000	.085	.000
England	.101	.000	.074	.000
Canada	.089	.000	.070	.000
US	.078	.000	.068	.000
Singapore	.070	.000	.069	.000
Germany	.063	.000	.054	.000

Note: The numbers in this table are derived from data in Table F-11 of the *Technical Supplement*.

the Soviet Union. Esprit de corps also positively influences work centrality in England, Japan, Singapore, Poland, Israel, and the Soviet Union. Workload is a significant positive predictor of work centrality in five of nine countries: the United States, England, Japan, Israel, and the Soviet Union.

Summary: Satisfaction, Stress, and Centrality

The quality of work conditions impacts teachers' overall job satisfaction across all cultures, accounting for between 27.3 percent (England) and 12.1 percent (the Soviet Union) of the variance in ratings of overall job satisfaction. Considering the seven aspects of working conditions, support from colleagues, parents, and community is a particularly strong predictor of overall job satisfaction for teachers in all nine countries, as is autonomy in work and esprit de corps in eight countries. Workload and economic incentives have mixed ramifications across countries. Physical resources and professional support are not significant contributors to overall job satisfaction for teachers in most countries, with the exception of Germany. Incongruities between ratings of the importance and extent of presence of work conditions are not significantly predictive of overall job satisfaction in most countries. This finding does not support Kalleberg's (1977) theory of job satisfaction, which promotes the notion that one must have job-related rewards that relate to the values of the individual.

Work conditions hold mixed powers across countries in the prediction of job-related stress, with the accounted variance ranging from a low of 4.2 percent of the variance to a high of 18.1 percent of the variance in job-related stress. Incongruence between condition importance and presence significantly predicts increased stress in every country but Singapore, where the influence is in the same direction but insignificant. Workload emerges as another positive predictor of stress.

Work conditions account for between 5.4 percent and 18.2 percent of the variance in the work centrality score. The incongruity index demonstrates universal power in predicting work centrality of teachers across countries, but the direction of influence changes from country to country for reasons not understood. The expected positive influences were found for autonomy in all countries, but not quite strong enough to be statistically significant in Japan, Canada, and Israel. Similarly esprit de corps had a positive influence in all countries, but it was not quite strong enough to be of statistical significance in the United States, Germany, and Canada.

There are no universal patterns linking various working conditions to overall job satisfaction, job-related stress, and work centrality across the nine countries studied, but there are useful trends. To produce satisfied teachers, one should try to increase positive support, autonomy, and esprit de corps. To decrease teacher stress, try to reduce incongruence and workload. Last, for dedicated, work-centered teachers, attempt to decrease incongruence and increase autonomy and esprit de corps. In general, *work conditions hold the power to predict overall job satisfaction of teachers to a moderate extent, and to a lesser extent, to impact the job-related stress and work centrality of teachers in diverse cultural contexts.*

CLOSING THOUGHTS

What issues arise from the data on working conditions? What universal and country-specific insights are particularly valuable and useful to policy makers and administrators? Comparing these national constituencies, what differences and likenesses are most important?

First, as a profession, teachers universally and across diverse cultures receive and value support for their work from parents, community, or colleagues. This finding strongly suggests that regardless of national setting, teachers benefit from recognition of their work. Teachers in diverse cultures universally benefit from public acknowledgment that their profession is necessary to educate citizens, advance culture, and improve the economic viability and social well-being of one's nation. Thus, all countries should focus on efforts to recognize the contributions of teachers.

Second, the major finding that autonomy, as a dimension of teachers' work life, universally has a strong impact on quality of work life relates to the debate over the impact of organizational structure of education—centralization or decentralization (Berman, 1987; Reed, 1986; Shields, 1989). These data indicate that a majority of teachers across cultures enjoy significant freedom to experiment and express creativity and diversity by using different teaching strategies and ideas, and by deciding *how* to teach. This finding does not address the debate over *what* to teach, which relates back to the issue of centralization versus decentralization.

While teachers universally have some autonomy in their work, it is not universally valued as important for their job satisfaction. However, this process dimension of work has greater implications for attracting, recruiting, developing, encouraging, and retaining teachers (Chapman & Hutcheson, 1982; Faber, 1984; Dworkin, 1987). Professional activities should be geared toward a continuous renewal of teachers, appreciating the fact that attending to autonomy in work may not result in increased job satisfaction ratings. However, increased autonomy most assuredly will reduce job-related stress and burnout, as well as improve student learning, an aspect of work which does impact teachers' job satisfaction. This might suggest that collaborative relationships between universities and schools would benefit teachers.

Third, professional support (specifically professional, consultative, clerical, and technical support), meaningful professional and supervisory interactions, and staff meeting time, are all important process dimensions of working conditions. With the exception of teachers in England, Japan, and Singapore, teachers generally are not getting necessary professional support. This is a disappointing finding. The psychosocial and intellectual demands of teaching are so great that adequate professional support is a necessary condition in order to reduce stress, increase work centrality, and decrease teacher burnout and attrition. The general absence of professional support and the universal lack of importance attached to it for job satisfaction by teachers depicts teaching as an isolated profession. Clearly, the physical settings where teaching occurs (classrooms), the social organization of most classrooms within schools (one teacher–multiple students), and the scheduling of professional time in schools fosters the professional isolation of teachers. Getting professional support is a challenge, or even an impossibility (Duke, 1987; Russell, Altmaier, & Van Velzen, 1987). However, as teachers are increasingly pressured to educate students who are able to function successfully in team settings, it is ironic that teachers find themselves as professional loners, in situations that do not reinforce collegial, supervisory, or clerical support—in short, a team effort. This is an area of teachers' work life that should be examined and addressed by administrators and policy makers.

Fourth, teachers, policy makers, and administrators are particularly attentive to the issue of workload, specifically class size, the number of free periods during the day, the amount of after-school work, and clerical and administrative demands of teachers. The teachers studied across cultures give highly variable assessments of the reasonableness of these aspects of work. The cross-cultural findings suggest that teachers work within highly variable time structures, in a wide range of class sizes, and have varying degrees of after-school and administrative demands. Workload proves to be a work dimension that evades universal statements about its impact on job satisfactions, stress, and work centrality. Workload was predictive of both job satisfaction and work centrality in only half the countries studied. In all countries with the exception of Singapore, Poland, and the Soviet Union, increased workload creates greater job stress for teachers. Administrators and policy makers, who have the greatest power to structure teachers' work environments, should study country-specific data when addressing teacher workload.

Fifth, esprit de corps is closely associated with ratings of professional support. This has to do with principals' successes in promoting positive collegial relations and staff morale (Werner, 1982; Duke, 1988, 1989). Sadly, the North American and Western European teachers studied here experience deprivation in this regard. Teachers in those countries indicate that their work environments have leaders who are relatively less successful in getting staff to work together and in creating positive staff morale. Esprit de corps is predictive of job satisfaction and creates work centrality; in addition, this work dimension predicts the stress of teachers in six of nine countries. There is a clear message that teachers want pleasant, professional work climates, and look to principals to facilitate those work dimensions.

Sixth, teachers generally give moderate ratings of the quality of the physical resources afforded them and attach moderate importance to having adequate physical resources in relation to job satisfaction (Louis & Smith, 1990). Despite the push to improve the physical resources afforded to teachers and classrooms, there is little relation to improved teacher job satisfaction, stress, or work centrality.

Seventh, economic incentives, such as pay, benefits, and promotion opportunities, have increasingly become the focus of national efforts to improve teacher recruitment and retention. Teachers across the countries studied agree that teaching does *not* provide strong or acceptable economic incentives. However, in only five of nine countries do teachers associate economic incentives with overall job satisfaction, and it only is associated with job-related stress for teachers in England and Canada. Focusing on economic incentives is not likely to predict teachers' work centrality either; economic incentives contribute to work centrality only in England, Canada, and the Soviet Union. Surprisingly, increasing economic incentives in order to retain teachers in the profession, increase teacher job satisfaction, or reduce teacher stress is not likely to be fruitful.

Eighth, the cross-cultural data from this study indicate that generally males and females, married and unmarried, share equal evaluations and value judgments of their working conditions. Generally, adjustments in working conditions should be more sensitive to the age of the teacher than to the gender or marital status of the teacher. Interactive dynamics of these three demographic variables are culturally sensitive, and changes in policy or work rewards or demands should be analyzed in relation to age of the work force (Gibson & Klein, 1970; Swanson-Kauffman, 1987).

Ninth, and last, one of the most interesting findings relates to the issue of incongruity, or giving teachers the kind of working conditions they value as important for their job satisfaction (Sergiovanni, 1967; Hofstede, 1980; Schmitt & Pulakos, 1985; MacQueen & Ignatovich, 1986). Regarding the seven aspects of work conditions that were examined, the teachers in the country ranking in the top position on the extent of presence of a work condition also had lower ratings of the importance of that condition for their job satisfaction. So, when teachers had high ratings in the amount of presence of working conditions, it appears that they attributed less value to that specific work condition for their job satisfaction. This is a condition of saturation. The phenomenon associated with saturation raises an interesting question with regard to job satisfaction theory (Festinger, 1957, 1964; Chapman & Lowther, 1982; Caplan, 1987; Poppleton & Riseborough, 1989). It appears that teachers universally and from diverse cultures devalue those work conditions that they find satisfactory. Simply put, *saturation leads to devaluation*. It appears that once individuals experience positive ratings of a working condition, the value they assign to the condition for their job satisfaction lessens. *These findings also suggest that people may assign greater importance to that which they do not have, and less importance to that which they do have.* Prior research on job satisfaction has not specifically studied the phenomenon of satisfaction leading to devaluation of specific aspects of work life. This would be an interesting and fruitful area for future, cross-cultural research with regard to teacher job satisfaction.

REFERENCES

Adams, J. S. (1963). Towards an understanding of equity. *Journal of Abnormal and Social Psychology, 67*, 422–436.

Berman, D. M. (1987). Educational reform in postwar Japan or the "Japanization" of American education. *Forum, 15* (2), 22.

Caplan, R. D. (1987). Person–environment-fit in organizations: Theories, facts, and values. In A. W. Riley and S. J. Zaccaro (Eds.), *Occupational stress and organizational effectiveness*. New York: Praeger.

Chapman, D. W.; and Hutcheson, S. M. (1982). Attrition from teaching careers: A discriminant analysis. *American Educational Research Journal, 19* (1), 93–105.

Chapman, D. W.; and Lowther, M. A. (1982). Teachers' satisfaction with teaching. *Journal of Educational Research, 74* (4), 241–247.

Duke, D. L. (1987). *School leadership and instructional improvement*. New York: Random House.

Duke, D. L. (1988). Why principals consider quitting. *Phi Delta Kappan, 70* (4), 308–312.

Duke, D. L. (1989). The aesthetics of leadership. In J. L. Burdin (Ed.), *School leadership: A contemporary reader*. Newbury Park, CA: Sage.

Dworkin, A. G. (1987). *Teacher burnout in public schools*. New York: State University of New York Press.

Erlandson, D. A.; and Pastor, M. C. (1981). Teacher motivation, job satisfaction, and alternatives—Directions for principals. *NASSP, 65* (442), 5–9.

Faber, B. A. (1984). Teacher burnout: Assumptions, myths, and issues. *Teachers College Record, 86*, 321–338.

Festinger, L. (1957). *A theory of cognitive dissonance*. Evanston, IL: Row, Peterson.

Festinger, L. (1964). *Conflict, decision, and dissonance*. Stanford, CA: Stanford University Press.

Gibson, J.; and Klein, S. (1970). Employee attitudes as a function of age and length of service. *Academy of Management Journal, 13*, 411–425.

Guttentag, M.; and Secord, P. F. (1983). *Too many women? The sex ratio question*. Newbury Park, CA: Sage.

Hackman, J. R.; and Oldham, G. R. (1980). *Work redesign*. Reading, MA: Addison-Wesley.

Hearn, J.; Sheppard, D. L.; Tancred-Sheriff, P.; and Burrell, G. (Eds.). (1989). *The sexuality of organization*. Newbury Park, CA: Sage.

Herzberg, R.; Mausner, B.; and Snyderman, B. (1959). *The motivation to work*. New York: John Wiley & Sons.

Hess, B. B.; and Ferree, M. M. (Eds.). (1987). *Analyzing gender: A handbook of social science research*. Newbury Park, CA: Sage.

Hofstede, G. (1980). *Culture's consequences: International differences in work-related values*. Newbury Park, CA: Sage.

Holdaway, E. (1978). Facet and overall satisfaction of teachers. *Educational Administration Quarterly, 14* (7), 30–34.

Hoppock, R. (1935). *Job satisfaction.* New York: Harper.

Johnson, D. J. (1987). Effect of selected variables related to faculty on faculty satisfaction with the administrator. *Education, 107* (4), 406–416.

Kahn, R. L.; and Boulding, E. (Eds.). (1964). *Power and conflict in organizations.* New York: Basic Books.

Kalleberg, A. L. (1977). Work values and job rewards: A theory of job satisfaction. *American Sociological Review, 42*, 124–143.

Katz, D.; and Kahn, R. (1978). *The social psychology of organization.* New York: John Wiley & Sons.

Lawler, E. E. (1973). *Motivation in work organizations.* Monterey, CA: Brookes-Cole.

Lawler, E. E.; and Hall, D. T. (1970). Relationship of job characteristics to job involvement, satisfaction, and intrinsic motivation. *Journal of Applied Psychology, 54*, 305–312.

Lortie, D. C. (1975). *School teacher: A sociological study.* Chicago: University of Chicago Press.

Louis, K. S.; and Smith, B. (1990). Teacher working conditions. In P. Reyes (Ed.), *Teachers and their workplace: Commitment, performance, and productivity.* Newbury Park, CA: Sage.

MacQueen, L. W.; and Ignatovich, R. R. (1986). *An importance-method approach to overall and job-facet satisfaction of teachers.* Paper presented at the annual meeting of the American Educational Research Association, San Francisco, CA, April.

Maslow, A. H. (1970). *Motivation and personality.* New York: Harper and Row.

MOW International Research Team. (1987). *The meaning of work.* Orlando, FL: Academic Press.

Nias, J. (1981). Teacher satisfaction and dissatisfaction: Herzberg's "two-factor" hypothesis revisited. *British Journal of Sociology of Education, 2* (3), 235–246.

Pastor, M. C.; and Erlandson, D. A. (1982). A study of higher order need strength and job satisfaction in secondary public school teachers. *The Journal of Educational Administration, 20* (2), 172–183.

Poppleton, P. (1990). *The work perceptions of secondary teachers in England: Similarities and differences with four other countries—U.S., Japan, Singapore, and West Germany.* Paper presented at the American Educational Research Association Conference, Boston, April 16–21.

Poppleton, P.; and Riseborough, G. (1988). *Teaching in the U.K. in the mid-1980s: Secondary teachers' perceptions of their working conditions, roles, classroom practices, and job satisfactions.* Paper presented at the American Educational Research Association Conference, New Orleans, April 5–8.

Poppleton, P.; and Riseborough, G. (1989). Rewards and values in secondary school teachers' perceptions of their job satisfaction. *Research Papers in Education, 4*, 71–95.

Postlethwaite, T. N. (1988). *The encyclopedia of comparative education and national systems of education.* New York: Pergamon Press.

Reed, S. R. (1986). *Japanese prefectures and policymaking.* Pittsburgh, PA: University of Pittsburgh Press.

Riseborough, G.; and Poppleton, P. (1991). Veterans versus beginners: A study of teachers at a time of fundamental change in comprehensive schooling. *Educa-*

tional Review, 43 (1), 307–334.

Russell, D. W.; Altmaier, E.; and Van Velzen, D. (1987). Job-related stress, social support, and burnout among classroom teachers. *Journal of Applied Psychology, 72* (2), 269–274.

Schaffer, R. (1955). Job satisfaction as related to need satisfaction in work. *Psychological Monographs, 67* (364), 14.

Schmitt, N.; and Pulakos, E. D. (1985). Predicting job satisfaction from life satisfaction: Is there a general satisfaction factor? *International Journal of Psychology, 20* (2), 155–167.

Sergiovanni, T. (1967). Factors which affect satisfaction and dissatisfaction of teachers. *The Journal of Educational Administration, 5* (1), 66–82.

Shields, J. J., Jr. (Ed.). (1989). *Japanese schooling: Patterns of socialization, equality, and political control.* University Park: Pennsylvania State University Press.

Swanson-Kauffman, K. M. (Ed.). (1987). *Women's work, families, and health.* New York: Hemisphere Publishing.

Weick, K. E. (1966). The concept of equity in the perception of pay. *Administrative Science Quarterly, 11*, 414–439.

Werner, W. W. (1982). How the principal spells "R-E-L-I-E-F" for teacher burnout. *American Secondary Education, 12* (2), 13–16.

6

Teaching Practices

Allen Menlo

This chapter reports the results of comparisons between the nine countries regarding their secondary teachers' perceptions of their classroom practices. Sixteen practices are involved, and their difficulty, use, importance for teacher job satisfaction and importance for student learning and development are explored. In addition, several indexes of broad practice, developed from combinations of the sixteen practices, are examined regarding their influence on each other and upon the overall job satisfaction, work centrality, and job-related stress of the teachers. Further, the influence of three demographic variables of gender, age, and marital status on the practice indexes is investigated. (See Figure 6.1 for a display of all the variables examined in this chapter, including an identification of the individual practices, which are combined to comprise each index.)

Similarities and differences between and across countries are searched for significant configurations, relationships and patterns, and where possible, these are sociopsychologically interpreted and discussed. In addition, questions are put forth regarding the place occupied by individual countries within the comparisons. These questions are intended as stimulus for further integrative discussion in Chapter 8. This places the dynamics of teaching practice within nine countries in the context of comparison with each other, which allows for the emergence of universal and country-specific meanings of teaching from those who know it most intimately—the teachers themselves. The schema in Figure 6.1 provides a conceptualization of the practices section of the overall study discussed in this book.

Figure 6.1
Conceptual Schema for the Teaching Practices Section of the Overall Study

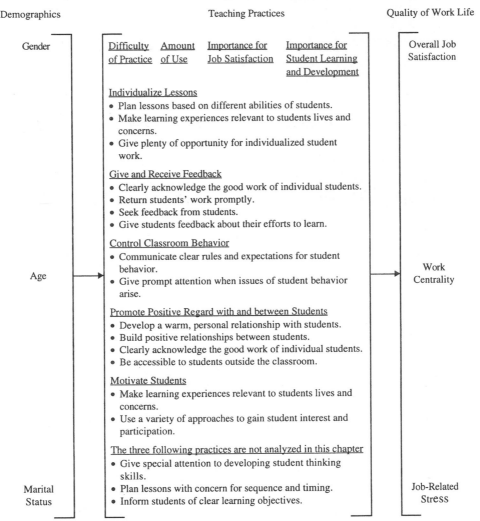

Demographics   Teaching Practices   Quality of Work Life

Gender

Difficulty   Amount   Importance for   Importance for
of Practice of Use   Job Satisfaction Student Learning
                                        and Development

Overall Job
Satisfaction

Individualize Lessons
• Plan lessons based on different abilities of students.
• Make learning experiences relevant to students lives and
  concerns.
• Give plenty of opportunity for individualized student
  work.

Give and Receive Feedback
• Clearly acknowledge the good work of individual students.
• Return students' work promptly.
• Seek feedback from students.
• Give students feedback about their efforts to learn.

Control Classroom Behavior
• Communicate clear rules and expectations for student
  behavior.
• Give prompt attention when issues of student behavior
  arise.

Age   Work
                                                                            Centrality

Promote Positive Regard with and between Students
• Develop a warm, personal relationship with students.
• Build positive relationships between students.
• Clearly acknowledge the good work of individual students.
• Be accessible to students outside the classroom.

Motivate Students
• Make learning experiences relevant to students lives and
  concerns.
• Use a variety of approaches to gain student interest and
  participation.

The three following practices are not analyzed in this chapter
• Give special attention to developing student thinking
  skills.
Marital   Job-Related
Status   • Plan lessons with concern for sequence and timing.   Stress
          • Inform students of clear learning objectives.

RATIONALE FOR FOCUSING ON TEACHING PRACTICES

The structure of all systems of elementary and secondary education appears to be based on the strong belief that something significant happens when teachers meet students in classrooms. Consequently, for several years in the United States there has been a continuing interest in extrapolating from psychological knowledge those teaching practices that are most promotive of student learning. These identifications of classroom practices have varied from broad statements of general practice (e.g., Burton, 1958; Watson, 1960; Dill, 1990) to quasiprescriptive statements of rather specific practices (e.g., Kounin, 1970; Hunter & Russel, 1981; Doyle, 1986). It seems useful to augment and enrich this knowledge and information, especially from a cross-cultural vantage point. This study provides an opportunity to do that through its examination of the difficulty, use, and importance for student learning and development of sixteen practices, as perceived by teachers in nine countries. Alternatively, attention has been called to the need for defining the knowledge base to be communicated to teachers in order to increase the likelihood of success in their practice (Holmes Group, 1988). It has been further suggested (Menlo & Marich, 1988) that a determination of those practices that teachers view as essential for student learning may be a rich, untapped resource of information which can be translated into areas and pieces of behavioral science knowledge that undergird the practices. Also, while we have learned much from prior studies about the contributions of work conditions and teacher attitudes toward the quality of teachers' working life (Holdaway, 1978; Kottkamp, Provenzo, & Cohn, 1986), the present study of the effect of teachers' practices on the three dimensions of the quality of working life (work satisfaction, work centrality, and job stress) is unique.

PRIOR RESEARCH ON TEACHING PRACTICES

Understandably, most of the studies on classroom practices have related to the learning and development outcomes for students rather than the learning and development and quality of professional life for the teacher. The literature on classroom practices in relation to effective classrooms is impressive, usually detailing the effects of good teaching on students' achievement. Experimental and qualitative studies and international comparisons have established the same patterns of relationship between instructional practices of teachers on the one hand and student achievement gains on the other (Peterson & Walberg, 1979; Everston, 1985; Peterson & Fennema, 1986; Rosenshine & Stevens, 1986; Brophy, 1988; Anderson & Postlethwaite, 1989; Walberg, 1990).

It seems important to note, though, that teachers' practices also have outcomes for teachers which may be interrelated with or independent of student outcomes. From a perspective of continuing professional education and adult development, it seems appropriate to view the practice experiences of teachers in schools and the outcomes of these experiences for teachers as legitimate issues of educational concern. For instance, it has been determined that when teachers are helped to be more competent in such practices as maintaining time-on-task, using a variety of teaching methods, communicating clear expectations to students, adjusting levels of instruction to levels of student comprehension, and giving students clear feedback on test performance and homework assignments, then positive consequences occur for both student and teacher. Not only does the achievement of students increase across subject domains and grade levels, but the sense of self-efficacy and job satisfaction improves for teachers (Gage & Giacona, 1980: Emmer, Everston, Clements, Sanford, & Worsham, 1981; Good, 1983; Gage, 1984; Gage & Berliner, 1984; Rosenholtz, 1989). In addition, the methods that teachers use in the classroom, their selection of material, and the monitoring and control of the students' behavior have been demonstrated to influence the extent and nature of their satisfaction (Holdaway, 1978; Cooper, Burger, & Seymour, 1979). The teachers' sense of autonomy in classroom practice has also been shown to be a major source of satisfaction (Lee, Dedrick, & Smith, 1990). Teachers whose practices reflect that they know their subject matter, plan ahead, are well organized, present lessons in a clear manner, and assign tasks that students can do are also known to have a high sense of efficacy and job satisfaction and are evaluated positively by their peers (Ashton & Webb, 1986).

Teachers whose classroom management practices bring about orderly behavior also show feelings of high efficacy and satisfaction (Kounin, 1970; Everston, 1985; Doyle, 1986; Newmann, Rutter, & Smith, 1989). On the other hand, practices that lead to a lack of control tend to be promotive of a low sense of efficacy and to dissatisfaction (Blase, 1981; Feitler & Tokar, 1981; Greenberg, 1984; Sizer, 1984; Litt & Turk, 1985; Rosenholtz, 1989). It is also known that teachers whose classroom practice experiences have brought them to feel frightened about losing control are the most insecure about changing their practices (Hand & Treagust, 1994; Jofili & Watts, 1995). Teachers with high self-efficacy create a rich rapport with their students and apply consistent and clear rules (Ashton & Webb, 1986). Teachers with feelings of efficacy and job satisfaction tend to feel more warmly toward their students (Greenwood & Soar, 1973). Teachers regard their relations with students and the practices they use to bring them about as the most important factor in their attitude toward teaching (Lortie, 1975; Holdaway, 1978; Kottkamp, Provenzo, & Cohn, 1986; Prick, 1989). This finding was corroborated cross-culturally by analyzing teachers' responses in interviews conducted by the Consortium for Cross-Cultural Research in Education in five countries (Evers & Engle, 1989).

Findings from other countries confirm and extend the U.S. findings. Japanese teachers who developed personal and warm relationships with students reported greater job satisfaction, and those who were more critical of their students and of their personal relationships with students reported less job satisfaction (Ninomiya & Okato, 1988). Also, the general tendency for Japanese teachers to be clear on rules for classroom conduct and provide feedback to students about their work has been related to a high-sense of work centrality (Ninomiya & Okato, 1989). Singapore teachers regarded rapport with students and the use of a variety of teaching methods as very important to their job satisfaction. Also, those with a high need for control of student behavior appeared to have a high sense of work centrality (Lau, 1968; Soh, 1984). Studies on classroom practices in England indicated that teachers in general feel strong concern about the relevance of content to the lives of their students (Broadfoot, Osborn, Gilly, & Paillet, 1987), and that in ten good secondary schools, teachers were concerned about proper student behavior and about the development of positive study habits and healthy personality (Department of Education and Science, 1977). Practices which have been found to produce high satisfaction in British teachers are the development of warm relationships with students and between students and providing feedback to students (Poppleton, 1988; Poppleton & Riseborough, 1990). In addition, British teachers who were more involved in providing individualized programs for students appeared to express higher levels of both work centrality and stress, and teachers who placed higher value on practices as a source of satisfaction showed greater involvement in their work (Poppleton & Riseborough, 1989). In one study, West German teachers showed conflict between external demands for more diligence and discipline of students and their own wishes to provide more choice and freedom (Lissman, 1983). West German teachers who gave much time to planning lessons based on different abilities of students, using a variety of teaching methods, making learning experiences relevant to students, and giving prompt attention to student behavior showed higher levels of investment in their work. Also, German teachers indicated that the building of rapport with students is very important to their job satisfaction (Lissmann & Gigerich, 1989).

The foregoing discussion has called attention to the fact that most prior research on teacher practices has related practice to student achievement. Following that, a sample has been provided of the smaller number of studies that have concerned themselves with the effects of practice jointly on outcomes for students and teachers, or on just the outcomes for teachers.

THE TEACHING PRACTICES SECTION OF OUR PRESENT STUDY

Research Questions

This section of the overall study focused on teacher practices: how they were affected by demographics, and how they affected teachers' quality of work life. The research was guided by five major research questions:

1. How do teachers compare across the nine countries regarding
   a. the difficulty they experience with their practices?
   b. the extent to which they use their practices?
   c. the importance that the doing of their practices has for their job satisfaction?
   d. the importance of their practices for bringing about their students' learning and development?
2. How do teachers compare across the nine countries regarding the influence of gender, marital status, and age on the difficulty, use, importance for job satisfaction, and importance for student learning and development of their practices?

3. How do teachers compare across the nine countries regarding the extent to which their use of their practices is influenced by the practices' difficulty, the practices' importance for job satisfaction, and the practices' importance for student learning and development?

4. How do teachers compare across the nine countries regarding the influence of the difficulty of their practices on their overall job satisfaction, the centrality of their work in their lives, and their experience of job-related stress?

5. How do teachers compare across the nine countries regarding the influence of the use of their practices on their overall job satisfaction, the centrality of their work in their lives, and their experience of job-related stress?

Responses to Research Question 1: Teachers' Perceptions of the Difficulty, Use, and Importance of Their Practices

This question concerns the ways in which teachers from the nine different countries are similar and dissimilar in their perceptions of the difficulty, use, and importance of their practices. One way to answer this question is to examine each country's T deviation from the grand mean of all nine countries together. If, on the basis of a 3-point effect size, categories of T deviation are established, where 3.00 and above = *HIGH*; 1.50 to 2.99 = *high*; −1.49 to 1.49 = *MID*; −1.50 to −2.99 = *low*; and −3.00 and below = *LOW*; then easily visible comparisons can be made between teachers from the nine countries. Table 6.1 has been constructed using this procedure.

Table 6.1 advises us that, in general, teachers from Poland appear to view their practices at a level of difficulty higher than the views of practice difficulty held by teachers in any of the eight other countries. Teachers in Germany and Canada appear to be quite the opposite, seeing their practices as the least difficult. In addition, the German teachers appear to have a remarkably consistent low profile in regard to all four aspects of their practice, possibly signaling a less challenging outlook on the established procedures and methods of teaching; that is, they are not viewed as being highly important for promoting either the learning of students or the job satisfaction of the teacher. Even though these methods and procedures are relatively easy to perform, why bother?

The Polish teachers, who appear to regard their practices as having the highest difficulty, also seem the most challenged to use and master them. On the other hand, the Canadian teachers may have the most comforting time of all, since they appear to view their practices as being highly important, and, with the accompanying LOW difficulty of their practices, they are highly engaged in practice use. It is additionally interesting to note that where there is high attribution of importance of practice in both student learning and teacher job satisfaction (Canada and the Soviet Union), there is also HIGH use.

It is somewhat intriguing to focus on the two rows of difficulty and use across countries in Table 6.1. Poland is the only country in which HIGH difficulty of practices and HIGH use of practices appear to exist. This could

Table 6.1
Cross-Country Comparison of the Overall Difficulty, Use, and Importance of Teaching Practices

Practice Dimension Means	US	England	Germany	Japan	Singapore	Canada	Poland	Israel	USSR
Difficulty of Practice Use	low	MID	LOW	high	low	LOW	HIGH	MID	low
Amount of Practice Use	HIGH	high	LOW	LOW	MID	HIGH	HIGH	low	HIGH
Importance for Job Satisfaction	MID	MID	LOW	MID	MID	high	high	LOW	HIGH
Importance for Student Learning	MID	high	LOW	MID	high	high	MID	LOW	high

Note: The categories in this table are derived from data in Table G-1 of the *Technical Supplement*.

be viewed as a "heroic" stance in teaching—practices are highly difficult and yet highly pursued. The stances of all other countries in Table 6.1 could be viewed as "nonheroic," where greater use occurs with less difficult practices (United States, England, Singapore, Canada, and the Soviet Union), or where practices are more difficult than the level of use they get (Japan and Israel), or where levels of difficulty and use other than HIGH–HIGH are congruent (Germany). Are secondary teachers in Poland "heroic"; if so, are they self-perceived and socially perceived as "heroic"; or is heroism not even a relevant concept here and HIGH use in the face of HIGH difficulty has some other meaning? It is interesting to note that the characterization, here, of Polish teachers as "heroic" is akin to a characterization in previous research (Poppleton, Deas, & Pullin,1987) of U.S. teachers in socially disadvantaged schools as having the "Alamo complex" or an attitude of "us against the world." While these are only two examples, it raises the question to what extent the arousal of persistence in the face of strong difficulty is a near-universal resource acquired from many teacher education and teacher socialization programs, or to what extent it is determined by cultural variation in teacher education and socialization.

An examination of Table 6.1 also raises the question of the roles of difficulty and importance as antecedents to use. How do the conditions of difficulty level and the pair of importances for own job satisfaction and student learning interrelate in the teacher's own determination of their levels of use? Is there an undergirding, behavioral science formula that interrelates these three components as sources of influence on use? One thing that appears to be clear is that, at the individual country level, there is either no discrepancy between the importance of practices for teacher job satisfaction and the importance of practices for student learning development (United States, Germany, Japan, Canada, and Israel), or very little discrepancy (England, Singapore, Poland, and the Soviet Union). Therefore, strong conflicts between loyalties to self and colleagues and loyalties to students in determining the use of a practice seem unlikely with teachers in all countries.

A reasonable question that would seem to arise from the examination of Table 6.1 is, if teachers in Germany and Japan indicate, as they do, that the sixteen practices are very low in their daily use, what then are the components that comprise their everyday practice? Another way to respond to Research Question 1 is to examine each country's mean t-scores for the five practice areas (indexes). These scores were constructed by translating actual index (raw) scores of all countries into standard t-scores based on where each country index score lies within the range of index scores in just that country. This approach "equalizes" the index scores of all countries, and each country, then, has the same midpoint score, the same upper and lower limit scores, and the same set of potential score occupancies. It allows for a comparison of where each country index score is in relation to other index scores within that country. It also allows for a comparison of scores between countries, as long as one remembers that what is being compared is not the actual scores, but the standing of a score among a number of scores within one country to the standing of a score among a number of scores in another country. A minimum three-point difference between any two scores is deemed to be both educationally important and well beyond the usual (0.05) statistical significance. T-score means with these characteristics are represented in Tables 6.2, 6.3, 6.4, and 6.5.

Table 6.2 provides information for an answer to the question, In what ways are the difficulty levels of the five areas (indexes) of practice similar and different across the nine countries? The five scores in each country were ranked according to their size, and the ranks were entered into the table. The underlining of a rank indicates that it has an educationally important difference between itself and the rank of immediate successive size.

As can be seen in Table 6.2, teachers in all nine countries experience the practice areas of individualizing lessons for their students and motivating them to learn as their two most difficult areas of teaching. In seven of the nine

Table 6.2
Within-Country Ranking of Teachers' Difficulty with Their Areas of Practice

Indexes: Practice Difficulty	US	England	Germany	Japan	Singapore	Canada	Poland	Israel	USSR	All
Individualize Lessons	1.0	1.0	1.0	1.0	1.0	1.0	1.0	2.0	1.5	1.0
Give and Receive Feedback	3.5	3.0	4.5	4.5	3.5	4.5	2.5	5.0	3.5	3.0
Control Classroom Behavior	5.0	4.0	2.5	4.5	3.5	3.0	5.0	4.0	3.5	3.0
Promote Positive Regard	3.5	5.0	4.5	3.0	5.0	4.5	4.0	3.0	5.0	3.0
Motivate Students	2.0	2.0	2.5	2.0	2.0	2.0	2.5	1.0	1.5	2.0

Note: Ranks of 1 represent the highest score and 5 the lowest. Underlined ranks are based on scores that differed from the next smaller score by an educationally significant effect size (3 or more t-scores). The numbers in this table are derived from data in block 1 of Table G-2 in the *Technical Supplement*.

countries the individualizing of lessons by the specific practices of planning lessons based on the different abilities of students, increasing the relevancy of learning experiences to students' lives and concerns, and building in plenty of opportunity for individualized student work is clearly the toughest single challenge. The other three practice areas of giving and receiving feedback with students, controlling classroom behavior, and promoting positive regard with and between students appear to trail unsystematically with less difficulty. It would seem that the two most difficult areas of teacher practice are less influenced by variation in culture than by their own universal complexity.

Table 6.3 is responsive to the question, In what ways are the use levels of the five areas of teacher practice similar and different across the nine countries?

There appears to be a pattern here for the teachers in all countries, except the Soviet Union, to direct most or the second most of their broad practice efforts with students toward the management of student classroom behavior through the specific practices of communicating clear rules and expectations and giving prompt attention when issues of student behavior arise. And, on the other hand, they all appear to give least effort toward purposive planning to accommodate individual differences between students. It is understandable that the practice area which teachers across all countries indicate as the most difficult to master is also the one which they seem to avoid the most. At the same time, this may indicate an area of challenge in professional development that somehow has universally not received sufficient attention from those responsible for preservice, in-service, and continuing education for secondary teachers, or from the teachers themselves who may sense their own need for revisiting a particular practice area.

Table 6.3
Within-Country Ranking of Teachers' Amount of Use of Their Areas of Practice

Indexes: Amount of Use of Practice	US	England	Germany	Japan	Singapore	Canada	Poland	Israel	USSR	All
Individualize Lessons	5.0	5.0	5.0	5.0	5.0	5.0	5.0	4.5	5.0	5.0
Give and Receive Feedback	2.5	3.0	3.5	3.0	3.0	3.0	3.5	1.0	2.0	3.0
Control Classroom Behavior	1.0	1.0	1.0	1.0	1.5	1.0	1.0	2.0	4.0	1.0
Promote Positive Regard	4.0	2.0	3.5	2.0	1.5	2.0	2.0	3.0	1.0	2.0
Motivate Students	2.5	4.0	2.0	4.0	4.0	4.0	3.5	4.5	3.0	4.0

Note: Ranks of 1 represent the highest score and 5 the lowest. Underlined ranks are based on scores that differed from the next smaller score by an educationally significant effect size (3 or more t-scores). The numbers in this table are derived from data in block 2 of Table G-2 in the *Technical Supplement*.

The high use of classroom control has been documented in interviews with U.S. teachers (Menlo & Marich, 1988), who provide the rationale that it is difficult for teachers to be certain of teaching any subject matter until the students are personally, interpersonally, and situationally ready to give their attention to the learning activity at hand. And, yet, it is most interesting to note that, for Soviet teachers, their practice area of greatest use is the promotion of positive regard through the specific practices of developing warm, personal relationships with students, building positive relationships between students, acknowledging the good work of students, and being accessible to students outside the classroom. In addition, their lower order use of classroom control practices is at a level that has a significant educational difference from their promotion of positive regard. What cultural or sociopsychological dynamics might explain this phenomenon between Soviet teachers and students?

Table 6.4 speaks to the question, In what ways are the five areas of teacher practice similar and different across the nine countries in regard to their importance for the teacher's job satisfaction?

Once again, a pattern of sorts appears to emerge in Table 6.4. Teachers in all countries except the Soviet Union seem to indicate that the area of practice that holds the first or second greatest potential for bringing them job satisfaction is the control of classroom behavior—being able to move students to a state of their committing their fullest attention to the learning task of the moment. This behavior management practice seems to have the lowest priority for reaching job satisfaction for the Soviet teachers. For them, the most favored route toward job satisfaction seems to be a combination of promoting positive regard and generating motivation. Note, also, that the Japanese teachers most highly favored route is the promotion of positive regard.

Table 6.4
Within-Country Ranking for How Important the Five Index Areas of Practice Are for the Teachers' Job Satisfaction

Indexes: Practice Importance for Job Satisfaction	US	England	Germany	Japan	Singapore	Canada	Poland	Israel	USSR	All
Individualize Lessons	5.0	5.0	3.0	5.0	5.0	5.0	5.0	4.5	<u>3.5</u>	5.0
Give and Receive Feedback	<u>3.5</u>	4.0	5.0	4.0	<u>3.0</u>	<u>4.0</u>	4.0	2.0	<u>3.5</u>	4.0
Control Classroom Behavior	<u>1.0</u>	<u>1.0</u>	1.0	2.0	1.0	<u>1.0</u>	2.0	2.0	5.0	1.0
Promote Positive Regard	<u>3.5</u>	2.5	4.0	1.0	<u>3.0</u>	2.5	2.0	4.5	1.5	2.5
Motivate Students	2.0	2.5	2.0	3.0	<u>3.0</u>	2.5	2.0	2.0	1.5	2.5

Note: Ranks of 1 represent the highest score and 5 the lowest. Underlined ranks are based on scores that differed from the next smaller score by an educationally significant effect size (3 or more t-scores). The numbers in this table are derived from data in block 3 of Table G-2 in the *Technical Supplement*.

What emerges as the least favored route to job satisfaction for teachers in seven of the nine countries is the practice area of individualizing learning—that practice area which can be recalled as the most difficult to implement across all countries.

The last question under Research Question 1 is, In what ways are the five areas of teacher practice similar and different across the nine countries in regard to their importance for student learning and development? Table 6.5 speaks to this question.

One observation in Table 6.5 is that there appears to be less agreement across the countries regarding the contribution of the five practice areas toward student learning and development than there is toward teacher job satisfaction (Table 6.4). In one sense, this seems somewhat strange since what might enthuse a teacher would seem to be more subject to individual teacher attitude, style, and background, and what might facilitate learning would seem to be more a matter of consensual behavioral science knowledge. But, then, studies in search of the truth about teaching and learning seem to go on and on without consensus at levels below generality. The two tables of practices important for job satisfaction and practices important for student learning and development may provide testimony that it is still easier to know what excites the teacher than what facilitates the learner.

Another observation is that the rankings in Table 6.5 are based on successive t-scores, which have very little difference of an educational or statistically significant nature between them. Keeping this fact in mind, one can still observe that the teachers from the United States, Canada, England, and Singapore identify the control of classroom behavior as the most important practice area for student learning and development; teachers from Japan iden-

Table 6.5
Within-Country Ranking for How Important the Five Index Areas of Practice Are for Student Learning and Development

Indexes: Practice Importance for Student Learning	US	England	Germany	Japan	Singapore	Canada	Poland	Israel	USSR	All
Individualize Lessons	4.0	3.5	1.0	4.0	3.5	5.0	2.0	3.5	<u>3.5</u>	3.0
Give and Receive Feedback	4.0	3.5	5.0	5.0	3.5	4.0	4.5	2.0	<u>3.5</u>	5.0
Control Classroom Behavior	1.0	1.0	3.0	2.5	1.0	1.0	2.0	5.0	5.0	3.0
Promote Positive Regard	4.0	5.0	4.0	1.0	3.5	2.5	4.5	3.5	1.5	3.0
Motivate Students	2.0	2.0	2.0	2.5	3.5	2.5	2.0	1.0	1.5	1.0

Note: Ranks of 1 represent the highest score and 5 the lowest. Underlined ranks are based on scores that differed from the next smaller score by an educationally significant effect size (3 or more t-scores). The numbers in this table are derived from data in block 4 of Table G-2 in the *Technical Supplement*.

tify the promotion of positive regard with and between students as being most important; teachers from Germany identify the accommodation of individual differences and motivation of students as the most important; the Israeli teachers identify the motivation of students as most important; the Soviet teachers view the practice areas of motivation and promotion of positive regard as equally most important; and the teachers from Poland spread their views of what is most important over the three practice areas of individualizing learning, controlling classroom behavior, and motivation. Is the transfer of knowledge and practice in education greatest between the United States, Canada, England, and Singapore? If so, which are the directions of import and export? What is to be learned across borders and by what means? What are the sources of the different views about the nature of teaching and learning in each culture and how permeable or impermeable are the views? Many important questions about the present status and the diffusion of educational knowledge and practice with and between countries emerge from the contents of Table 6.5.

Those countries in which there appears to be a clear statement of which practice area is *least* important as a source of student learning are the following: England—promotion of positive regard; Germany and Japan—feedback to and from students; Canada—individualization of learning; and Israel and the Soviet Union—control of classroom behavior.

Two parting observations: Most cross-country agreement about the importance of practice areas for student learning and development appear to occur at the second level of importance, and this points to the area of motivating students. When the responses of teachers to the question of how important is each of the five areas of practice for bringing about student learning and development are treated as a total sample (the overall picture), motivation of students appears highest and giving and receiving feedback with students appears lowest.

Responses to Research Question 2: The Ways in Which the Teachers' Gender, Age, and Marital Status Affected the Difficulty, Use, and Importance of Their Practices

This question concerns the ways in which the gender, marital status, and age of teachers in the nine countries affect their perceptions of the difficulty, use, and importance of their practice areas. The usual three-point difference between scores was employed to determine instances in which gender, marital status, or age level of teachers are a source of influence on their perceptions of the difficulty, use, or importance of their practices areas.

The Influence of Gender. Table 6.6 identifies the instances in which either female (F) or male (M) teachers were the dominant influence and instances where neither was dominant (blank). An examination of Table 6.6 advises that in the United States men teachers appear to find the individualization of student learning more difficult than women teachers do. In Ger-

Table 6.6
Within-Country and Across-Country Comparisons of Gender Influences on Five Indexes in Each Practice Dimension

Practice Dimension Indexes	US	England	Germany	Japan	Singapore	Canada	Poland	Israel	USSR	TOTALS	
Difficulty of Use										Female	Male
Individualize Lessons	M	...	...	...	...	...	...	...	...	0	1
Give and Receive Feedback	...	...	...	...	...	...	...	...	...	0	0
Control Class Behavior	...	...	F	...	...	...	...	...	...	1	0
Promote Positive Regard	...	...	...	...	...	...	...	...	...	0	0
Motivate Students	...	...	...	...	...	M	...	...	...	0	1
Amount of Use										Female	Male
Individualize Lessons	F	...	...	...	...	...	...	...	...	1	0
Give and Receive Feedback	...	...	...	F	...	...	...	...	...	1	0
Control Class Behavior	...	...	...	...	...	...	...	F	...	1	0
Promote Positive Regard	...	...	...	...	...	...	F	...	F	2	0
Motivate Students	...	...	...	...	...	F	...	...	...	1	0
Importance for Job Satisfaction										Female	Male
Individualize Lessons	F	F	...	F	...	...	...	...	F	4	0
Give and Receive Feedback	...	...	...	...	...	...	...	...	F	1	0
Control Class Behavior	F	...	F	...	...	...	...	...	...	2	0
Promote Positive Regard	...	...	...	F	...	...	...	...	F	2	0
Motivate Students	...	...	...	F	...	...	...	...	F	2	0
Importance for Student Learning										Female	Male
Individualize Lessons	F	F	...	...	...	...	...	...	F	3	0
Give and Receive Feedback	F	...	...	F	...	...	...	...	F	3	0
Control Class Behavior	F	...	...	...	...	...	...	F	...	2	0
Promote Positive Regard	...	...	...	F	...	...	...	...	...	1	0
Motivate Students	...	...	...	F	...	...	...	...	...	1	0
Totals for Countries										Female	Male
Total Female Dominant	6	2	2	7	0	1	1	2	7	28	...
Total Male Dominant	1	0	0	0	0	1	0	0	0	...	2
Total Dominant/Max. Possible	7/20	2/20	2/20	7/20	0/20	2/20	1/20	2/20	7/20	30/180	

Note: The symbol F or M in a cell indicates the dominance of female or male gender categories, respectively, for the index and country concerned. The data in this table are derived from Tables G-3 through G-6 of the *Technical Supplement*.

many, women teachers appear to find the control of student behavior more difficult than men teachers do. In Canada, men teachers appear to find the motivation of students more difficult than women teachers do. With all other practice areas in all countries, men and women teachers do not appear to differ in their perception of the practice areas' difficulty.

Men and women teachers in England, Germany, and Singapore do not appear to differ in the extent to which they use their five practice areas. When a difference in the extent of use of their practice areas does occurs, it is the women teachers who appear to outpractice the men.

The countries and practice areas in which women outpractice men are the individualization of learning in the United States, the giving and receiving of feedback in Japan, the motivation of students in Canada, the promotion of positive regard in Poland, the control of student behavior in Israel, and the control of student behavior and the promotion of positive regard in the Soviet Union.

Overall, in the majority of instances, men and women teachers across the nine countries do not differ in the importance they place on their areas of practice for achieving job satisfaction. But, while there are no differences between men and women teachers on this issue in Singapore, Canada, Poland, and Israel, there is in one out of five instances in England and in Germany, two out of five in the United States, three out of five in Japan, and four out of five in the Soviet Union. In all instances of difference, it is the women teachers rather than the men who attribute to their practices more potential for providing job satisfaction.

The dominance of women in sensing the potential of job satisfaction through engagement in teaching practices is true for engagement in the practice of individualizing learning in the Soviet Union, Japan, England, and the United States; the controlling of classroom behavior in the United States and Germany; promoting positive regard in Japan and the Soviet Union; and motivating students and exchanging teacher–student feedback in the Soviet Union.

Overall, in the majority of instances, men and women teachers across the nine countries do not differ in the importance they place on their practices for bringing about student learning and development. But, while there are no differences between women and men teachers on this issue in Singapore, Canada, and Poland, there is in one out of five instances in England and Israel, two out of five in the Soviet Union, and three out of five in the United States and Japan. In all instances of difference, again it is the women teachers rather than the men who attribute to their practices more potential for bringing about student learning and development. The only country in which teachers' perspectives on their practices appear to be free of influence by gender (i.e., women's and men's perspectives do not differ) is Singapore.

The ascendance of women in relating the importance of teaching practices to the learning of students is true in the areas of individualization of learning in the United States, England, and the Soviet Union; the exchange of teacher–student feedback in the United States, Japan, and the Soviet Union; the control of classroom behavior in the United States and Israel; and the promotion of positive regard and the motivation of students in Japan.

In eight instances, women teachers accentuated the linking of a teaching practice area to both student learning outcomes and teacher job satisfaction (individualization of learning in United States, England, and the Soviet Union; teacher–student feedback in the Soviet Union; control of behavior in the United States; and promoting positive regard and motivating students in Japan). Does this double attribution of power to a practice area increase the motivation of a teacher to perform that practice?

In six instances, women teachers accentuated the linking of a teaching practice only to teacher job satisfaction (individualizing learning in Japan; con-

trolling classroom behavior in Germany; and motivating students in the Soviet Union), or only to student learning and development (giving and receiving feedback in the United States and Japan, and controlling classroom
behavior in Israel). Does this create a conflict in values or divided loyalties
between the teacher's job satisfaction aspirations and the teacher's aspirations for student learning? For instance, if a teacher views a practice area as
contributing more to the teacher's own job satisfaction than to student learning (or vice versa), what forces determine the direction of the teacher's resultant behavior?

One final observation regarding the power of gender to differentiate teachers views of their practices is that it appears to be strongest in the Soviet
Union and weakest in Singapore. Further, this differentiation seems to occur
most in views regarding the potential of practices for bringing about the benefits of teacher satisfaction and student learning; and least in views regarding
the difficulty of putting the practices into action.

The Influence of Age. Table 6.7 shows how the age level of teachers in
each country influenced the teachers' difficulty with each of their five broad
practices, the teachers' use of these practices, the importance teachers placed
on these practices for their own job satisfaction, and the importance they
placed on these practices for the learning and development of their students.
The instances are identified in which teacher age groups of younger (Y: under 35 years old), midrange (M: 35 to 49 years old), or elder (E: over 49 years
old) was the dominant influence and instances where there were no differences (blank) in influence. The last row summarizes the total number of instances in which the young, midrange, and elder age groups of teachers have
dominant influence. The last column summarizes the total number of times
there are differences between age levels in each country.

In thirty out of forty-five instances, young, midrange, and elder age groups
do not differ in the extent of difficulty they experience with their five areas of
practice. In the fifteen other instances across the nine counties, there are eleven
in which younger teachers have more difficulty with a practice area than do
elder teachers, and there are four in which elder or midrange teachers have
more difficulty.

The younger teachers in Singapore, Poland, and the Soviet Union have
more trouble than elders in individualizing learning; the younger teachers in
Germany, Japan, Canada, and Poland have more trouble with controlling classroom behavior; and the younger teachers in Poland and the Soviet Union
have more trouble with motivating students.

In Israel, it is only the elder and midrange teachers who indicate the most
difficulty, and that is in the practice areas of giving and receiving feedback and
promoting positive regard and motivating students. Elder teachers in Germany
also indicate more difficulty than younger ones in the practice of feedback. In
contrast to Israel, in Poland and the Soviet Union, it is only the younger teachers who indicate the greater difficulty. Where difficulty does occur in higher

Table 6.7
Within-Country and Across-Country Comparisons of Age Influences on Five Indexes in Each Practice Dimension

Practice Dimension Indexes	US	England	Germany	Japan	Singapore	Canada	Poland	Israel	USSR	TOTAL Young	Mid	Elder
Difficulty of Use:										Young	Mid	Elder
Individualize Lessons	...	...	...	...	Y	...	Y	...	Y	3	0	0
Give/Receive Feedback	...	...	E	...	...	...	...	E	Y	1	0	2
Control Class Behavior	...	...	Y	Y	...	Y	Y	...	...	4	0	0
Promote Positive Regard	...	...	...	...	...	...	Y	E	...	1	0	1
Motivate Students	...	...	...	...	...	...	Y	M	Y	2	1	0
Amount of Use										Young	Mid	Elder
Individualize Lessons	...	...	...	E	...	...	E	...	E	0	0	3
Give/Receive Feedback	...	E	...	E	E	...	...	...	E	0	0	4
Control Class Behavior	...	...	...	E	...	E	...	Y	...	1	0	2
Promote Positive Regard	...	...	...	...	...	...	...	...	...	0	0	0
Motivate Students	...	...	Y	...	...	...	...	...	E	1	0	1
Importance for Job Satisfaction										Young	Mid	Elder
Individualize Lessons	...	...	...	...	...	...	E	...	...	0	0	1
Give and Receive Feedback	...	...	...	...	...	...	...	...	...	0	0	0
Control Class Behavior	...	E	...	E	...	...	E	...	E	0	0	4
Promote Positive Regard	...	E	...	...	...	Y	...	M	...	1	1	1
Motivate Students	...	...	Y	...	...	...	E	...	...	1	0	1
Importance for Student Learning										Young	Mid	Elder
Individualize Lessons	...	Y	Y			...	E	...	...	2	0	1
Give/Receive Feedback	...	...	...	...	...	...	E	...	...	0	0	1
Control Class Behavior	...	E	...	...	...	...	E	Y	E	1	0	3
Promote Positive Regard	...	...	...	...	E	...	...	Y	...	1	0	1
Motivate Students	...	Y	Y	...	...	...	E	Y	...	`3	0	1
Totals for Countries										Young	Mid	Elder
Younger Age Dominant	0	2	5	1	1	2	4	4	3	22	...	...
Medium Age Dominant	0	0	0	0	0	0	0	2	0	...	2	...
Older Age Dominant	0	4	1	4	2	1	8	2	5	...	...	27
Total Dominant/Max. Possible	0/20	6/20	6/20	5/20	3/20	3/20	12/20	8/20	8/20		51/180	

Note: The symbol Y, M, or E in a cell indicates the dominance of young, midrange, or elder age groups, respectively, for the index and country concerned. The categories in this table are derived from data in Tables G-7 through G-10 of the *Technical Supplement*.

amounts, it appears to occur most often with younger teachers and mainly in the practice areas of classroom control and individualizing learning.

It is interesting that age level of teachers appears to have no significant influence on difficulty with practice in the United States or England. Are the number and kind of professional development opportunities, younger–older colleague mentoring programs, or preprofessional training courses in these two countries a part of the explanation?

In just twelve of the forty-five instances, age appears to affect the extent to which teachers use their areas of practice. In the other thirty-three, age does not play a role. In Japan, Poland, and the Soviet Union, the elder teachers spend more time individualizing learning with their students than do the younger teachers. In England, Japan, Singapore, and the Soviet Union, the elder teachers spend more time than the younger ones in giving and receiving feedback. It is in Japan and the Soviet Union where the elder teachers appear to be the greater users of their practice areas, and it is in the United States where extent of practice use is not related to teacher age at all. The one area of practice that appears to be used with equal frequency by all age levels in all countries is the promotion of positive regard with and between students. Does this represent a value position of teachers of all age levels across all countries?

Age level appears to have a very limited and spotty effect on teachers' expectations of job satisfaction from engagement in their areas of practice. In fact, teachers of all age levels in each country appear to agree on the extent of satisfaction gained from mutual feedback with students. The more outstanding findings are that, in four of the nine countries (England, Japan, Poland, and the Soviet Union), it is the elder teachers who see the greater possibilities of deriving satisfaction from controlling classroom behavior. It is decidedly the elder teachers in Poland who see the greater potential of reaping satisfaction from their areas of practice. And, whether teachers are younger or elder in the United States or Singapore, they have similar expectations for satisfaction from all their areas of practice. So, while age does not appear as a significant influence on levels of satisfaction derived from using one's professional practices, when differences do occur, they are more likely to favor the elder teachers. It may be fruitful to explore more deeply this occurrence of elder teachers being more likely to expect satisfaction from their practices than younger teachers, this occurrence being most associated with teachers in Poland. A parting observation is that, among the U.S. teachers, there appear to be no instances in which teachers' age level is promotive of differences in the difficulty or use of their practices or in the importance placed on their practices for deriving their own job satisfaction or bringing about student learning and development—a phenomenon of no age bias. Generally speaking, younger and elder teachers do not have a great number of disagreements on how important their areas of practice are for facilitating the learning and development of students. Their views are similar in thirty-one of the forty-five instances. This is an item of interest in and of itself—that age of teachers does not appear to have far-reaching impact on the beliefs they hold about the power of their practices to promote student learning and development. In addition, this is true across a number of different countries.

Some of the fourteen differences in opinion on the importance of practices for student learning and development, though, are also of interest in regard to the countries in which they occur and the areas of practice involved. For instance, the most age-related disagreements within a country occur in Poland; the elder teachers there attach more importance to four of the five practice areas than do younger teachers (individualizing learning, feedback, classroom control, and motivation). Of interest also, is the practice area of their agreement—the promotion of positive regard. In contrast to the teachers in

Poland, where elder members attribute the greater power to their practice areas for bringing about student learning and development, in Israel it is the younger teachers who see the greater power of their practices for student learning and development. Why does the optimism about practices rest more with elder teachers in Poland and younger teachers in Israel?

In three countries—the United States, Canada, and Japan—there appear to be no cross-age disagreements at all regarding the extent of contribution of the five practice areas to student learning and development. These would seem to be ideal settings for cross-age teacher mixes in team teaching.

The Influence of Marital Status. The findings regarding the effects of marital status on practices (which appear in detail in Tables G-11 through G-14 of the *Technical Supplement*) do not contain the extent of diversity to warrant a full display via a table. It is clear that the marital status of teachers generally plays an unimportant role in influencing how they relate to their teaching practices. In all nine countries, married and unmarried teachers use each of their practice areas to similar extents and see them as having similar importance for facilitating their students' learning and development.

In Singapore, though, unmarried teachers appear to have greater difficulty than married teachers in individualizing student learning. In Canada, the unmarried teachers see the promoting of positive regard with and between students as a greater source of job satisfaction than married teachers do.

The case in England is perhaps of greater interest. Married teachers in England experience three of their five areas of practice as contributing more to their job satisfaction than their unmarried English colleagues do. They appear to have a greater sense of optimism about the satisfaction they can derive from giving and receiving feedback with their students, from motivating their students to learn, and from promoting positive regard between themselves and their students and between their students. This is very unlike teachers in the other countries. How does having or not having a wife–husband relationship relate to the extent of satisfaction derived from teaching practice in England?

In summary, responses to Research Question 2 advise us that teachers' views of their practices are most impacted by gender differences in the Soviet Union and least impacted in Singapore; most impacted by age differences in Poland and least in the United States; and mildly influenced or not influenced at all by marital status across all nine countries.

Responses to Research Question 3: The Ways in Which the Difficulty and Importance of the Teachers' Practices Affected Their Use

This question explores how much the teachers' use of their practices in each of their nine countries was influenced by the level of difficulty of the practices, the likelihood that the doing of the practice would provide the teachers with feelings of satisfaction, and the probability that the practices would help their students in their learning and development. In a sense, this question assesses the weight of each of three work values (the challenge of difficulty, job satisfaction for the teacher, and outcome benefits for the student) in teachers' decisions to use their various practices.

In order to provide a representation of the study data from which answers to this question could be drawn, Table 6.8 was constructed. To do this, the relevant correlations were identified for each country, rounded to two digits, and entered into Table 6.8. All correlations are statistically significant except Israel's very interesting, almost nonexistent difficulty–use correlation. In order to determine educationally important differences between the correlations, each correlation was transformed into a (standardized) z_r score (McCall, 1980, pp. 94–105, 374) and educationally important differences of 0.06 or more (effect size of 0.03 × 2 for 2-tailed test) were noted. In Table 6.8, educationally important differences exist between all correlations whose ranks are *not* tied. The development of mean correlations for the all-country measures conformed to the rules for back-transformation from standard score (z_r) to correlation (r).

What is before us in Table 6.8, then, is a ranking of one to three for the order in which teachers' use of their practices in each of the nine countries is influenced most to least by the difficulty of their practices, the importance of the doing of their practices for their own job satisfaction, and the importance of their practices for bringing about learning and development in their students. Thus, Table 6.8 speaks to the question of what are the similarities and differences in the influence these three variables have on the use of practice across the nine countries. Note that the inverse relationship between practice difficulty and practice use; the greater the difficulty, the less the use.

An initial observation based on the all countries row of Table 6.8 is that, in the overall study population of more than 7,000 teachers, the teachers were more likely to base their extent of use of a practice on the amount to which it contributes to either their own job satisfaction or the learning and development of their students than how difficult the practice is to execute. That is, level of difficulty is secondary to teacher job satisfaction and student learning and development as a determiner of practice use.

While the foregoing appears to be true when the total population of teachers from the nine countries is considered together, it also appears to hide the opposite, separate-country character of teachers in Singapore, England, and Japan, where the extent of use of a practice appears to have been determined more by the practice's level of difficulty than its perceived importance for either job satisfaction or student learning and development. Thus, the general engagement in practice in these three countries might be characterized as having been determined more by the avoidance of difficulty than the production of teacher or student benefits.

By the same means of deduction, the use of a practice by teachers in Poland and Israel appears to have been determined by the effect of the process or consequences of the practice on the job satisfaction of the teacher more

Table 6.8
**Within-Country and Across-Country Comparisons of How Much Teachers'
Use of Practices Is Influenced by the Practice Difficulty, Importance for Job
Satisfaction, and Importance for Student Learning and Development**

COUNTRY	Difficulty Influence on Use (All Negative Correlations)	Importance For Job Satisfaction Influence on Use	Importance For Student Learning and Development Influence on Use
US	Rank = 3 Corr = -.45	Rank = 1.5 Corr = +.59	Rank = 1.5 Corr = +.55
England	Rank = 1 Corr = -.53	Rank = 2.5 Corr = +.37	Rank = 2.5 Corr = +.34
Germany	Rank = 3 Corr = -.32	Rank = 2 Corr = +.54	Rank = 3 Corr = +.60
Japan	Rank = 3 Corr = -.47	Rank = 2 Corr = +.43	Rank = 1 Corr = +.35
Singapore	Rank = 1 Corr = -.62	Rank = 2.5 Corr = +.46	Rank = 2.5 Corr = +.45
Canada	Rank = 2 Corr = -.60	Rank = 2 Corr = +.61	Rank = 2 Corr = +.60
Poland	Rank = 3 Corr = -.28	Rank = 1 Corr = +.56	Rank = 2 Corr = +.46
Israel	Rank = 3 Corr = -.10	Rank = 1 Corr = +.48	Rank = 2 Corr = +.42
USSR	Rank = 3 Corr = -.38	Rank = 1.5 Corr = +.46	Rank = 1.5 Corr = +.47
All Countries	Rank = 3 Corr = -.43	Rank = 1.5 Corr = +.51	Rank = 1.5 Corr = +.47

Note: The data in this table are derived from Table G-15 of the *Technical Supplement*.

than either its perceived importance for student learning and development or
its level of difficulty. Thus, the engagement in practices in these two countries might be characterized as having been decided more on the basis of
teacher satisfaction benefits than either student benefits or avoiding difficulty.

In passing, it is probably the distinctly low influence of difficulty in Poland
and the noninfluence of it in Israel, that helps mask the difference of Singapore,
England, and Japan within the total population of teachers. Another interesting masking of a country difference in the context of the total population of
all countries is the case of Canada, where the teachers appear to value each of
these three forces toward practice use without either of them being favored.

Other configurations of influence on practice use can be seen with Germany, where teachers' use of their practices appears to be related more to
their students' learning and development than to their own job satisfaction or

the avoidance of difficulty (the only country where this configuration is so clearly communicated); and with teachers in the United States and the Soviet Union, where benefit to teacher and benefit to student seem to be the equally stronger determiners of practice use than avoidance of difficulty.

A final observation of interest is that deriving a sense of job satisfaction is never the least powerful force toward the use of a practice; it is always the first or second powerful influence in each country. That is, the importance of having a job-satisfied situation as a means to get teachers to exploit the full range of their practices is always there, being either of primary or secondary, but not tertiary, importance.

Responses to Research Question 4: The Ways in Which the Difficulty of the Practices Affected the Teachers' Job Satisfaction, Work Centrality, and Job-Related Stress

This question concerns the ways in which the levels of difficulty teachers have with their practices affect their satisfaction with their overall job, the centrality of their work in their lives, and their job-related stress.

In order to provide a representation of the study data from which answers to this question could be drawn, Tables 6.9, 6.10, and 6.11 were constructed using a procedure similar to that used in the construction of Table 6.8.

What is portrayed in the upper half of the first row in Table 6.9 is each of the nine countries' ranking for the extent to which teachers' overall job satisfaction is influenced by total practice difficulty. Notice that all influences are negative; the greater the difficulty, the less the overall job satisfaction. In the lower half of the first row is the correlation behind each ranking, including the mean correlation between overall job satisfaction and practice difficulty for all countries combined. In each country's column are the rankings for the extent to which overall job satisfaction in that country is negatively influenced by the difficulty of each of the five practice areas.

Notice, also, that all of the correlations in the first row of Table 6.9 (ranging from −0.13 to −0.31) would be considered, statistically, to be quite modest. For instance, by squaring the correlation coefficient of 0.31, a coefficient of determination (Kerlinger, 1973, p. 88) of 0.10 is calculated, which advises that only 10 percent of the variance in teachers' work satisfaction is associated with or determined by the variance in practice difficulty. So, even though the authenticity of all nine correlations is confirmed by eight of them being statistically significant at the 0.01 level and one at the 0.05 level, the extent to which the presence of practice difficulty determines the presence of work satisfaction is limited. At the same time, the same expert opinion (Kerlinger, 1973, pp. 200–201) warns that not exploring a statistically significant correlation above 0.10 may result in the loss of a valuable lead for theory and subsequent research. Social science field theory (Cartwright, 1951) provides further rationale for giving serious attention to factors of limited power in the

Table 6.9
Within-Country and Across-Country Comparisons of How Much Teachers'
Job Satisfaction Is Influenced by the Difficulty of Their Practices

Practice Difficulty and Satisfaction	US	England	Germany	Japan	Singapore	Canada	Poland	Israel	USSR	All
Total Difficulty and Job Sat. r =	-.24	-.31	-.26	-.31	-.24	-.28	-.23	-.13	-.24	-.25
Rank Order of Correlations	6.5	2.5	2.5	2.5	6.5	2.5	6.5	9.0	6.5	...
Rank Order of Correlations for Difficulty Indexes with Job Sat.										
Individualize Lessons	4.0	3.5	3.0	5.0	2.0	4.0	2.5	1.5	2.5	3.5
Give and Receive Feedback	4.0	3.5	5.0	3.0	4.5	2.0	2.5	4.0ns	2.5	3.5
Control Classroom Behavior	4.0	3.5	3.0	3.0	2.0	2.0	5.0ns	1.5	5.0	3.5
Promote Positive Regard	1.5	1.0	1.0	1.0	2.0	2.0	2.5	4.0ns	2.5	1.0
Motivate Students	1.5	3.5	3.0	3.0	4.5	5.0ns	2.5	4.0ns	2.5	3.5

Note: ns = not significant at the 0.05 level. The data in this table are derived from Tables G-16 and G-17 of the *Technical Supplement*.

determination of human actions. If one acknowledges that any situation involving persons has a field of personal, interpersonal, and situational forces impinging on the persons, and that examining the effects of almost any of these forces on the actions of the persons provides us with information helpful toward understanding them, then real forces of any size become avenues for acquiring knowledge about those persons separately or in comparison to others who are also being studied in similar ways. It should also be pointed out that the larger correlations occurring under Research Question 3 came from the examination of relationships between single items in a common context and adjacent to each other in the questionnaire, while Research Question 4 examined relationships between single and multiple item variables in noncommon contexts and distant from each other in the questionnaire.

With the immediately foregoing information as groundwork, we continue with responses to Research Question 4. The same groundwork applies also to the analyses under Research Question 5.

Several interesting findings appear to speak out from Table 6.9. The most striking finding is that, when teachers from all nine countries are considered together, it is the teacher's difficulty with the practice of promoting positive regard with and between students that has the strongest negative influence on the teacher's overall job satisfaction. What seems almost equally striking is that, when the countries are considered comparatively, the teachers in Israel are distinctly different from all the others, whose overall job satisfaction is most destroyed when they have difficulty with promoting positive regard. Any difficulty Israeli teachers have in promoting positive regard has no significant association with their overall job satisfaction. And further, the general influence of practice difficulty on Israeli teachers' overall job satisfaction is distinctly the very lowest (ninth) in comparison to the other eight countries.

This last finding seems quite consistent with Israeli teachers' low job-related stress level as cited in Chapter 3; that is, difficulty in practice does not have high potential for Israeli teacher stress and its impact on overall job satisfaction. Within this phenomenon, there may be some important insights to be learned from Israeli teachers regarding cognitive and affective mechanisms for negotiating sources of difficulty-related stress.

Another interesting and somewhat puzzling observation from Table 6.9 is the very low impact of difficulty in the control of classroom behavior on overall job satisfaction for teachers in the Soviet Union and Poland. The case of the Soviet Union seems understandable, since Soviet teachers have already indicated the low level of importance of classroom control for job satisfaction in Table 6.4.

One explanation of this phenomenon for Soviet teachers is that, in the Soviet Union, the nature of classroom discipline was a function of edict by a totalitarian government. Expected behavior in school was clearly and officially communicated to parents and students. Enforcement of the expectations and control of any modifications in actual behavior reflected the harsh perspectives of totalitarianism in which teachers were in the informal role of quasiofficers. Our interviews with Soviet teachers advised us that, for teachers, the students' understanding of expected behavior was "taken care of" before school attendance, and it had not become a priority issue in relationship to their own sense of professional satisfaction. There was little manifest difficulty with classroom control, and, further, if it did occur, it was not viewed as having teacher origin.

But, the Polish teachers' responses in Table 6.4 indicate that classroom control is within their first order of importance for job satisfaction. What psychological mechanism possibly springs from Polish culture, which allows teachers to view their classroom control efforts as important for their own job satisfaction and yet not have it impacted when they have difficulty with these efforts? Or, is this phenomenon more realistically explained by the interpretation of Table 6.1, in which Polish teachers not only view their practices as highly difficult, but they also "heroically" pursue their use? So, while difficulty is recognized, it is overcome by strenuous effort; that is, difficulty only means the acceptable hard work and challenge that precludes a negative impact on overall job satisfaction.

Another, more direct explanation of this apparent discrepancy is that there is a real difference between the concepts of job satisfaction and overall job satisfaction—the former being just one dimension or component of the latter. As measured in this study, this is actually the case. A teacher's own experience of the importance of a practice for the teacher's *job* satisfaction is accessed by the single question, "How important is doing this for my job satisfaction?" while the larger concept of *overall job* satisfaction, which is analytically interrelated here to practice difficulty, is accessed by the composite of four questions concerning *satisfaction with present job, enjoyment of teaching as an occupation, congruity of initial expectation and present experience*, and *likelihood of entering teaching once again*. It undoubtedly seems important to differentiate between satisfaction with a teacher's narrower image of *job* and broader image of *overall job*, even though the components of the broader image can be both pragmatically and theoretically related to the one component of the narrower image.

Table 6.10 speaks to the part of Research Question 4 that asks about the effect of practice difficulty on work centrality. Each cell in the farthest right column brings into focus the effect of difficulty of total practice and of each area of practice on the centrality of work in the lives of teachers in all nine countries combined. The six NOs in the first row indicate that, in general, there is no statistically significant evidence that how difficult teachers find their practices influences how central their work is in their lives. The six rows of cells press the question of relationship between practice difficulty and work centrality a little further and surface any individual country patterns that may be contrary to the general, overall picture.

It is somewhat interesting, then, to note that this appears to be the case for Singapore, Japan, and the Soviet Union. The correlation coefficient for the relationship between total practice difficulty and work centrality for each of the three countries is small but statistically significant (Singapore: $r = 0.16$, significance $= 0.01$; Japan: $r = 0.11$, significance $= 0.01$; Soviet Union: $r = 0.07$, significance $= 0.05$). Since expert advice (Kerlinger, 1973, pp. 200–201) suggests that most rs of 0.10 or less hold too little certainty for interpretation, only the columns for Singapore and Japan will be considered here. So, in a sea of NO relationships between practice difficulty and work centrality for all other countries, Singapore teachers' responses appear to indicate that they may have a mild predisposition (five low but significant rs) for their investment in their work to be subdued when faced with difficulty in executing any or all of their practices. The Japanese teachers' investment and involvement with their work also appear to have this potential for waning when faced with practice difficulty, but for them it is related to difficulty with three rather than with all five practice areas. How to account for this slightly higher vulnerability to practice difficulty by teachers from the two Asian countries? If real, it would seem to have implications for the content and skill aspects of inservice education and training for teachers in those countries. Reeducation aimed at changing behavior and attitude embedded in culture would be quite a challenge.

Table 6.11 addresses the last part of Research Question 4, which inquires about the effect of practice difficulty on job stress. Once again, the first row presents the correlations and the ranks which arise from these correlations for the relationship between total practice difficulty and job-related stress for

Table 6.10
Within-Country and Across-Country Comparisons of Whether the Teachers' Work Centrality Is Influenced by the Difficulty of Their Practices

Practice Difficulty and Centrality	US	England	Germany	Japan	Singapore	Canada	Poland	Israel	USSR	All
Is there a relationship?	NO	NO	NO	YES	YES	NO			NO	YES	NO
Total Difficulty and Centrality r =	...	...	...	-.11	-.16	...	...	...	-.07	...
Is there a relationship between Difficulty Indexes and Centrality?										
Individualize Lessons	NO	NO	NO	NO	YES	NO	NO	NO	NO	NO
Give and Receive Feedback	NO	NO	NO	YES	YES	NO	NO	NO	YES	NO
Control Classroom Behavior	NO	NO	NO	YES	YES	NO	NO	NO	YES	NO
Promote Positive Regard	NO	NO	YES	YES	YES	NO	NO	NO	YES	NO
Motivate Students	NO	NO	NO	NO	YES	NO	NO	NO	NO	NO

Note: The categories in this table are derived from data in Tables G-16 and G-17 of the *Technical Supplement*.

teachers in each of the nine countries and for teachers in all nine countries combined.

An immediate observation is that all of the ten correlation coefficients, ranging from 0.11 to 0.26, are relatively small and the presence of total practice difficulty determines only 4 percent (r^2) of the presence of overall stress. This is a very interesting and meaningful finding, since knowing that the major components of one's daily work are hard to master would seem to be a more sizable source of job stress. Perhaps there is more to be understood here than meets the eye, especially since this relatively small impact of practice difficulty is true not only for all teachers combined, but for the teachers in each separate country as well.

Does this finding mean that the "mission" nature of work for many teachers places *difficulty* in the domain of challenge and motivation, creating a motivational eustress rather than a debilitating distress? Or, could it be that, while teachers recognize the demanding nature of their work, they also feel competent to handle it, and thus are not anxiety-ridden over its twists and turns? It also seems possible that the greater difficulty teachers find in other areas of their work outside of classroom practice make classroom practice appear relatively less difficult. Whatever the case, this finding does seem to indicate that there are a number of other factors, in addition to practice difficulty that determine the amount and nature of job stress that teachers experience.

A further observation in Table 6.11 is that each of the five practice areas do not differ in their influence on overall stress for the nine countries (last column). Also, Canadian and Polish teachers both rank lowest of all countries in the extent to which practice difficulty affects stress.

Table 6.11

**Within-Country and Across-Country Comparisons of How Much Teachers'
Job-Related Stress Is Influenced by the Difficulty of Their Practices**

Practice Difficulty and Stress		US	England	Germany	Japan	Singapore	Canada	Poland	Israel	USSR	All
Total Difficulty and Stress	r=	+.16	+.26	+.20	+.25	+.25	+.11	+.13	+.24	+.17	+.20
Rank Order of Correlations		6.0	2.5	6.0	2.5	2.5	8.5	8.5	2.5	6.0	...
Rank Order of Correlations for Difficulty Indexes with Stress											
Individualize Lessons		2.0	2.0	1.5	2.0	2.0	3.5ns	3.0	1.5	3.0	3.0
Give and Receive Feedback		4.5	2.0	4.0	4.5	4.5	1.0	1.5	4.0	3.0	3.0
Control Classroom Behavior		2.0	2.0	1.5	2.0	4.5	3.5ns	4.5ns	4.0	3.0	3.0
Promote Positive Regard		2.0	4.5	4.0	2.0	2.0	3.5ns	4.5ns	4.0	3.0	3.0
Motivate Students		4.5	4.5	4.0	4.5	2.0	3.5ns	1.5	1.5	3.0	3.0

Note: ns = not significant at the 0.05 level. The data in this table are derived from Tables G-16 and G-17 of the *Technical Supplement*.

Responses to Research Question 5: The Ways in Which the Teachers' Use of Their Practices Affected Their Job Satisfaction, Work Centrality, and Job-Related Stress

This question concerns the ways in which different levels of practice use affect teachers' overall job satisfaction, centrality of their work in their lives, and their experience of job-related stress. In the service of responding to the first part of this question, Table 6.12 was constructed in the same manner as the immediately preceding tables.

In all countries together, there is a modest, positive relationship (r = 0.21) between the teachers' overall use of the range of their practices and their feeling satisfied with their overall job. It is of interest that this overall positive effect of practice use on overall job satisfaction is similar to the overall negative effect of practice difficulty on satisfaction (r = –0.25, Table 6.9). As a reminder, while both use and difficulty of practice are relatively small-size determiners of level of overall job satisfaction, they come through as real forces in this regard.

Information in Table 6.12 also indicates that the teachers' practice area of promote positive regard with and between students is clearly the strongest determiner of overall job satisfaction level across all teachers together and for teachers in each country except Israel and the Soviet Union. That is, when teachers are trying to develop mutually respectful and valued relationships within the learning environment, in seven out of nine countries, this appears to arouse within themselves a greater feeling of satisfaction than they experience with their other practice areas. For Israel, a relationship between total

Table 6.12
Within-Country and Across-Country Comparisons of How Much Teachers'
Overall Job Satisfaction Is Influenced by the Amount of Use of Their Practices

Amount of Use vs. Satisfaction	US	England	Germany	Japan	Singapore	Canada	Poland	Israel	USSR	All
Total Amt. of Use and Job Sat. r=	+.24	+.26	+.20	+.25	+.21	+.25	+.20	ns	+.25	+.21
Rank Order of Correlations	3.0	3.0	7.0	3.0	7.0	3.0	7.0	9.0	3.0	...
Rank Order of Correlations for Amount Indexes with Satisfaction										
Individualize Lessons	4.5	2.5	3.0	4.5	2.5	4.5	3.5	3.5ns	1.5	3.5
Give and Receive Feedback	1.5	4.5	3.0	2.5	2.5	2.0	3.5	3.5ns	3.5	3.5
Control Classroom Behavior	4.5	4.5	5.0ns	2.5	5.0	2.0	3.5	1.0	5.0ns	3.5
Promote Positive Regard	1.5	1.0	1.0	1.0	2.5	2.0	1.0	3.5ns	3.5	1.0
Motivate Students	3.0	2.5	3.0	4.5	2.5	4.5	3.5	3.5ns	1.5	3.5

Note: ns = not significant at the 0.05 level. The data in this table are derived from Table G-17 of the *Technical Supplement*.

practice use and satisfaction appears nonexistent (r = –0.01). In other words, it appears that satisfaction with one's overall job, for Israel's teachers, comes almost totally from sources other than their engagement in their classroom teaching practices. Yet, the single practice area of control classroom behavior has a statistically significant (albeit small; r = –0.16) *inverse* relationship with satisfaction. This is to say, the more Israeli teachers spend time controlling classroom behavior, the less satisfied they feel. So, while none of their classroom practices appear to contribute positively to their overall job satisfaction, their exercise of control over classroom behavior does contribute negatively.

For the Soviet Union teachers, satisfaction appears to be most positively stimulated when they are individualizing learning and motivating students. How to explain Israeli teachers' not acquiring satisfaction from their engagement in teaching practices, and the Soviet teachers' difference from other teachers in the practices that arouse their satisfaction?

The second part of Research Question 5, concerning the extent to which teachers' use of their practices affects the extent to which their work is central in their lives, is responded to by Table 6.13. A beginning observation is that, in the overall context of our nine countries, how much teachers engage in all their practices appears to determine slightly over 6 percent (r^2) of how much teaching is an important part of their lives. This is a small but real force in the obviously wide array of forces acting upon work centrality. Out of the five practice areas that comprise total practice, it is the promotion of positive regard with and between students that appears to have the strongest effect upon teachers' sense of work centrality, and the controlling of classroom behavior that has the weakest effect. It is most interesting that the promotion of

Table 6.13
Within-Country and Across-Country Comparisons of How Much Teachers'
Work Centrality Is Influenced by the Amount of Use of Their Practices

Amount of Use and Centrality	US	England	Germany	Japan	Singapore	Canada	Poland	Israel	USSR	All
Total Amt. of Use and Centrality r=	+.23	+.18	+.29	+.30	+.27	+.16	+.32	+.23	+.31	+.25
Rank Order of Correlations	6.5	8.5	3.0	3.0	3.0	8.5	3.0	6.5	3.0	...
Rank Order of Correlations for Amount Indexes with Centrality										
Individualize Lessons	3.5	1.5	1.5	4.5	4.0	2.0	4.0	2.5	5.0	3.0
Give and Receive Feedback	1.5	3.5	3.5	2.0	4.0	4.5ns	1.5	2.5	1.5	3.0
Control Classroom Behavior	5.0ns	5.0ns	5.0	2.0	1.5	4.5ns	4.0	5.0ns	3.5	5.0
Promote Positive Regard	1.5	1.5	1.5	2.0	1.5	2.0	1.5	1.0	1.5	1.0
Motivate Students	3.5	3.5	3.5	4.5	4.0	2.0	4.0	4.0ns	3.5	3.0

Note: ns = not significant at the 0.05 level. The data in this table are derived from Table G-17 of the *Technical Supplement.*

positive regard is also the strongest promoter of overall job satisfaction, as is controlling classroom behavior the weakest promoter (Table 6.12); that difficulty with being successful at promoting positive regard is the strongest deterrent to satisfaction; and difficulty with controlling classroom behavior is among the lowest (Table 6.9).

It is recognized that when work, in general, becomes a central issue for a person, it can have either positive or negative implications; as is clarified in Chapter 3, it depends on whether the person's preoccupations are consumingly worrisome or rewardingly challenging. Since the practices fostering work centrality, here, are also the practices associated with fostering work satisfaction, the kind of centrality being promoted takes shape as more challenging than worrisome.

The response to the third part of Research Question 5, regarding the extent to which teachers' use of their practices bears on the amount of their job-related stress, is contained within Table 6.14. Each of the cells in the first row indicate whether the use of the total practice of teachers in a country affects their experience of job-related stress. If the cell's correlation coefficient was 0.10 or below, the answer is NO; if the coefficient is above 0.10 and statistically significant, the answer is YES. The same procedure was used in each of the following rows for each of the practice areas. The upper right corner cell advises us that when all nine countries are considered together, how much teachers engage in their overall practice has no meaningful effect on the extent to which they experience job-related stress. Following that first observation, there is the clear picture of Singapore's teachers who, in deviation from all other eight countries, show a small but stable relationship between their

Table 6.14
Within-Country and Across-Country Comparisons of Whether the Job-Related Stress of Teachers Is Influenced by the Amount of Use of Their Practices

Amount of Use and Stress	US	England	Germany	Japan	Singapore	Canada	Poland	Israel	USSR	All
Total Amt. of Use and Stress r=	...	...	...	...	+.26	...	...	...	...	...
Is there a relationship	NO	NO	NO	NO	YES	NO	NO	NO	NO	NO
Is there a relationship between Amount of Use Indexes and Stress										
Individualize Lessons	NO	NO	NO	NO	YES	NO	NO	NO	NO	NO
Give and Receive Feedback	NO	NO	NO	NO	YES	NO	NO	NO	NO	NO
Control Classroom Behavior	NO	NO	NO	NO	YES	NO	NO	YES	NO	NO
Promote Positive Regard	NO	NO	NO	NO	YES	NO	NO	NO	NO	NO
Motivate Students	NO	NO	NO	NO	YES	NO	NO	NO	NO	NO

Note: The categories in this table are derived from data in Table G-17 of the *Technical Supplement*.

practice use—both overall and each practice area—and their experience of stress. Doing one's teaching practices in Singapore accounts for almost 7 percent $(0.26)^2$ of the stress the teachers experience. While this may sound a little strange, our observations and interviews with teachers in Singapore informed us of their high academic interschool competitiveness; and it seems reasonable to expect a sense of risk in the very act of teaching.

It can also be recalled that the Singapore teachers were different from teachers in the other eight countries in the larger extent to which the centrality of work in their lives was subdued by the extent of the work's perceived difficulty. This would seem to mean that there is, for Singapore teachers more than for teachers in other countries, an element of risk to the practice of teaching and a reduction of its take-home saliency in reaction to its difficulty.

REFLECTIONS

In the first section of this chapter, a context was provided for the content of a report on the classroom-practices part of our international study of teacher work life. The second section contained the report of the research findings with limited accompanying commentary, so as to help the findings have unfettered visibility. This third section is not intended to summarize the overall findings, formulate statements of knowledge from the findings, or develop particular recommendations. For the careful reader, the first possibility could be a redundancy; and the second and third possibilities are to occur in Chapter 8, where formalized statements of knowledge and their practice and policy implications will be drawn from the study as a whole. What is intended here is some reflective discourse on a few of the key issues raised by the findings on classroom practices.

One reflection concerns the approach we have taken in the analysis of data on classroom practices within our "small world" of nine countries. The analyses have allowed us to view teachers' practices both from a large-size, whole-system perspective in which the national constituencies are undifferentiated, and from a large-size, whole-system perspective in which the national constituencies are seen in comparison to each other. One insight which has emerged from this simultaneous experience is that the undifferentiated view can preclude us from understanding the symmetrical or universal aspects of teaching practice across the countries and the asymmetrical or unlike aspects of teaching practices between the countries. Both symmetry and asymmetry are important sources for understanding the nature of teaching practices and the work lives of teachers who use them, thus pointing up the usefulness of multidimensional, international–cross-cultural comparison.

Another reflection is that it is helpful to understand how work values impinge upon the extent to which teachers put each of the classroom practices in their repertoire into use, and that, while the values may be universal, their patterns of priority consideration may be different in different countries. For instance, with the three work values presented to teachers in the practices part of this study—challenge of difficulty, job satisfaction for the teacher, and outcome benefits for the student—there were five different patterns of influence of these values on practice use. These variations, seemingly linked to different countries, become important pieces of information in developing strategies for increasing the use of various practices in different settings. What is still to be learned from future research on values affecting practice use is the level of awareness or consciousness at which such values operate in teachers' decision making on how much of which practices to use. Whatever the results, they will be rich "grist for the mill" in teacher professional development programs.

Still another reflection is that, in light of the finding that the overall job satisfaction of teachers is a persistently ongoing, necessary condition for the teacher's full engagement in good practice, it is very discouraging that the psychosocial, logistical, and professional–personal development factors affecting teacher satisfaction with their work experience remain as unattended as they are in schools, leaving us bereft of a condition necessary for practice use. As indicated in Chapter 3 in this study's findings regarding the quality of teacher work life, overall job satisfaction across all countries, as well as overall job satisfaction in each country, is the lowest of this study's three measures of quality. Other observers of teacher job experience have noted that the arrangements for teachers to do their professional work in schools are setups for failure (McLaughlin, Pfeifer, Swanson-Owens, & Yee, 1986). It is understandable, then, that the condition of stress is higher than the condition of satisfaction. And it would seem to follow that professional designers of the ideal school day would be well advised to explore what the day would look like if it were planned to be entirely in the service of teachers using a wide repertoire of practices most fully and creatively. How different and how similar would the design be in each country? How can teachers and other education professionals, in countries where the higher job satisfaction requisite for the best use of practice already exists, advise teachers in countries with lower job satisfaction, and how can these ideas be creatively adapted across cultures?

An area of practice that would seem to deserve special attention is the area of individualizing lessons, which comprises three specific practices aimed at shaping instruction to the different abilities, life experiences, and concerns of students. This practice area is viewed by teachers as the most difficult in eight of the nine countries and second most difficult in the ninth. At the same time, it is least used by teachers in all countries, least important for job satisfaction in seven of the nine, and on the lower side of satisfaction in the two other countries. Yet, it runs the range from most important to least important for contributing positively to student learning and development. For a practice area long touted as the sine qua non of modern education, this could be described as an unhappy state of affairs. What imagery do teachers in each country have of this practice area, and what are their understandings of its purpose, methods, and rationale? What are the sources of its perceived difficulty, and is its low use a function of its perceived difficulty or its attributed low potential for deriving job satisfaction? If the concept of accommodation of individual differences is still valid for the facilitation of student learning and development, then it would seem to be a ripe candidate for the continuing education agenda for teachers, as well as its meaning and use being a focus for further study.

It is most interesting to observe how teachers from each and all the countries relate to the practice area which we have labeled promote positive regard with and between students. As a broad practice, this involves the building of a network of authentic care and support between all persons in the classroom. The more the teacher has learned the competencies of facilitating constructive interaction, the greater likelihood that this outcome will occur. The way teachers relate to this practice area is of particular interest since, as pointed out in a recent authoritative report of the U.S. National Institute of Mental Health (Basic Behavioral Science Task Force, 1996), there is extensive scientific evidence of a strong linkage between good relationships and overall well-being, particularly psychological well-being. These studies have made clear the importance of friendship and social support at all age levels, and how lack of social support and instability of support networks affect young people's sense of personal control and responsibility for their decisions. So, the classroom practice area of promoting positive regard represents a major mental health contribution by teachers to young people's lives. Attention has also been called to the critical importance of social interaction to the development of cognitive processes, such as in mature writing (Mac Arthur, 1995). It is interesting, therefore, to observe that teachers in seven of the nine countries derive their major sense of satisfaction from carrying it out. In addition, the use of this practice area appears to be one of the strongest arousers of the centrality of work in teachers' lives in all nine countries, as well as not being a stimulus for stress in eight of the nine countries. The finding that most teachers tend to react to their building of a support system in their classrooms by feeling more satisfied, more involved, and less stressed would seem to give strong testimony to most teachers' ability to translate research-based and/or experiential knowledge into practices that are in the best service of the psychological health and academic learning of their students.

It is a complex enlightenment to observe how a practice area by itself can depict both near-universality across countries and uniqueness for a particular country, and, when combined with another reinforcing practice area, reveal a preoccupation for still another particular country. This appears to be the case for the practice area of control classroom behavior. For teachers in all countries except the Soviet Union, it is the practice area of first or second most frequent use and the first or second highest source of satisfaction. In this instance, while the teachers in eight countries are joined by their primary attachment to the act of control, teachers in the Soviet Union stand out in their primary attachment to the somewhat opposite action of supportiveness. When the act of student control is linked conjointly to the stimulation of student motivation, which has been viewed as two reinforcing sides of the same coin (Curwin & Mendler, 1988, p. 189), the U.S. teachers stand out from all the other countries in their using the two practice areas more than teachers in any of the other countries and experiencing these practice areas as the most important for both their own job satisfaction and their students' learning and development.

Placing, side by side, information on how the same set of classroom practices used by teachers in several different countries and examining the information on each country in the context of comparison to the information on each and all other countries, as well as all countries in comparison to each other, and all countries together as a single "small world" system, allows one to make discoveries about the function of the practices themselves, about the character of the teachers who use them, about dimensions of culture in each country, about the universality of teaching across countries, and the nature of teaching within countries. To the composer of the foregoing sentence, its multidimensionality and length beg for reconstruction. But, the sentence has been left as is—as one means of conveying to the reader a small sense of both the rich potential and the unyielding complexity of international–cross-cultural, comparative, collaborative research on teaching.

REFERENCES

Anderson, L. W.; and Postlethwaite, N. T. (1989). What IEA studies say about teachers and teaching. In A. C. Purves (Ed.), *International comparisons and educational reform*. Alexandria, VA: Association for Supervision and Curriculum Development, Donnelly and Sons.

Ashton, P. T.; and Webb, R. B. (1986). *Making a difference: Teacher's sense of efficacy and student achievement*. Research on Teaching Monograph Series. New York: Longman.

Basic Behavioral Science Task Force of the National Advisory Mental Health Council. (1996). Basic behavioral science research for mental health: Family processes and social networks. *American Psychologist, 51* (6), 622–630.

Blase, J. J. (1981). A qualitative analysis of sources of teacher stress. *American Educational Research Journal, 23* (1), 13–40.

Broadfoot, P.; Osborn, M.; Gilly, M.; and Paillet, A. (1987). Teachers' conceptions of their professional responsibility: Some international comparisons. *Comparative Education, 23*, 287–301.

Brophy, J. (1988). Research linking teacher behavior to student achievement: Potential implications for instruction of Chapter 1 students. *Educational Psychologist, 23*, 235–286.

Burton, W. H. (1958). Basic principles in a good teaching–learning situation. *Phi Delta Kappan, 39*, 242–248.

Cartwright, D. (1951). Field theory in social science: Selected theoretical papers by Kurt Lewin. New York: Harper and Row.

Cooper, H. M.; Burger, J. M.; and Seymour, G. E. (1979). Classroom context and student ability: Influence on teacher perceptions of classroom control. *American Educational Research Journal, 16*, 189–196.

Curwin, R. L.; and Mendler, A. N. (1988). *Discipline with dignity*. Alexandria, VA: Association for Supervision and Curriculum Development.

Department of Education and Science. (1977). *HMI Series, Matters for Discussion: Ten good schools—A secondary school inquiry*. London: Crown Copyright.

Dill, D. D. (Ed.). (1990). *When teachers need to know: The knowledge, skills, and values essential to good teaching*. San Francisco: Jossey-Bass.

Doyle, W. (1986). Classroom organization and management. In M. Wittrock (Ed.), *Handbook of research on teaching*. New York: Macmillan.

Emmer, E. T.; Everston, C. M.; Clements, B. S.; Sanford, J. S.; and Worsham, M. E. (1981). *Organizing and managing the junior high classroom*. Austin: Austin Research and Development Center for Teacher Education, University of Texas.

Evers, T. B.; and Engle, J. M. (1989). *What teachers tell us about students and learning*. Paper presented at the annual meeting of the American Educational Research Association, San Francisco, CA, March 27–31.

Everston, C. (1985). Training teachers in classroom management: An experimental study in secondary school classrooms. *Journal of Educational Research, 79*, 51–59.

Feitler, F.; and Tokar, E. B. (1981). *Teacher stress: Sources, symptoms, and job satisfaction*. Paper presented at the annual meeting of the American Educational Research Association, Los Angeles, CA, April 13–17.

Gage, N. L. (1984). What do we know about teaching effectiveness? *Phi Delta Kappan, 66*, 87–93.

Gage, N. L.; and Berliner, D. C. (1984). *Educational psychology* (3d ed.). Boston: Houghton Mifflin.

Gage, N. L.; and Giacona, R. (1980). *The causal connection between teaching practices and student achievement: Recent experiments based on correlational findings*. Technical report, Stanford University Center for Educational Research, Stanford, CA.

Good, T. L. (1983). *Classroom research: A decade of progress.* Paper presented at the annual meeting of the American Educational Research Association, Montreal, Canada, April 11–15.

Greenberg, S. F. (1984). *Stress and the teaching profession.* Baltimore: Paul H. Brooks.

Greenwood, G. E.; and Soar, R. (1973). Some relationships between teacher morale and teacher behavior. *Journal of Educational Psychology, 64,* 105–108.

Hand, B.; and Treagust, D. F. (1994). Teachers thoughts about changing to constructive teaching–learning approaches within junior secondary science classrooms. *Journal of Education for Teaching, 20,* 97–112.

Holdaway, E. (1978). Facet and overall satisfaction of teachers. *Educational Administration Quarterly, 14* (1), 30–47.

Holmes Group, Midwest Region. (1988). *Three goals of the Holmes Group: A compendium of related issues.* Columbus, Ohio: Holmes Group Midwest Office.

Hunter, M.; and Russell, D. (1981). *Planning for effective instruction: Lesson design in increasing your teaching effectiveness.* Palo Alto, CA: Learning Institute.

Jofili, Z.; and Watts, M. (1995). Changing teachers thinking through critical action research. *Teachers and Teaching: Theory and Practice, 1* (2), 213–227.

Kerlinger, F. N. (1973). *Foundations of Behavioral Research* (2d ed.). New York: Holt, Rinehart and Winston.

Kottkamp, R. B.; Provenzo, E. F.; and Cohn, M. (1986). Stability and change in a profession: Two decades of teacher attitudes, 1964–1984. *Phi Delta Kappan, 67* (8), 559–567.

Kounin, J. (1970). *Discipline and group management in classrooms.* New York: Holt, Rinehart and Winston.

Lau, H. (1968). *Why teach? A study of motives for teaching as a career.* Singapore: Teachers Training College.

Lee, V. E.; Dedrick, R. F.; and Smith, J. B. (1990). The effect of the social organization of schools on teacher efficacy and satisfaction. *Sociology of Education, 64* (July), 190–208.

Lissmann, H. J. (1983). *Teachers experience with good and poor instructional practice in a German school.* Paper presented at the annual meeting of the Society for Cross-Cultural Research, Washington, D.C., February 18–20.

Lissmann, H. J.; and Gigerich, R. (1989). *The centrality of work in teachers' lives: A report on the West German findings.* Paper presented at the annual meeting of the American Educational Research Association, San Francisco, CA, March 27–31.

Litt, M. D.; and Turk, D. C. (1985). Sources of stress and dissatisfaction in experienced high school teachers. *Journal of Educational Research, 18* (3), 178–185.

Lortie, D. (1975). *Schoolteacher: A sociological study.* Chicago: University of Chicago Press.

MacArthur, C. A. (1995). Contributions from research on instruction. *Issues in Education, 1* (2), 215–218.

McCall, Robert B. (1980). *Fundamental statistics for psychology* (3d ed.). New York: Harcourt Brace Jovanovich.

McLaughlin, M. W.; Pfeifer, R. S.; Swanson-Owens, D.; and Yee, S. (1986). Why teachers won't teach. *Phi Delta Kappan, 67* (6), 420–426.

Menlo, A.; and Marich, M. (1988). *Teacher wisdom as a source for the knowledge base of teacher education.* Paper presented at the Midwest Regional Holmes Group Conference, Chicago, IL, May 13–15.

Newmann, F. M.; Rutter, R. A.; and Smith, M. S. (1989). Organizational factors that affect schools' sense of efficacy, community, and expectations. *Sociology of Education, 62*, 221–238.

Ninomiya, A.; and Okato, T. (1988). *Teachers practices, work conditions and satisfaction in Japan.* Paper presented at the annual meeting of the American Educational Research Association, New Orleans, LA, April 5–9.

Ninomiya, A. and Okato, T. (1989). *The centrality of work in teacher's lives in Japan.* Paper presented at the annual meeting of the American Educational Research Association, San Francisco, CA, March 27–31.

Peterson, P. L.; and Fennema, E. (1986). Teacher–student interaction and sex-related differences in learning mathematics. *Teaching and Teacher Education, 2* (1), 19–42.

Peterson, P. L.; and Walberg, H. J. (Eds.). (1979). *Research on teaching.* Berkeley, CA: McCutchan.

Poppleton, P. (1988). Teacher professional satisfaction. *Cambridge Journal of Education, 15,* 5–16.

Poppleton, P.; Deas, R.; and Pullin, R. D. (1987) The experience of teaching in disadvantaged areas in the United Kingdom and the USA. *Comparative Education, 23*, 305–315.

Poppleton, P.; and Riseborough, G. (1989). Teaching in the UK in the mid-1980s: Secondary teachers' perceptions of their satisfactions. *Resources in Education, 94* (3), 298–623.

Poppleton, P.; and Riseborough, G. (1990). Teaching in the mid-1980s: The centrality of work in secondary teachers' lives. *British Educational Research Journal, 16* (2), 105–124.

Prick, L. G. M. (1989). Satisfaction and stress among teachers. *International Journal of Educational Research, 13* (4), 363–376.

Rosenholtz, S. J. (1989). *Teachers' workplace: The social organization of schools.* New York: Longman.

Rosenshine, B.; and Stevens, R. (1986). Teaching function. In M. Wittrock (Ed.), *Handbook of research on teaching.* New York: Macmillan.

Sizer, T. R. (1984). *Horace's compromise.* Boston: Houghton Mifflin.

Soh, K. (1984). Why teach? Motives for teaching re-visited. *Singapore Journal of Education, 6*, 34–37.

Walberg, H. (1990). Productive teaching and instruction: Assessing the knowledge base. *Phi Delta Kappan, 71,* 470–478.

Watson, G. (1960). What psychology can we feel sure about? *Teachers College Record, 60*, 253–257.

7

Multivariate Influences on Quality of Work Life

LeVerne S. Collet

This chapter is concerned with a country-to-country comparison of the influence of antecedent variables on the perceived quality of teachers' work life. Antecedent variables in this context consist of all variables except QWL measures. The analysis begins with the hypothetical model presented in Figure 7.1, which shows the variable relationships and functions within the multiple regression. As conceptualized in this model, influence flows through a time-related chain running from the independent variable (country) through moderator variables (demographics) and mediating predictor variables (roles, conditions, and practices) to affect the criterion variables (QWL). The important notion here is that demographics have both a direct and indirect effect on the QWL variables. The labels moderator, predictor, and criterion are used to suggest a simple predictive relationship rather than the causal relationship implied by the dependent-variable terminology. This chapter documents country similarities and differences in the combined effects of moderators and predictors on criterion variables and evaluates the influence model in Figure 7.1.

It is important to place the contents of this chapter in context. Chapters 2 through 6 focus on the relationship between *pairs* of boxes in Figure 7.1. Chapter 7 is concerned with the combined influence of variables from all antecedent domains (preceding boxes) on quality of work life, which is operationally defined by three QWL indexes: overall job satisfaction, work centrality, and job-related stress.

The chapter analyses will serve both practical and theoretical goals. The practical goal is to conduct a cross-cultural comparison of both the *combined* and the *unique* effects of variables from all antecedent domains (preceding

Figure 7.1
Hypothesized Chain of Influence among Variable Domains

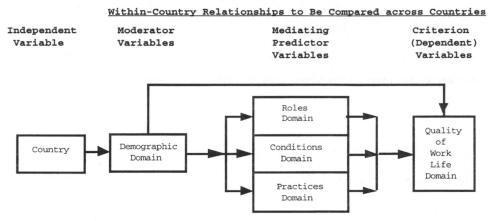

boxes) on the QWL indexes. The combined-effects comparison will document country-to-country similarities and differences in the power of the entire set of antecedent variables to predict (account for) variations in the QWL indexes. The unique-effects comparison seeks to determine how much each antecedent variable contributes to the overall prediction in each country.

The theoretical goals of Chapter 7 are to (1) determine whether the pattern of results is consistent with the chain of influence posited by Figure 7.1, and (2) compare the predictive patterns in our cross-cultural findings to established patterns reported in the literature. Since the available quoted research was conducted in the United States, this latter goal becomes a test of whether the relationships found in American research are replicated in all nine countries.

It is important to notice that this assessment of a variable's influence on QWL indexes is substantively different here than prior assessments of the same variable. Analyses in previous chapters measured the influence of each separate predictor variable on QWL indexes one at a time rather than entering all predictors together. This ignores the fact that predictors are usually correlated, causing their influences to overlap. For example, there are seven predictor indexes in the conditions domain, each of which accounts for a significant amount of the QWL variation. But because these predictors are correlated with one another, all seven indexes together account for only a little more QWL variation than any one index taken separately. To put it another way, part of the influence of each predictor is due to a common shared factor.

In this chapter, the effect of correlations among predictors is explicitly controlled by first entering a dimension mean that measures common-factor effects, and then entering predictor indexes one at a time and measuring how much additional (unique) QWL variation is accounted for by each added predictor. This provides a cross-cultural comparison that documents country-to-country similarities and differences in both the shared and unique influence of individual predictor variables on the three QWL indexes *within* the combined prediction. For each predictor variable, the comparison attempts to answer three questions: How much of the variation in QWL indexes is uniquely accounted for by this predictor variable, and how much is accounted for by a common factor shared with other predictors in this domain? Does the direction and magnitude of this predictor's influence on QWL indexes change from country to country? Do the observed influences of the predictor agree with the relationships found in previous (American) research?

RESEARCH METHOD

The goals described necessarily involve the use of multiple regression statistics. In multiple regression terms, the task is to find the combination of variables that provides optimum predictions of overall job satisfaction, work centrality, and job-related stress. As defined here, an optimum prediction must (1) use the same predictors for all indexes in each country (this is essential for comparability); (2) provide a multiple R that is equivalent to (i.e., not significantly lower than) the maximum attainable R (to be established by trial and error); and (3) involve no more than 35 predictors. The last criterion was based on a regression rule of thumb that says there must be at least ten times as many cases as predictors to have a reliable solution. Since the smallest sample (Israel) had roughly 350 cases, this rule suggested a 35 predictor limit.

The variables available for regression analysis are listed in Table 7.1, grouped by domain and level of aggregation. Notice that each item in the roles and conditions domains had two response dimensions (A and B) and each item in the practices domain had four response dimensions (A, B, C, and D). The dimension name "Amount" refers to amount of use of the characteristic identified by the relevant questionnaire items(s), "Difficulty" refers to its difficulty of use, "ImportJS" refers to its importance for job satisfaction, and "ImportSL" refers to its importance for student learning. Acronyms for dimension means use the first four letters of the domain preceded by an M and followed by the dimension letter. The acronyms for incongruence means follow a similar pattern, but end with two dimension letters indicating the order of subtraction; for example, BA = B–A. Incongruence means refer to the average difference in item rating for a pair of dimensions.

An extensive series of experimental regressions clearly supported the selection of an "optimum" set of predictors consisting of 35 variables: 3 demographic indexes, 8 dimension means, 6 dimension incongruence means, and the 18 amount indexes from domains 2, 3, and 4. The 35 selected variables have been underlined in Table 7.1. The meanings of the indexes in each domain are defined in context during the presentation of results.

Table 7.1
Variables Available for Analysis Classified by Domain and Function (Underlined Indexes and Means Are Included in the "Optimum Prediction" of Quality of Work Life)

Function	Modifier	Dependent		Mediating Dependent		Mediating Dependent				Dependent
Domain Number	(1)	(2)		(3)		(4)				(5)
Domain Name	Demographics (3 items)	Roles and Responsibilities (18 items)		Work Conditions (33 items)		Teaching Practices (16 items)				Quality of Work Life (8 items)
Dimension Letter	...	(A)	(B)	(A)	(B)	(A)	(B)	(C)	(D)	...
Dimension Name	...	Amount	ImportJS	Amount	ImportJS	Difficulty	Amount	ImportJS	ImportSL	...
Number of Indexes	3	5	5	7	7	6	6	6	6	3
Dimension Means	...	MRoleA	MRoleB	MCondA	MCondB	MPracA	MPracB	MPracC	MPracD	...
Incongruence Means	...		MRoleBA		MCondBA	MPracBA	MPracCB	MPracCD	MPracDB	...

Note: Amount refers to the amount or prevalence of a characteristic; Difficulty indicates its difficulty of use; ImportJS refers to its importance for job satisfaction; and ImportSL refers to its importance for student learning. Acronyms for dimension means are formed using the first four letters of the domain name preceded by an M and followed by the dimension letter. Acronyms for incongruence means are similar except they end in two dimension letters indicating the dimensions being compared.

Regression Procedure

The three QWL indexes were each regressed on the thirty-five optimum predictors to test the overall strength of prediction for each country. To assess the viability of the theoretical model, it was important to test the effects of each predictor domain and of components within domains in the order specified by the model. Rather than letting the computer decide the order in which predictors were entered (as in the popular stepwise regression), the ENTER command was used to add predictors (or blocks of related predictors) one at a time in a prescribed order, and to test the amount of improvement in multiple R attributable to each successive entry. In this respect, it must be recognized that order of entry affects the size of the increment attributed to each predictor or block of predictors. Therefore, the order of entry should be determined by defensible theoretical relations among domains.

In these analyses, domains were entered in ascending order of their vulnerability to manipulation by individual teachers. It was argued that demographics were the least vulnerable, and should be entered first. Roles, which were in general considered to be an attribute of the position to which a teacher was hired, often a central office rather than a school prerogative, were entered second. Conditions were somewhat more vulnerable to school-level (or teacher–group) manipulation, and were entered third. Practices were considered to be under the direct control of the teacher and therefore entered fourth. All findings reported in the results section derive from this prescriptive-entry procedure, and must be interpreted with that in mind.

RELEVANT RESEARCH AND THEORY

The three indexes of quality of work life represent three conceptually different but interrelated aspects; they are not intended as a comprehensive definition. A brief review of the theory and research dealing with the expected relationships of the optimum predictors to these three indexes is necessary to guide the analysis and assist in the interpretation of the findings presented in this chapter. The material cited here was distilled from 286 articles selected from a comprehensive electronic search of research and theory published between 1967 and 1996, inclusively.

Definitions of QWL Indexes

The analysis presented in this chapter derives from relationships among various conceptual attributes of the three QWL indexes used as criterion (dependent) variables. What follows is a brief description of the characteristics of overall job satisfaction, work centrality, and job-related stress that influence the research considered relevant for review. (A broader discussion of the theoretical issues related to these constructs appears in Chapter 3.)

Overall Job Satisfaction. The term overall job satisfaction in this study has a meaning consistent with its common definition in the literature as an affective state that results when an educator evaluates his or her day-to-day work experience (Hoy & Miskel, 1987, p. 401; Knoop, 1995b). The emphasis on ongoing day-to-day experience is critically important for developing expected relationships with predictor variables.

Work Centrality. Important aspects of the expectations for prediction of work centrality depend on its close conceptual relationship to the terms "job commitment" and "organizational commitment." A brief summary of the logical connections among these constructs is necessary to justify the approach taken here.

Paullay, Alliger, and Stone-Romero (1994) categorized three definitions of the term "work centrality" that are often used interchangeably in the literature as: Protestant work ethic (PWE), work centrality (WC), and job involvement (JI). PWE definitions involve an intrinsic value for work learned from parents and supported by religion that comes with the individual to the workplace. Work centrality definitions emphasize beliefs that individuals have regarding the importance of work that are socialized by the family but may be modified over time by the work environment. This is closely parallel to the central life interests construct (CLI) developed by Dubin (1956). Job involvement definitions, on the other hand, emphasize the degree to which one is physically and cognitively engaged in and preoccupied by job-related activities and the degree to which one finds these activities rewarding or satisfying. Job involvement is considered to be socialized primarily by cumulative exposure to work conditions and assignments (Knoop, 1995a; Knoop, 1995b; Paullay, Alliger, & Stone-Romero, 1994; Knoop, 1986).

The terms "job commitment" and "organizational commitment" as used by Dubin, Champoux, and Porter (1975) involve both the perceived importance of work and broad participation in work activities; this usage overlaps with both the JI and WC definitions of work centrality given above. Similarly, the term "teacher commitment" used in a comprehensive review of research by Firestone and Pennell (1993, pp. 490–491) involves high importance (intrinsic worth) attached to teaching activities and extensive use of good teaching strategies as well as a "partisan, affective attachment to the goals of (the teaching profession and/or the school)." Although the emphasis on goals is unique, the first two elements of this definition clearly overlap with the WC and JI definitions of work centrality, respectively. Similarly, the term "organizational commitment" as used by Glisson and Durick (1988, pp. 64–65) consists of (1) a strong belief in an organization's goals, and (2) willingness to exert considerable effort in (performing job activities). The second part of this definition clearly overlaps with the JI definition of work centrality previously given and implies an overlap with the WC definition as well. Consequently, these commitment articles are directly relevant to the development of expectations for work centrality.

Job-Related Stress. Stress has historically been used as an umbrella term for an individual's psychological response to negative stimuli in the environment (Kahn, Wolfe, Quinn, Snoek, & Rosenthal, 1964). In a comprehensive review published in the *International Journal of Stress Management*, Landy, Quick, and Kasl (1994) evaluated the research evidence accumulated over the last thirty years for a long list of environmental stressors. This study uses the Landy and colleagues definition of stress: an individual's psychological response to the stressors found in the work environment. Only the stressors which had strong research support in the literature are considered relevant to this analysis.

Expected Regression Outcomes

The research most relevant to the proposed analysis are studies that used some form of multiple regression to establish the unique contribution of each available predictor. Ideally, these studies should use the same set of predictors with each criterion (satisfaction, centrality, and stress) to determine changes in the order of importance and effectiveness of predictors from index to index. Unfortunately, very few of the studies used a multiple regression approach, and no study used the same set of variables to predict all three indexes. But the review did identify seven major predictors of both satisfaction and centrality, and there was one comprehensive multiple-regression study that used the same set of predictors with the two criterion variables. However, there was little correspondence between these common predictors and the predictors of stress. Consequently, the findings regarding predictors of satisfaction and centrality are presented together with a separate presentation of the findings for stress.

The remainder of this section is organized under two headings: expectations for overall job satisfaction and work centrality, and expectations for job-related stress. In each section, selected study findings related to the targeted criterion variable(s) are presented followed by a statement of the *expected* relationships, with equivalent variables selected from our set of optimum predictors. These expectations are parenthesized and printed in italics to set them apart from the reviewed material. The term expectation is used rather than hypothesis to emphasize the post-hoc, nonexperimental nature of this study and the tentativeness of using findings from American research to anticipate and explain the results from other cultures.

Expectations for Overall Job Satisfaction and Work Centrality. Glisson and Durick (1988) conducted a canonical-regression study in which the same set of variables was used to predict both job satisfaction and organizational commitment. Because it was established in the previous section that the organization commitment variable contained a JI component similar to that used in our index of work centrality, Glisson and Durick's findings are the most relevant evidence available for establishing the expected effectiveness of predictors for overall job satisfaction versus work centrality.

Glisson and Durick began by making a critically important distinction between the two dependent-variable constructs: they modeled satisfaction as a function of job experiences on a day-to-day basis, and commitment (and, by overlap, work centrality) as a function of beliefs about the organization derived from long-term exposure to the work involved. This critical JS–WC distinction allowed them to hypothesize a differential weighting of common predictors for satisfaction and commitment (centrality), which they subsequently tested and confirmed. In the following list of expected effects, the findings from the Glisson and Durick are used as a primary source to establish the direction of influence of predictors on overall job satisfaction and work centrality and the *relative* strength of the prediction for the two criterion variables. Studies that confirm the expected influence of predictors for each variable separately are reported as supporting evidence. Predictors for which there was incomplete or contradictory evidence were excluded from this list of expectations.

1. The breadth of involvement in complex work activities and the perceived significance of work tasks were strong positive predictors of work

centrality and somewhat weaker positive predictors of job satisfaction (Glisson & Durick, 1988). One study (Billingsley & Cross, 1992) provides separate support for the positive influence on both satisfaction and centrality.

(Our role amount mean [a measure of involvement in all school roles] and our role importance mean [a measure of task significance] were expected to be strong positive predictors of work centrality and somewhat weaker positive predictors of overall job satisfaction.)

2. Ambiguous role definitions and role conflicts were found to have a strong negative influence on job satisfaction and a smaller negative influence on work centrality (Glisson & Durick, 1988; Miskel & Ogawa, 1988; Hoy & Miskel, 1987). Two studies (Billingsley & Cross, 1992; Mannheim & Cohen, 1978) support the positive influence of ambiguity on satisfaction, and three studies (Billingsley & Cross, 1992; Mannheim & Cohen, 1978) support its positive influence on centrality.

(Our role incongruity mean [the absolute difference between the role importance and role amount means], analogous to role ambiguity, was expected to have a negative influence on overall job satisfaction and a weaker negative influence on work centrality.)

3. The use of a variety of complex technical skills was one of the strongest positive predictors of satisfaction in human service organizations and a somewhat weaker positive predictor of centrality (Glisson & Durick, 1988). One study (Billingsley & Cross, 1992) provides separate support for the positive influence of complex skill practice on both satisfaction and centrality.

(Our practice amount mean [a measure of the overall use of a variety of well-regarded teaching skills] was expected to be a positive predictor of overall job satisfaction and a somewhat weaker positive predictor of work centrality.)

4. Demographic variables such as age, sex (maleness), and marital status (being married) were found to have small, positive influences on job satisfaction and positive-but-trivial influences on work centrality (Glisson & Durick, 1988). Three studies (Grau, Chandler, Burton, & Kolditz, 1991; Aranya, Kushnir, & Valency, 1986; Wright, King, & Berg, 1985) support the positive influence of demographics on satisfaction, and six studies (Mannheim, 1993; Grau et al., 1991; Aranya et al., 1986; Mannheim & Angel, 1986; Wright et al., 1985; Mannheim, 1975) support their weak positive influence on centrality.

(In our study, age, being male, and being married were expected to be weak positive predictors of overall job satisfaction and even weaker predictors of work centrality.)

5. Support of colleagues, particularly the principal, have been found to increase job satisfaction and school commitment (work centrality) and to de-

crease stress (Littrell, Billingsley, & Cross, 1994). Similarly, collaboration (participation) with other workers has been found to have a moderate positive effect on satisfaction and a larger positive effect on centrality (Glisson & Durick, 1988). One study (Firestone & Pennell, 1993) supports the positive influence of collaboration on both satisfaction and centrality. Participation in decisions has been found to have a similar effect (Hoy & Miskel, 1987, p. 402). Three studies (Knoop, 1995a, 1995b; Munene & Azuka, 1991) support the positive influence of participation on satisfaction and four studies (Knoop, 1986, 1995a, 1995b; Munene & Azuka, 1991) support its positive influence on centrality.

(Our role index 3 [amount of shared management] was expected to be a positive predictor of overall job satisfaction and a stronger positive predictor of work centrality. Condition index 1 [amount of colleague and administration support] was also expected to be a positive predictor of overall job satisfaction and a stronger positive predictor of work centrality.)

6. Lack of an orderly environment (poor classroom discipline) significantly reduces satisfaction but has little or no effect on centrality (there was no regression evidence by Glisson and Dureck, 1988, but the relative effectiveness of predictions can be inferred from the critical JS–WC distinction. One study (Firestone & Pennell, 1993) supports both the negative influence of disorder on satisfaction and no influence on centrality.

(Our practice index 3 [use of behavior control], practice index 5 [use of student motivation], and practice index 6 [use of content to motivate] were all expected to be negative predictors of overall job satisfaction and unrelated to work centrality.)

7. Inadequate classroom resources significantly lowered satisfaction but had little effect on centrality (there was no regression evidence by Glisson & Dureck, 1988, but the relative effectiveness of predictions can be inferred from the critical JS–WC distinction). Again, one study (Firestone & Pennell, 1993) supports both the negative influence of inadequate resources on satisfaction and no influence on centrality.

(Our condition amount mean [the average presence of positively-stated work conditions], a measure of resource adequacy, was expected to be an extremely powerful positive predictor of overall job satisfaction and essentially unrelated to work centrality. In addition, condition index 3 [adequate economic incentives] and condition index 5 [adequate physical resources] were expected to be strong positive predictors of overall job satisfaction and essentially unrelated to work centrality.)

8. Autonomy, defined as a worker's freedom to schedule work and determine work procedures, has been shown to have a positive influence on job

satisfaction and a stronger positive influence on work centrality (there was no regression evidence by Glisson & Dureck, 1988, but the relative effectiveness of predictions can be inferred from the critical JS–WC distinction). Three studies (Lam, Foong, & Moo, 1995; Cheng, 1994; Wright et al., 1985) support the positive influence of autonomy on satisfaction, and six studies (Lam et al., 1995; Cheng, 1994; Mannheim & Dubin, 1986; Mannheim & Angel, 1986; Wright et al., 1985; Mannheim, 1983) support its strong positive influence on centrality.

(Our condition index 2 [teacher autonomy] was expected to be a strong positive predictor of work centrality and a weaker predictor of overall job satisfaction.)

9. Human service organizations in general have been found to have relatively low levels of job satisfaction (Glisson & Durick, 1988). However, this does not appear to be true for teachers: Several studies found that 80 to 85 percent of teachers report that they are satisfied or very satisfied, and that less than 10 percent report dissatisfaction (Hoy & Miskel, 1987, p. 402). There was no corresponding data on absolute levels of centrality.

(Because of similarities in the structure and content of items in the two scales used in our study, the mean of raw-score responses for both overall job satisfaction and work centrality were expected to be at or above 3.0 on a 4-point scale; both distributions were therefore expected to have a strong negative skew.)

10. Overwork has been found to have a negative influence on job satisfaction and, because of its indirect association with role conflict, a small negative influence on work centrality (there was no regression evidence by Glisson & Dureck, 1988, but the relative effectiveness of predictions can be inferred from the critical JS–WC distinction). Support for the satisfaction prediction comes from the fact that overwork and high activity levels produce dissatisfaction, which negatively influences job satisfaction (Landy, Quick, & Kasl, 1994). In addition, overwork has been defined as an indirect, quantity versus quality type of role conflict (Kahn & Byosiere, 1990); this suggests a strong negative influence on satisfaction and a somewhat weaker negative influence on centrality (see the support for role conflict effects in item 2).

(Our condition index 6 [reasonable workload] was expected to be a strong positive predictor of overall job satisfaction and a weaker positive predictor of work centrality.)

11. Research indicates that stable personal variables and longer-term work-role characteristics have a stronger influence on centrality than on satisfaction, and that short-term, less-stable working conditions have a stronger influence on satisfaction than on centrality (Glisson & Durick, 1988, direct evidence from tables 3, 4, and 5). There are no supporting studies for this expectation.

(Roles variables were more personal and long term than conditions variables; consequently it was expected that conditions would be the dominant predictor of overall job satisfaction, with roles in second place, but that roles would be the dominant predictor of work centrality, with conditions in second place.)

Expectations for Job-Related Stress. The following findings are generally paraphrased from the Landy and colleagues (1994) article with additional citations to document important original sources. Notice that the findings have been numbered continuously from the previous set in order to simplify references to expectations in subsequent sections.

12. Poor physical accommodations and/or an inadequate supply of necessary resources have generally been experienced as stressful. However, it is important to note that these effects are moderated by a comparative rather than an absolute evaluative frame (i.e., how comfortable or efficient are my surroundings compared to those of my friends and coworkers [Landy et al., 1994]).

(Our condition index 5 [adequate physical resources] was expected to be a strong negative predictor of job-related stress.)

13. Although poor pay and/or inadequate benefits (e.g., medical and retirement) would seem to be natural suspects, there has been little consideration of the role financial rewards of these types might play as stressors (Landy et al., 1994). However, personal interviews with teachers in countries experiencing widespread economic hardship suggest a great deal of associated personal stress.

(Our condition index 3 [the adequacy of economic incentives] was therefore expected to be a strong negative predictor of job-related stress in the affected countries and a weaker negative predictor in less-affected countries.)

14. Poor interpersonal relations with coworkers or, more particularly, with a supervisor were generally experienced as stressful (Landy et al., 1994). There is also increasing evidence (Kahn & Byosiere, 1990) that social support (e.g., friends and family outside the workplace) can help reduce stress in the workplace.

(Our condition index 1 [support from colleagues, administrators and parents] was expected to be a strong negative predictor of job-related stress; condition index 4 [professional support] was expected to be a somewhat weaker negative predictor of job-related stress.)

15. Role conflict or role ambiguity and a closely related stressor, workload (or more precisely, work overload) have been found to increase stress (Landy et al., 1994). Overwork is included here because it is better defined as a conflict of quality versus quantity because of time demands (Kahn & Byosiere, 1990).

(A reasonable workload [condition index 6] was expected to be a strong negative predictor of job-related stress. Three role components were expected to be positive predictors of job-related stress: the role ambiguity mean, because it is analogous to role conflict as used previously; the role amount mean, because the time pressures of increased role involvement are stressful; and the role importance mean, because more important roles are more stressful.)

16. Research indicates that (the perception of) participation in decision making (PDM) reduces worker stress (Landy et al., 1994). However, it is not clear whether this results from an increased sense of empowerment or a reduction in uncertainty.

(Our role index 3 [prevalence of shared management] was expected to be a strong negative predictor of job-related stress.)

17. Many research findings have emphasized the critical role of uncertainty with respect to personal or job security or to the attainment of important personal goals as a major source of stress (Landy et al., 1994). Perceived uncertainty is so important that several investigators (McGrath, 1976; Schuler & Jackson, 1986; Jackson, 1989) believe it is a unifying theme for all stress research. Other research (Moses & Lyness, 1988) has found that individuals vary in their ability to cope with uncertainty. There has been a good deal of speculation that people can adapt to uncertainty by increasing their tolerance for ambiguity, but there is as yet no supporting research.

(As argued in item 13, teachers in many countries faced great economic and social uncertainty, which was expected to increase job-related stress. Because our optimum predictors contained no measure of uncertainty, the multiple R would be artificially depressed. Therefore lower values of multiple R were expected in the affected countries.)

18. Firestone and Pennell (1993) reviewed a number of studies in which a disorderly environment (poor discipline) produced a strong "aversive work condition"—an obvious equivalent of stress.

(In our study, student discipline appears only in the practice domain. Practice index 3 [use of behavior-control practices], practice index 5 [use of student motivation skills], and practice index 6 [use of motivation through content], all indirect measures of the need for discipline, were expected to be positive predictors of job-related stress. Since three of the six practice indexes had similar expectations, the practice amount mean was expected to be a strong positive predictor of job-related stress.)

SUMMARY AND DISCUSSION OF RESULTS

This section begins with a presentation of the results of the regressing the three QWL indexes on the thirty-five variables in the optimum predictor set in each of the nine countries. Next, it summarizes the findings from explicit comparisons of observed results to the corresponding theoretical expectations and provides an interpretive discussion of findings. The discussion is divided into seven sections: (1) regression results, (2) strength of "optimum" predictions, (3) comparing domain influences, (4) relationships among criterion variables, (5) evidence for the chain of influence model, (6) effects of demographics, and (7) evaluation of expected relationships.

Regression Results

Since the results to be discussed are interrelated, it would be highly redundant to have a separate table for each discussion topic listed above. Therefore, complete regression tables for overall job satisfaction, work centrality, and job-related stress are presented here in Tables 7.2, 7.3, and 7.4, respectively. Because the results discussed in most of the following sections refer back to these tables, it is useful to explore the information presented in more detail.

Notice that each of these three tables is divided into five blocks. The first block presents the multiple R on line 1, the percentage of variance accounted for (R squared expressed as a percent) on line 2, the raw-score mean and skewness index of the criterion on lines 3 and 4, the number of cases with scores on all 35 predictors on line 5, and the rank order of the multiple R within the nine countries on line 6.

The next four blocks present the percentage of variance, which can be uniquely attributed to each of the four predictor domains in the order of their entry into the regression equation: demographics (lines 7 to 10), roles (lines 11 to 16), conditions (lines 17 to 22), and practices (lines 23 to 29). The first line in each block presents the percentage of criterion variance accounted for by the entire domain, and the last line of each block presents the rank order (largest to smallest) of index effects. Each of the intervening lines (between first and last) presents the influence percentage uniquely attributable to a particular domain component. The roles, conditions, and practices domains each contain four components assessing the influence of the amount mean, importance mean(s), incongruence mean(s), and the combined index variables from the amount dimension. The practice domain has a practice difficulty mean as an additional component.

Notice that the influence percentages for all domain components except the combined indexes are preceded by either a plus sign to indicate a positive (increasing) effect on the criterion or a minus sign to indicate a negative (decreasing) effect. It is also important to recognize that overall job satisfaction and work centrality have a positive valence in which higher scores are more desirable, while job-related stress has a negative valence in which lower scores are more desirable. The following sections present results in the order listed. The meaning of each component or index is explained in context.

Table 7.2

Percentage of Overall Job Satisfaction Variance Attributable to Various Domain Components within Each Country

Regression of Overall Job Satisfaction	US	England	Germany	Japan	Singapore	Canada	Poland	Israel	USSR
1. Multiple R with All 35 Predictors	0.5866	0.6123	0.4729	0.5239	0.4895	0.5518	0.5974	0.6391	0.4847
2. Total Variance Accounted for (R², in %)	34.4**	37.5**	22.4**	27.5**	24.0**	30.5**	35.7**	40.8**	23.5**
3. Raw Score Mean for Job Satisfaction	3.30	2.91	2.90	2.82	3.10	3.65	2.91	2.84	3.02
4. Skewness Index for Job Satisfaction	-0.94	-0.65	-1.11	-0.30	-0.56	-1.41	-0.65	-0.48	-0.62
5. Number of Complete Cases	848	621	651	1238	849	356	616	285	1118
6. Rank Order of Country R's	4	2	9	6	7	5	3	1	8
7. Demographic Domain Total (in %)	1.8*	3.0*	0.7	3.1*	1.5*	0.7	2.0*	2.4	3.6*
8. Married Status: with Yes + (in %)	+0.2	-0.2	+0.3	+0.1	+0.7*	+0.0	+0.1	+0.6	+0.5
9. Age Category (in %)	-0.5	-0.0	+0.3	+2.3*	-0.5	-0.0	+0.8*	-1.1	+1.85*
10. Gender: with Male + (in %)	-1.2*	-2.8*	-0.1	+0.7	+0.4	-0.7	-1.1*	-0.6	-1.3*
11. Roles Domain Total (in %)	10.8*	10.6*	6.0*	5.9*	4.4*	8.5*	11.4*	10.2*	11.5*
12. Overall Amount Mean (in %)	+7.6*	+8.2*	+1.5*	+3.7*	+3.9*	+6.4*	+10.0*	+8.8*	+9.2*
13. Overall Importance Mean (in %)	-0.0	-0.0	-0.4	+0.2	+0.1	-0.8	+0.0	-0.3	+0.8*
14. Incongruence Mean (in %)	-0.0	-0.1	-2.9*	-0.0	-0.1	-0.2	-0.4	-0.1	+0.0
15. Combined Amount Indexes (in %)	3.1*	2.2*	1.2	1.9*	0.4	1.0	1.1	1.0	1.5*
16. Rank Order of Index Betas	34152	21354	45231	24513	32154	45312	31524	23514	51432
17. Conditions Domain Total (in %)	19.2*	21.7*	13.2*	13.4*	15.7*	19.4*	19.9*	18.5*	5.3*
18. Overall Amount Mean (in %)	+15.7*	+20.4*	+8.9*	+11.8*	+13.9*	+17.8*	+17.4*	+14.9*	+3.7*
19. Overall Importance Mean (in %)	-1.2	-0.1	-1.0*	-0.1	-0.1	-0.1	-0.0	-0.3	-0.0
20. Incongruence Mean (in %)	+0.0	+0.0	+0.0	-0.2	+0.3	-0.1	-0.2	-0.0	+0.0
21. Combined Amount Indexes (in %)	2.3*	1.2	3.2*	1.3*	1.4	1.5	2.3*	3.2*	1.6*
22. Rank Order of Index Betas	1234576	2561743	2164573	1637542	2635741	6714253	4325617	4271365	4251367
23. Practices Domain Total (in %)	2.6*	2.2*	2.5*	5.1*	2.4*	1.9	2.3*	9.7*	3.1*
24. Overall Amount Mean (in %)	+0.9*	+0.5*	+0.6*	+3.0*	+0.2	+0.3	+0.4	-3.5*	+0.5*
25. Combined Importance Means (in %)	-0.1	-0.0	-0.2	-0.1	-0.8*	+0.1	+0.1	-0.9	-0.1
26. Practice Difficulty Mean (in %)	-0.1	-0.3	-0.3	-0.6*	-0.0	-0.2	-0.5*	-0.2	-0.5*
27. Combined Incongruence Means (in %)	0.0	0.3	0.2	0.5	1.2*	0.4	0.4	0.7	1.2*
28. Combined Amount Indexes (in %)	1.5*	1.0	1.2	0.8*	0.2	0.8	1.0	4.5*	0.9
29. Rank Order of Index Betas	165234	246531	642153	421653	246351	143562	463521	341256	654132

Note: *p 0.05; **p 0.01.

198

Table 7.3
Percentage of Work Centrality Variance Attributable to Various Domain Components within Each Country

Regression of Work Centrality	US	England	Germany	Japan	Singapore	Canada	Poland	Israel	USSR
1. Multiple R with All 35 Predictors	0.4556	0.5598	0.4776	0.4996	0.4359	0.4424	0.5792	0.5842	0.5272
2. Total Variance Accounted for (R², in %)	20.5**	31.3**	22.8**	25.0**	19.0**	19.6**	33.6**	34.1**	27.8**
3. Raw Score Mean for Work Centrality	3.62	3.62	3.06	3.36	3.44	3.59	3.44	3.48	3.58
4. Skewness Index for Work Centrality	-1.40	-1.71	-1.73	-0.61	-0.96	-2.00	-1.35	-0.82	-1.35
5. Number of cases complete	848	621	651	1238	849	356	616	285	1118
6. Rank Order of Country R's	7	3	6	5	9	8	2	1	4
7. Demographic Domain Total (in %)	0.7	2.2*	1.4*	0.8*	0.2	2.5*	2.5*	4.7*	5.9*
8. Married Status: with Yes + (in %)	-0.1	+0.2	+0.7*	-0.0	+0.1	-0.5	+0.0	+1.6*	-0.0
9. Age Category (in %)	+0.0	+1.6*	+0.3	+0.8*	+0.0	+0.0	+2.5*	-0.4	+1.1*
10. Gender: with Male + (in %)	-0.6	-0.4	-0.5	-0.0	+0.0	-2.0*	-0.0	-2.7*	-4.7*
11. Roles Domain Total (in %)	12.7*	20.7*	14.8*	9.4*	9.9*	7.6*	23.7*	14.1*	11.0*
12. Overall Amount Mean (in %)	+6.3*	+9.7*	10.0*	+5.6*	+5.4*	+6.5*	+9.9*	+6.2*	+4.3*
13. Overall Importance Mean (in %)	+5.5*	+10.5*	+2.4*	+2.9*	+2.8*	+0.3	+12.7*	+5.9*	+5.1*
14. Incongruence Mean (in %)	+0.0	-0.3	+0.0	+0.0	+0.4	-0.1	-0.1	+0.5	-0.0
15. Combined Amount Indexes (in %)	0.9	0.2	2.4*	0.8	1.3*	0.7	1.0	1.4	1.6*
16. Rank Order of Index Betas	32154	31452	14253	45213	43125	21435	54213	23451	41235
17. Conditions Domain Total (in %)	2.6*	3.7*	2.2*	6.4*	4.5*	4.3*	3.3*	10.7*	5.8*
18. Overall Amount Mean (in %)	-0.2	-0.0	+0.1	+0.7*	+0.9*	+0.0	+0.4	-0.4	+0.0
19. Overall Importance Mean (in %)	+1.0*	+0.9*	+0.4	+0.6*	+1.5*	+0.3	+1.9*	+1.2*	+2.7*
20. Incongruence Mean (in %)	-0.0	-0.0	+0.0	-0.9*	+0.2	-0.0	+0.4	-0.8	+0.2
21. Combined Amount Indexes (in %)	1.4	2.8*	1.7	4.2*	1.8*	4.0*	0.6	8.2*	2.9*
22. Rank Order of Index Betas	6435271	6452731	6257314	6314572	4237561	1635427	7456213	6745321	2517346
23. Practices Domain Total (in %)	4.7*	4.7*	4.4*	8.3*	4.4*	5.3*	4.0*	4.7*	5.2*
24. Overall Amount Mean (in %)	+0.9*	+0.1	+2.3*	+2.3*	+1.0*	-0.2	+1.2*	+1.3	+1.3*
25. Combined Importance Means (in %)	+1.8*	+2.6*	+1.2*	+3.4*	+1.2*	+2.8*	+0.9*	+0.1	+1.7*
26. Practice Difficulty Mean (in %)	+0.9*	+0.6*	+0.0	+0.2	+0.2	+0.2	+0.3	+0.4	+0.4*
27. Combined Incongruences (in %)	0.3	0.2	0.2	1.4*	0.4	0.6	0.7	1.1	0.4
28. Combined Amount Indexes (in %)	0.8	1.2	0.7	1.1*	1.6*	1.5	0.9	1.9	1.4*
29. Rank Order of Index Betas	152643	512436	342615	354612	351642	164325	216543	514362	126534

Note: *p 0.05; **p 0.01.

Table 7.4
Percentage of Job-Related Stress Variance Attributable to Various Domain Components within Each Country

Regression of Job-Related Stress	US	England	Germany	Japan	Singapore	Canada	Poland	Israel	USSR
1. Multiple R with All 35 Predictors	0.3953	0.5019	0.4563	0.4204	0.4400	0.4863	0.3623	0.5651	0.4282
2. Total Variance Accounted for (R², in %)	15.6**	25.2**	20.8***	17.7**	19.4**	23.7**	13.1**	31.9**	18.3**
3. Raw Score Mean for Job-Related Stress	3.31	3.32	2.97	3.24	3.14	3.10	3.03	2.56	3.27
4. Skewness Index Job-Related Stress	-0.84	-0.94	-0.74	-0.66	-0.43	-0.68	-0.75	-0.02	-0.88
5. Number of Cases Complete	848	621	651	1238	849	356	616	285	1118
6. Rank Order of Country R's	8	2	4	7	5	3	9	1	6
7. Demographic Domain Total (in %)	0.4	2.2*	1.2*	1.9*	0.5	2.4*	0.7	0.9	2.5*
8. Married Status: with Yes + (in %)	-0.2	+1.0*	-0.7*	-0.1	+0.2	-1.2*	-0.2	-0.0	-0.0
9. Age Category (in %)	+0.0	+1.2*	+0.0	-0.9	+0.0	-0.4	+0.5	-0.0	-0.2
10. Gender: with Male + (in %)	-0.1	-0.1	-0.6*	-0.9*	+0.3	-0.8	+0.0	-0.8	-2.3*
11. Roles Domain Total (in %)	2.9*	3.4*	5.7*	2.6*	9.5*	1.7*	2.6*	2.3*	3.6*
12. Overall Amount Mean (in %)	+0.0	+0.1	+2.2*	-0.1	+6.8*	+0.2	+1.2*	-0.1	+0.9*
13. Overall Importance Mean (in %)	+1.3*	+2.1*	+1.6*	+1.3*	+0.2	+0.0	+0.4	+0.1	+0.6*
14. Incongruence Mean (in %)	+0.2	-0.0	+0.2	-0.1	+0.0	-0.7	+0.1	+0.0	-0.1
15. Combined Amount Indexes (in %)	0.9	1.2*	1.7*	1.2*	2.5*	0.8	0.8	2.2*	2.0*
16. Rank Order of Index Betas	32145	43215	35421	25134	35412	45312	25143	23154	12534
17. Conditions Domain Total (in %)	9.8*	13.0*	11.6*	9.5*	4.7*	16.3*	5.5*	20.4*	6.7*
18. Overall Amount Mean (in %)	-7.8*	-7.1*	-3.9*	-7.0*	+2.8*	-7.0*	-3.8*	-6.6*	-3.4*
19. Overall Importance Mean (in %)	+0.4	+0.5	+2.9*	+0.8*	+0.2	+2.3*	+0.4	+3.3*	+0.9*
20. Incongruence Mean (in %)	+0.0	-0.0	-0.1	+0.1	+0.1	-0.2	+0.3	-0.1	+0.9*
21. Combined Amount Indexes (in %)	1.5*	5.5*	4.7*	1.6*	1.5*	6.8*	1.1	10.4*	1.6*
22. Rank Order of Index Betas	6452731	6134725	6521374	4613275	1762543	6431275	4213576	6312547	1352476
23. Practices Domain Total (in %)	2.6*	6.5*	2.3*	3.7*	4.7*	3.2*	4.4*	8.4*	5.5*
24. Overall Amount Mean (in %)	-0.0	-0.2	-0.1	-0.2	+1.7*	-0.1	+0.4	+1.8*	+0.2
25. Combined Importance Means (in %)	+0.2	+1.3*	+0.0	+0.6	+0.0	+2.3*	+0.1	-1.1	-0.1
26. Practice Difficulty Mean (in %)	+0.8*	+3.3*	+1.2*	+2.5*	-0.4*	+0.2	+2.2*	+2.8*	+3.9*
27. Combined Incongruences (in %)	0.3	1.3*	0.5	0.0	0.5	0.1	0.5	0.8	0.2
28. Combined Amount Indexes (in %)	1.2	0.4	0.5	0.4	2.1*	0.6	1.1	1.9	1.1
29. Rank Order of Index Betas	352416	651342	364215	451326	156342	265431	123564	364152	365142

Note: *p 0.05; **p 0.01.

Strength of Optimum Predictions

The optimum predictions for overall job satisfaction, work centrality, and job-related stress were operationally defined as the multiple R, obtained by regressing each criterion variable on the thirty-five "optimum" predictor variables. Ideally, with thirty-five predictors and theoretical reasons for believing that most of them had strong influence, one would hope to account for at least 50 percent of the criterion variance. This would require every multiple R to be greater than 0.70. However, the multiple Rs actually obtained in this study, although highly significant, were generally of moderate strength. The range and average of the obtained multiple Rs (with the corresponding percentage of variance accounted for in parentheses) are listed as follows (see block 1 of Tables 7.2, 7.3, and 7.4 for details).

- Multiple R for overall job satisfaction ranged from R = 0.47 (22.4%) to R = 0.64 (40.8%) and averaged R = 0.55 (30.3%).
- Multiple R for work centrality ranged from R = 0.44 (19.0%) to R = 0.58 (34.1%) and averaged R = 0.51 (26.0%).
- Multiple R for job-related stress ranged from R = 0.36 (13.1%) to R = 0.57 (31.9%) and averaged R = 0.45 (20.3%).

One suspected cause of the relatively low values of multiple R was the fact that the distributions of all three criterion variables had a strong negative skew in all countries (see line 4 of Tables 7.2, 7.3, & 7.4). To obtain a more accurate measure of relationship, the corresponding multiple R, percent of variance accounted for (R^2), and the skewness index values for each country were correlated across countries separately for each criterion. Positive correlations of R with skew and R^2 with skew were obtained for all three criterion variables, with the second correlation being slightly higher in all instances. The observed correlations for R^2 with skew were: r = 0.19 for overall job satisfaction; r = 0.21 for work centrality; and r = 0.60 for job-related stress. The combined results suggest that country to country variations in the amount of negative skew tend to be inversely proportional to R^2 for all three criterion variables: less skew produced larger Rs.

A similar relationship was found with many of the predictor variables, which also tended to have strong skews. On the basis of the pattern of results, it was concluded that skewed distributions somewhat depressed R in all countries and accounted for a small but significant amount of the country-to-country variations in the size of multiple R.

The bad effect of relatively low values of the multiple Rs caused by skewed distributions is that true relationships between individual predictors and the criterion are less likely to produce statistically significant influences. The good side, however, is that we can be more confident than usual that any significant results we do obtain are real.

Comparing Domain Influences

This section shifts away from a concern with the magnitude of multiple R in each country to a concern with the relative influence of each variable domain on criterion prediction in each country. The expected order of domain influence within optimum-predictions of each criterion was inferred from expectations 1, 2, 3, 4, and 9 versus 15 and 18. To simplify the definition of expected orders, the first letter will identify the domain: Demographics, Roles, Conditions, and Practices. The expected domain orders, listed in descending order of influence, and underlining the letters of domains for which the predicted rank is equivocal (reversible), are as follows: the expected domain order for overall job satisfaction is CRPD; the expected order for work centrality is RPCD; and the expected order for job-related stress is CPRD.

The observed order of domain influences on the three criterion variables in each country appears in Table 7.5 (see lines 7, 11, 17, and 23 of Tables 7.2, 7.3, and 7.4 for the actual percentages). When we compare the observed orders to the corresponding expected orders listed above, we notice that *if reversals of underlined domains are ignored* almost all of the results agree with the theoretical prediction. There is only one exception to expectation for overall job satisfaction (the Soviet Union), there are no exceptions for work centrality, and there are two exceptions for job-related stress (Singapore and Canada). However, because of the relatively small N in Canada, the RD reversal there is not statistically significant and has no theoretical importance.

The two significant exceptions to the expected order (the Soviet Union with overall job satisfaction, and Singapore with job-related stress) both involve a conditions versus roles reversal. A comparison of the percentages of criterion variance accounted for by conditions in the Soviet Union versus the corresponding percentages in other countries demonstrates that the CR reversal in the Soviet Union resulted from exceptionally poor prediction from the

Table 7.5
Observed Order of Domain Influence within the Optimum Prediction for Each QWL Index in Each Country

Criterion:	US	England	Germany	Japan	Singapore	Canada	Poland	Israel	USSR
Job Satisfaction	CRPD	CRDP	CRPD	CRPD	CRPD	CRPD	CRPD	CRPD	RCDP*
Work Centrality	RPCD	RPCD	RPCD	RPCD	RCPD	RPCD	RPCD	RCPD	RCDP
Job-Related Stress	CRPD	CPRD	CRPD	CPRD	RPCD*	CPDR*	CPRD	CPRD	CPRD

Note: First letters identify domains: Conditions, Demographics, Practices, and Roles; Departures from the predicted order are tagged with an asterisk (*); The influences of underlined domains are not significantly different—order is irrelevant.

conditions domain rather than from exceptionally good prediction from the roles domain.

Examination of the detailed results for job-related stress revealed a somewhat similar pattern involving Singapore. The influence of roles on job-related stress variance (9.5%) is fairly strong in Singapore compared to other countries, but the conditions influence (4.7%) is less than half the average for other countries. Colleagues from Singapore suggest that the connotative meaning of the term "stress" is different in Singapore than other countries, and that this explains the CR reversal here. A more detailed discussion of this explanation appears in a subsequent section.

The expectations and results are listed below in *descending* order of influence using the first letters to identify domains (Demographics, Roles, Conditions, and Practices) and underlining the letters of domains for which the predicted order is tied or equivocal.

- The expected CRPD order of domain influence on overall job satisfaction was confirmed in every country but the Soviet Union, where roles were more influential than conditions.

- The expected RCPD order of domain influence on work centrality was confirmed in all nine countries.

- The expected CPRD order of domain influence on job-related stress was confirmed in every country but Singapore, where roles were more influential than conditions or practices. (There was also a small insignificant difference between roles and demographics in Canada, but this was not considered theoretically relevant.)

The fact that the observed domain influences for most countries were in the expected order provides strong support for the prescribed order of predictor entry used in every regression, and for the chain of influence model in Figure 7.1.

Relationships among Criterion Variables

Some researchers have suggested causal relationships among stress, satisfaction, and centrality. Stress has been found to reduce personal well-being and satisfaction (Firestone & Pennell, 1993), and job satisfaction has been found to be a precursor of centrality (Marsh & Mannari, 1977; Williams & Hazer, 1986). However, other investigators have suggested that dissatisfaction is stressful (Landy et al., 1994), and that a central focus on work was a precursor to satisfaction (Bateman & Strasser, 1984). To quote Glisson and Durick (1988), "There continues to be a great deal of disagreement regarding any causal ordering."

The relationships among the criterion variables in our study were explored in two steps. First, the bivariate correlations among criterion variables were computed by country and analyzed for similarities and differences. Second,

within-country regressions of each criterion were computed with the predicted and residual scores for other two criterion variables added to the original thirty-five optimum predictors. It was argued that a significant improvement
attributable to the predicted versions of one criterion over the other would be
evidence for a causal ordering.

The results of the bivariate correlations in each country appear in Table
7.6. The correlation between overall job satisfaction and work centrality (Job
Sat–Work Cen) was positive and significant in all countries, and ranged from
+0.139 to +0.282. Similarly, the correlation of work centrality and job-related
stress (Work Cen–Stress) was positive and significant in all countries, but
slightly more variable ranging from +0.146 to +0.346. The correlation between overall job satisfaction and job-related stress (Job Sat–Stress) was considerably more variable, and even had one reverse direction. Singapore had a
significant positive correlation (+0.222), while the other eight countries had
significant negative correlations ranging from –0.072 to –0.326. In view of a
number of previous reversals of expectation involving job-related stress in
Singapore, this latter finding is considered to be quite important and will be
explored more fully in a subsequent section.

While there are significant differences in the size of the correlations across
countries and across variables within countries, the important observation for
this chapter is the fact that eight countries have the same pattern of relationships: High scores on overall job satisfaction go with high scores on work
centrality and low scores on job-related stress, but high scores on work centrality go with high scores on job-related stress. This is counterintuitive since
one would normally expect variables that are positively correlated to one another (satisfaction and centrality) to have the same relationship with a third
variable (stress)—either both positively related to it or both negatively related to it. Technically, an intransitive relationship in which two correlated
characteristics have reverse relationships with a third characteristic is only
possible when all of the correlations are relatively small. Psychologically,
however, it makes sense. The aspect of stress that signifies distress or apprehension creates a negative correlation with short-term satisfaction, while that

Table 7.6
Correlations among Pairs of Criterion Variables within Countries

Criterion Pair:	US	England	Germany	Japan	Singapore	Canada	Poland	Israel	USSR
Job Sat. – Work Cen.	+0.139*	+0.282*	+0.172*	+0.274*	+0.221*	+0.145*	+0.242*	+0.124*	+0.282*
Job Sat. – Stress	-0.233*	-0.254*	-0.161*	-0.326*	+0.222*	-0.235*	-0.176*	-0.293*	-0.072*
Work Cen. – Stress	+0.278*	+0.265*	+0.208*	+0.146*	+0.298*	+0.346*	+0.207*	+0.256*	+0.241*

Note: *p 0.05; **p 0.01.

aspect of stress which signifies eustress, challenge, or arousal creates a positive correlation with the longer-term centrality but has little influence on day-to-day satisfaction.

To provide a check on the possibility of a causal ordering of the three criterion variables, within-country regressions of each criterion were computed using the original thirty-five optimum predictors, and then the predicted and residual scores were saved. Subsequently a series of hierarchical regressions were run, adding the residual and predicted scores of the alternate criterion variables to the original optimum predictors. These enlarged predictor sets did *not* produce a significant increment in multiple R for any criterion. It was concluded that the regression analysis of our data provided no evidence for a causal ordering of the three criterion variables. Consequently, the three criterion variables are treated as related but separate facets of quality of work life.

Evidence for the Chain of Influence Model

The model in Figure 7.1 suggested that much of the effect of demographic variables on quality of work life would be passed through the mediating predictor variables; that is, the demographic variables would affect the mediating variables, and they, in turn, would affect quality of work life. The "passed through" influence is referred to as a mediated effect of demographics. Evidence for the existence of a mediated effect would provide support for the model.

A partial test of mediated demographic effects was made by regressing the amount and importance means for roles, conditions, and practices on demographics and saving the predicted and residual values. Subsequently, multiple regressions were computed within and across countries for each criterion by ENTERing first the six original dimension means, and then the six predicted versions of the (same) means. The nine-country regression was considered appropriate, because all means were standardized within each country. The individual country regressions were intended as a check on the nine-country result. Since the predicted means represented the mediated effects of demographics, a significant added effect for the set of six predicted means would be evidence that the hypothesized mediation actually occurred.

The addition of the predicted scores to the regression equation significantly increased the size of multiple R for all three criterion variables in all nine countries. This provides strong support for both a direct and indirect or mediated effect of demographics on all three criterion variables. The dual effect of demographics, in turn, provides strong support for the validity of the model presented in Figure 7.1.

Effects of Demographics

The review suggested that demographic variables would have a small but significant effect on satisfaction and stress, but less influence on work centrality. This generally proved to be the case in our data: Demographics typically accounted for about 2 percent of the variance in overall job satisfaction and job-related stress, but only about 1.4 percent of the work centrality variance. Country-to-country variations are most meaningfully explored as the individual effects of the three demographic indexes (marital status, age, and gender). These appear in the next three summary statements.

• The marital status of teachers was a dichotomous variable (1 = unmarried, 2 = married). Because married persons, on average, would have more intimate experience with children and should develop better communication and discipline skills, being married was expected to increase overall job satisfaction and work centrality and decrease job-related stress. In our study results, being married tended to

   a. Increase overall job satisfaction in Singapore, Israel, and the Soviet Union, as expected, but produced no change in the other countries (Table 7.2, line 8).

   b. Increase work centrality in Germany and Israel, as expected, but produced no significant effects in the other countries (Table 7.3, line 8).

   c. Decrease job-related stress in Germany and Canada, as expected, and unexpectedly increase job-related stress in England, but produced no change in the other countries (Table 7.2, line 8). Increased stress for English males is probably explained by threats to security during the 1983 to 1986 reforms that were felt particularly keenly by married men. See Chapter 2 for a full discussion of the reform effects.

• Teacher age would naturally be strongly correlated with amount of teaching experience, which could be expected to improve discipline skills and thus increase overall job satisfaction and work centrality and decrease job-related stress. In our study, increased age of teachers tended to

   a. Increase overall job satisfaction, as expected, in Japan, Poland, and the Soviet Union, but produced no change in the other countries (Table 7.2, line 9).

   b. Increase work centrality, as expected, in England, Japan, Poland, and the Soviet Union, but produced no change in the other countries (Table 7.3, line 9).

   c. Have no influence on job-related stress rather than the expected decrease in all countries but England, where stress unexpectedly increased (Table 7.2, line 9).

• Khan and Weiss (1973, p. 776) found that female teachers have more discipline problems, and are more likely to be disturbed by discipline problems than male teachers. Consequently, being male was expected to decrease job-related stress and increase overall job satisfaction and work centrality. In our study, being male tended to

   a. Unexpectedly increase overall job satisfaction in England, Poland, and the Soviet Union, but produced no change in other countries (Table 7.2, line 10).

   b. Unexpectedly decrease work centrality in Canada, Israel, and the Soviet Union, but produce no change in the other countries (Table 7.3, line 10).

   c. Decrease job-related stress, as expected, in Germany, Japan, and the Soviet Union, but produce no change in other countries (Table 7.4, line 10).

Summary of Demographic Effects. Given the relatively small effects of the entire demographic domain, it is not surprising that the individual marital status, age, and gender variables frequently had no significant effect. However, researchers in countries where one or more demographic variables had a strong effect may want to conduct additional research to determine the reach and cause of the effects. Such research would seem especially important in the Soviet Union where demographics accounted for 15.3 percent of the overall job satisfaction prediction, 21.0 percent of the work centrality prediction, and 13.6 percent of the job-related stress prediction.

Evaluation of Expected Relationships

An important goal of this chapter was to determine which of the theoretical relationships derived from the review appeared to have universal applicability and which were culturally specific. The discussion is divided into five subsections: accounting for common-factor relationships, expected effects of domain–dimension means, effects of predictors identified by prior research, exceptions and reversals, and a summary of the theoretical evaluation.

Accounting for Common-Factor Relationships. Because items and indexes within the roles, conditions, and practices domains were correlated, it was reasonable to expect that much—perhaps most—of their influence on quality of work life indexes might be accounted for by shared common factors. In each domain, the amount and importance dimension means were used as measures of commonality among the corresponding items and indexes.

In the regression analyses, a domain's amount means were entered first, importance means second, amount indexes third, and then the importance indexes. As it turned out, the importance indexes from all three domains failed to significantly improve the prediction of any criterion in any of the nine countries. Consequently, these indexes were dropped from the analyses, leaving only the common-factor importance means to represent the influence on criterion variables of all the importance variables in the roles, conditions, and practices domains.

To test the *relative* contribution of the common-factor amount mean in each domain, the amount of variation accounted for by the amount mean (its influence percentage) was divided by the total influence of that domain in each of the nine countries. The percentages of domain predictions attributed to common-factor amount means were as follows.

• The percentage of the role domain prediction attributable to the common factor were computed separately in all nine countries for each QWL index and yielded the following role amount attributions.

    a. For predicting overall job satisfaction, attributions ranged from 25.0 percent to 87.7 percent and averaged 72.6 percent (Table 7.2).

    b. For predicting work centrality, attributions ranged from 39.1 percent to 65.8 percent and averaged 54.3 percent (Table 7.3).

   c. For predicting job-related stress, attributions ranged from 2.9 percent to 71.6 percent and averaged 22.9 percent (Table 7.4).

• The percentage of the condition domain prediction attributable to the common factor were computed separately in all nine countries for each QWL index and yielded the following condition amount attributions.

   a. For predicting overall job satisfaction, attributions ranged from 69.8 percent to 94.0 percent and averaged 83.3 percent (Table 7.2).

   b. For predicting work centrality, attributions ranged from 1.2 percent to 20.0 percent and averaged 6.9 percent (Table 7.3).

   c. For predicting job-related stress, attributions ranged from 23.7 percent to 79.6 percent and averaged 55.1 percent (Table 7.4).

• The percentage of the practices domain prediction attributable to the common factor were computed separately in all nine countries for each QWL index and yielded the following practice amount attributions.

   a. For predicting overall job satisfaction, attributions ranged from 8.3 percent to 58.8 percent and averaged 26.0 percent (Table 7.2).

   b. For predicting work centrality, attributions ranged from 2.1 percent to 52.3 percent and averaged 23.4 percent (Table 7.3).

   c. For predicting job-related stress, attributions ranged from 1.9 percent to 36.2 percent and averaged 9.8 percent (Table 7.4).

These results provide ample evidence that the role amount, condition amount, and practices amount means represent common factors that are shared by all of the items and indexes in their respective domains, and that these common factors are frequently major predictors of quality of work life. The most important theoretical conclusion is that these results provide strong support for the use of the amount dimension means as measures of common factors. Since common factors are the most powerful predictors in every domain, it is important to extract and measure their effects before assessing the unique added effects of other dimension means and individual indexes.

Expected Effects of Domain–Dimension Means. Four dimension means from the roles and condition domains typically account a majority of the prediction attained with all thirty-five variables in the optimum regression of each criterion. These are the four dimension means: role amount, role importance, condition amount, and condition importance. On average, these variables account for 68 percent of the overall job satisfaction prediction, 53 percent of the work centrality prediction, and 45 percent the job-related stress prediction.

Each of the four variables had an expected effect derived from the review and evaluated by our analytic results on a country-by-country basis. In the following list, the term "universally significant" indicates statistically significant results in the expected direction in all nine countries; the term "universal trend" indicates results that are in the expected direction in all nine countries but are not statistically significant in one or more countries. All significant reversals of expectation are labeled "contradictions," and are specifically mentioned. References to the appropriate expectations and the table and line number of the corresponding results appear (in the order listed) in square brackets after each outcome statement.

- Increased involvement in a wide variety of teaching roles (higher role amount means) produced

  a. A strong, universally significant increase in teacher satisfaction. As expected, higher involvement increased satisfaction (expectation 1; Table 7.2, line 13).

  b. A strong, universally significant increase in teacher concentration on education-related activities (work centrality). As expected, higher involvement increased centrality (expectation 1; Table 7.3, line 13).

  c. An increase in teacher stress, as expected, in Germany, Singapore, Poland, and the Soviet Union, with weak imperceptible effects (0.2% or less) in every other country (expectation 15; Table 7.4, line 13).

- Role importance was expected to be a strong positive predictor of work centrality and a weaker positive predictor of overall job satisfaction (expectation 1). It was also expected to have a strong positive influence on job-related stress (expectation 15). However, increases in stress should also produce a corresponding *reduction* in satisfaction, tending to cancel the positive effect of task significance: Thus, the net expected effect should be a near-zero or perhaps even a negative influence of role importance on overall job satisfaction. Given this theoretical order of effects, the results for stress are presented first. Increases in the perceived importance of teaching roles (higher role importance means) produced

  a. A universal trend toward increased teacher stress in all nine countries, with significant increases in Germany, Japan, and the Soviet Union. As expected, the strain of more involvement produced more stress (distress) (expectation 15; Table 7.4, line 13).

  b. No perceptible effect on teacher satisfaction, as expected, in eight countries, and a small but significant increase (0.8%) in the Soviet Union (expectation 1; Table 7.2, line 13). It was argued that the negative influence of increased stress (distress) counteracted the positive influence of more significant tasks (as measured by average role importance) to produce these essentially null effects.

  c. A universally significant increase in teacher concentration on education-related activities (work centrality) (expectation 1; Table 7.3, line 13). As expected, the challenge aspects of stress (eustress) improved the longer-term centrality attitudes.

- A more positive work environment as defined by an increased presence of good work conditions (higher condition amount means) produced

  a. A strong, universally significant increase in teacher satisfaction. As expected, improvement in immediate day-to-day conditions increased job satisfaction (expectation 7; Table 7.2, line 18).

b. Small, mixed negative and positive influences on teacher concentration on education-related activities (work centrality); only two countries had significant influence percentages, and both of these were quite weak (Japan at 0.7% and Singapore at 0.9%). As expected, improvement in immediate work conditions had little effect on longer-term attitudes (expectation 1; Table 7.3, line 18).

c. A strong, significant decrease in teacher stress, as expected, in all countries but Singapore, where there was a significant contradictory increase in stress (expectations 12, 13, 14, 15, and 18; Table 7.4, line 18).

• The review contained no expectation for the influence of condition importance on overall job satisfaction, work centrality, or job-related stress. However, it is axiomatic that important conditions would produce more stress than unimportant ones: Therefore, condition importance was expected to be a positive predictor of job-related stress. Logically, an increase in job-related stress would be expected to produce a concomitant reduction in overall job satisfaction. For the longer-term attitudes, however, higher condition importance scores should serve as a stimulating goal, thus producing a positive influence on work centrality. Given this theoretical order of effects, the results for job-related stress are presented first. Increases in the perceived importance of positive work conditions (higher condition importance means) produced

a. A universal trend toward increased teacher stress in all nine countries. As expected, more important conditions tended to be more stressful (previous argument; Table 7.4, line 19).

b. A universal trend toward decreased teacher satisfaction in all nine countries, with a significant influence only in Germany. As expected, increased stress tended to reduce satisfaction (previous argument; Table 7.2, line 19).

c. A universal trend toward increased teacher concentration on education-related activities (work centrality). As expected, more important conditions tended to produce more work centrality (previous argument; Table 7.3, line 19).

The dimension means in the practices domain, although generally somewhat less influential than the roles and conditions means, together account for a significant chunk of the multiple regression prediction: On average, they account for an additional 5 percent of the overall job satisfaction prediction, an additional 13 percent of the work centrality prediction, and an additional 15 percent of the job-related stress prediction. Three dimension effects are summarized below: practice amount, practice importance, and practice difficulty.

• Increased use of good—well-regarded—teaching practices (higher practice amount means) produced

a. A trend toward increased teacher satisfaction, as expected, in all countries but Israel, where there was a significant and contradictory decrease in satisfaction (expectation 3; Table 7.2, line 24).

b. A trend toward increased teacher concentration on education-related activities (work centrality), as expected, in every country but Canada, where there was a small (0.2%) insignificant decrease in centrality (expectation 3; Table 7.3, line 24).

c. No significant change in stress, rather than the expected decrease in every country but Singapore and Israel, where significant contradictory increases occurred (expectation 3; Table 7.4, line 24).

- Unlike previous importance components, practice importance was the combined influence of two variables: the importance of the practice for job satisfaction and the importance for student learning. The review contained no research to support an expected effect of either variable. However, importance scores that were higher than the corresponding amount score generally indicates underuse of an important practice and should produce a mild increase in job-related stress. Mild increases in stress should produce a mild depression of overall job satisfaction. For the longer-term attitudes, however, higher importance scores should serve as a stimulating goal thus producing a positive influence on work centrality. Given this theoretical order of effects, the results for job-related stress are presented first. Increases in the perceived importance of using good teaching practices (higher practice importance means) produced

  a. A trend toward increased stress, as expected, in all countries but Israel and the Soviet Union, where there were small insignificant decreases (previous argument; Table 7.4, line 25).

  b. A weak trend to reduced teacher satisfaction, as expected, in every country but Canada and Poland, where there were weak insignificant increases (previous argument; Table 7.2, line 25).

  c. A universal trend toward increased teacher concentration on education-related activities (work centrality), as expected, in all nine countries (previous argument; Table 7.3, line 25).

- The review provided no expectation for the effects of practice difficulty. Intuitively, however, high levels of difficulty in using a teaching practice would be expected to increase job-related stress. If the rationale previously produced for practice importance also holds here, one would expect a corresponding decrease in job satisfaction with a concomitant increase in work centrality. Once again, it is appropriate to begin with an evaluation of the effects on job-related stress. Increased difficulty in using good teaching practices (higher practice difficulty means) produced

  a. A trend toward increased teacher stress, as expected, in all countries but Singapore, where there was an unexpected contradictory decrease in stress (previous argument; Table 7.4, line 26).

  b. A weak trend toward decreased teacher satisfaction, as expected, in all nine countries (previous argument; Table 7.2, line 26).

  c. A weak trend toward increased teacher concentration on education-related activities (work centrality) in all nine countries (previous argument; Table 7.3, line 26).

Although the overall results for the practice dimensions lean toward support for the theoretical structure, they tend to be weak and somewhat inconsistent. The weak magnitude of effects derives from the overlap of practice effects with the previously-entered roles and conditions components. Inconsistencies are probably explained by interactions of practice difficulty and practice importance, which were not accounted for in this analysis.

Effects of Predictors Identified by Prior Research. The review identified a number of specific job characteristics or conditions that had been found to affect the quality of a worker's life. In our study, these characteristics or conditions were assessed by individual index variables. Since each index is included *within* a dimension mean, it may not have a significant unique influence on the criterion variable, beyond the common-factor influence measured by the dimension mean. In this situation, evidence that a shared common factor produced the influence expected from an index, together with a significant bivariate correlation between the index and the criterion variable, is considered sufficient to confirm the expected relationship. However, it will be called a "trend," to distinguish it from the situation in which an index has a significant unique influence, in addition to the common-factor influence, measured by the corresponding amount dimension mean. Because tables of correlations and beta weights for each country are prohibitively large, only the expectations are documented here.

- Increased amounts of shared management (role index 3) produced
    a. A universal trend toward increased teacher satisfaction, as expected, in all nine countries (expectation 5).
    b. A universal trend toward increased teacher concentration on education-related activities (work centrality), as expected, in all nine countries (expectation 5).
    c. Neither a decrease in stress, as expected, nor an increase in any country (expectation 16).

- Increased support of colleagues, administrators, and parents (condition index 1) produced
    a. Universally significant increases in teacher satisfaction, as expected, in all nine countries (expectation 5).
    b. Universally significant increases in teacher concentration on education-related activities (work centrality), as expected, in all nine countries (expectation 5).
    c. A significant decrease in teacher stress, as expected, in all countries but Singapore, where there was an unexpected contradictory increase in stress (expectation 14).

- More adequate economic incentives (condition index 3) produced
    a. A universal trend toward increased teacher satisfaction, as expected, in all nine countries (expectation 7).
    b. A universal trend toward increased teacher concentration on education-related activities (work centrality), as expected, in all nine countries (expectation 7).
    c. A decrease in teacher stress, as expected, in all countries but Singapore, where it unexpectedly tended to increase teacher stress (expectation 13).

- More adequate physical resources (condition index 5) produced

  a. A universal trend toward increased teacher satisfaction, as expected, in all nine countries (expectation 7).

  b. A universal trend toward increased teacher concentration on education-related activities (work centrality), as expected, in all nine countries (expectation 7).

  c. A decrease in teacher stress, as expected, in all countries but Singapore, where it unexpectedly increased stress (expectation 12).

- Increased teacher autonomy (condition index 2) produced

  a. Universally significant increases in teacher satisfaction, as expected, in all nine countries (expectation 8).

  b. Universally significant increases in teacher concentration on education-related activities (work centrality), as expected, in all nine countries (expectation 8).

  c. A mild but insignificant reduction in stress, as expected, in every country but Singapore, which had a significant increase in stress (inferred from expectation 8).

- More reasonable workloads (condition index 6) produced

  a. Universally significant increases in teacher satisfaction, as expected, in all nine countries (expectation 10).

  b. Universally significant increases in teacher concentration on education-related activities (work centrality), as expected, in all nine countries (expectation 10).

  c. Significant decreases in teacher stress, as expected, in all countries but Singapore, where there was an unexpected contradictory increase in stress (expectation 15).

- Good discipline, inferred from the use of control and motivation techniques (practice indexes 3, 5, and 6), produced

  a. No perceptible effect rather than the expected increase in stress in all nine countries (expectation 18).

  b. A universal trend toward increased teacher satisfaction, as expected, in all nine countries (inferred from expectation 18).

  c. A universal trend toward increased teacher concentration on education-related activities (work centrality), as expected, in all nine countries (inferred from expectation 18).

One of the most surprising results of this analysis was the large number of theoretical relationships that were confirmed in all or almost all countries in our sample. The implications of these findings are discussed in the summary to this section. However, we must first consider the possible meaning of some exceptions and reversals of expectation that were found in the analysis.

Exceptions and Reversals. There were a number of instances where findings were insignificant and could neither confirm nor contradict the expected relations. These are considered problems of a lack of sensitivity in either the measurement instruments and/or the research design, and will be addressed as the implications for further research in a subsequent section. This section will deal with significant findings that constituted a contradiction of expectation.

Reverse Criterion Correlations. The finding that job-related stress was negatively correlated with overall job satisfaction (in all countries but Singapore) but positively correlated with work centrality was at first very puzzling, because overall job satisfaction and work centrality were positively correlated in all countries. Intuitively, one would expect two correlated variables (satisfaction and centrality) to have same-sign correlations with any third variable. (In fact, one can demonstrate mathematically that if the the correlation of two variables is high [0.80 or more], their correlations with any third variable *must* be in the same direction.) However, the observed opposite-sign correlations of stress with satisfaction and centrality *do* make psychological sense. The key to understanding this comes from the earlier definition of satisfaction as "a function of (day to day) job experience" and the internal-motivation aspect of centrality as "a function of (longer-term) beliefs about the organization." This definition suggests that the opposite-sign correlations with job-related stress are caused by its differing long- and short-term effects.

To see how this might work, consider the experience of men engaged in a difficult and dangerous team endeavor, such as an overland trek to the South Pole. Such a journey is inherently stressful, and the journals of participants invariably describe both individual discouragement and interpersonal conflicts that must have been enormously dissatisfying on a day-to-day basis. Yet these same sources almost always report that the shared trials actually strengthened their long-term regard for team members and their commitment to team goals. Job-related stress decreases immediate satisfaction, but in determining long-term attitudes, it operates as a challenge overcome, and thus has a positive rather than negative effect.

Applying this rationale to the criterion correlations, we would expect the correlation between job-related stress and overall job satisfaction (which is based on day-to-day job experience) to be negative because of the apprehension and anxiety (distress) aspects of stress. On the other hand, the correlation of job-related stress with work centrality, which is based on longer-term beliefs and attitudes, would tend to be positive because it relates more closely to the arousal and challenge (eustress) aspects of stress.

Practice Difficulty Reversal. A related phenomenon was that increased difficulty of a teaching practice tended to decrease overall job satisfaction but increase work centrality in all countries. For reasons already discussed, the positive influence of condition importance on work centrality at first seems counterintuitive. But, once again, this apparent anomaly is caused by the different long- and short-term effects of stress. The overall job satisfaction correlation is negative because it relates to the distress aspects of job-related stress, and work centrality is positively correlated because it relates to the eustress aspects of job-related stress.

Job-Related Stress Reversals in Singapore. In a number of instances, the component influence on job-related stress in Singapore was in the opposite direction to that predicted by the review, and opposite to the other eight countries. Opposite sign results with stress in Singapore were found for the influence of a more positive work environment (condition amount mean), the use of good practices (practice amount mean), the difficulty of using practices (practice difficulty mean), and for indexes measuring the support of colleagues and administrators, the adequacy of economic incentives, the adequacy of physical resources, and the reasonableness of workloads. On the other hand, Singapore's job-related stress results agreed with expectation and with the other eight countries with respect to the influence of broad involvement in a variety of teaching roles (the role amount mean), the perceived importance of broad involvement (the role importance mean), the perceived importance of positive work conditions (the condition importance mean), and the perceived importance of using good teaching practices (the practice importance mean).

One possible explanation for these puzzling inconsistencies was offered by a colleague from Singapore. He suggested that Singapore teachers, in general, tend to use the term "stress" to indicate eustress (challenge) rather than distress. As previously explained for criterion correlations and practice difficulty, job-related stress has both a distress and a challenge connotation in most countries. If job-related stress has only the challenge connotation for Singapore teachers, one would expect a *positive* correlation with immediate, day-by-day things, such as conditions and practices, as well as a positive correlation with the longer-term beliefs and attitudes in the roles domain and with the importance mean(s) in all other domains. A semantic shift such as this is much more likely when a criterion variable is based on responses to a single item, as it was in the case of the job-related stress measure used in this study. Although a connotative difference in the interpretation of the word "stress" appears to provide a logically consistent explanation of these phenomena, additional research using a multiitem measure of teacher stress is needed before we can say whether Singapore teachers interpret the stress *construct* as eustress, or just the word "stress" itself.

Reverse Dominant Predictor of Job-Related Stress. A closely related reverse anomaly was the fact that the role domain was the strongest predictor of job-related stress in Singapore, and the condition domain was the strongest predictor in every other country. This Singapore reversal would also be explained by a "challenge" interpretation of job-related stress unique to Singapore: By the line of argument developed in the previous section, roles variables, which tap longer-term beliefs and attitudes, would be strongly related to a challenge interpretation of job-related stress, while an anxiety–distress interpretation would be more affected by short-term work conditions. Further research using separate, carefully constructed measures of eustress and distress will be required to test the validity of this explanation.

Reverse Dominant Predictor of Overall Job Satisfaction. Glisson and Durick (1988) found that job satisfaction was influenced by short-term job conditions, and work centrality by global, longer-term thematic aspects of the work activities. In our study, work conditions represented day-to-day characteristics, and roles the thematic activities. Our condition domain was a stronger predictor of overall job satisfaction than the roles domain in every country but the Soviet Union. A subsequent cross-cultural comparison of the absolute influence percentages attributable to each domain demonstrated that the Soviet Union reversal was due to the extremely weak predictive power of conditions in that country, rather than the strong predictive power of roles.

A likely explanation for the weak conditions prediction is that teachers in the Soviet Union used a different interpretive frame for work conditions than teachers in other countries. As pointed out by Landy and colleagues (1994), the effects of (conditions) are moderated by a comparative rather than an absolute evaluative frame. That is, how satisfied one is by a set of conditions or how stressed by them is influenced more by how they compare to those of friends, coworkers, and perceived peers, than by the objective conditions themselves. It may be that smaller perceived differences among work groups caused teachers in the Soviet Union to place relatively less emotional value on work conditions. As a consequence, work conditions would be a weak predictor of overall job satisfaction and would likely be a weak predictor of work centrality and job-related stress as well. However, additional research will be required to confirm this explanation.

Importance of Incongruence. Incongruence variables, the absolute value of the difference between the standard-score means for the importance and amount dimensions, were expected to be strong positive predictors of job-related stress and strong positive predictors of satisfaction, because a short supply of important things and an oversupply of unimportant things are equally frustrating. But, despite the fact that some incongruence measures had significant influence on some criterion variables in some countries, incongruence was generally an impotent predictor. It turns out that this lack of power was a statistical artifact of the regression procedure we used rather than a weakness inherent in the incongruence construct. You will recall that we used a forced-entry regression procedure, and that within each domain, the amount mean was entered first, the importance mean second, and the incongruence mean third. Because of this forced order, the importance mean could have predictive influence only if it had a different standard score than the first-entered amount mean. In other words, it functioned as an algebraic or signed difference score (importance–amount). Because much of the potential effect of the incongruence score was "stolen" by a common-factor measured by the previously entered importance mean, incongruence measures were much less influential than expected.

The reader may have noticed that the negligible influence of incongruence discussed previously conflicts with Chapter 5, where various forms of condition incongruence were found to be significant predictors of overall job satisfaction and job-related stress. However, the conflict is more an illusion than a reality for two reasons. First, the incongruence measure in previous chapters was the *signed* difference in importance and amount ratings, while the *abso-*

lute value of that difference was used in this chapter. Second, regressions in previous chapters included incongruence as a predictor but *excluded* importance, whereas *both* variables were used as predictors in this chapter.

Summary of Theoretical Evaluation. It is obvious from reading the long list of findings above that most of the theoretical expectations were confirmed. The seven dimension means and the targeted indexes in the roles, conditions, and practices domains provide sixteen separate tests of expectation for each criterion variable. Counting each country as a replication, we obtain a total of 144 separate tests of expectation for each QWL criterion. Each test had four possible outcomes: The expectation was significantly confirmed by a unique effect; the expectation was confirmed as a trend (this includes the significant unique confirmations); the expectation was significantly contradicted by a unique effect; or the expectation was contradicted by a trend (this includes all the significant unique contradictions). The calculated percentage of tests with each outcome for each criterion are given in Table 7.7.

The percentage of confirmations for work centrality (99.3% confirmations by trend with 88.2% uniquely significant) is very impressive; of the 144 tests, only 1 was an opposite-of-expectation findings—an insignificant unique negative influence in Canada. The confirmation rates for overall job satisfaction (94.4% confirmations by trend with 83.3% uniquely significant) were almost as good; out of 144 tests, only 8 were opposite-of-expectation findings, and only 2 of these were uniquely significant. The confirmation rate for job-related stress (81.9% confirmations by trend with only 41.0% uniquely significant) was somewhat lower, but still reasonable at the trend level. What is of most concern here are the 12 significant reversals at the unique level. However, it is interesting that 9 of these occurred in Singapore. According to the argument presented in the section on job-related stress reversals in Singapore, it seems probable that the Singapore reversals would be removed if job-related stress were measured by a number of items using a variety of synonymous terms. In other words, if one discounts the semantic problem in Singapore, the actual confirmation rates for stress tests might be 89 percent by trend with

Table 7.7
Percentage of 144 Expected Influences Confirmed at Statistically Significant and Trend Levels for Each Quality of Work Life Index

Criterion	Expectation Significantly Confirmed	Expectation Trend Confirmed	Expectation Significantly Contradicted	Expectation Trend Contradicted
Overall Job Satisfaction	83.3	94.4	4.2	5.6
Work Centrality	92.4	99.3	0.0	0.7
Job-Related Stress	41.0	81.9	8.3	18.1

48 percent uniquely significant. No matter which summation is used, however, the results of this study provide strong support for the reviewed theory.
It also suggests that strong theory developed in one country, and operationally defined by broad-based, multiitem questionnaire items, can profitably be
used for cross-cultural research.

GENERAL CONCLUSIONS AND PRACTICAL IMPLICATIONS

Our study explicitly assumed that teachers who are more satisfied with
their job, more dedicated to their work (have greater work centrality), and
less stressed will perform better in the classroom, and thus produce better
educated students. If this assumption is valid, the regression results reported
in this chapter suggest some policies and actions that might be effective and
efficient means of improving education in the nine participating countries
particularly, and probably in other countries with similar characteristics.

The improvement of work conditions is likely to be the most efficient and
effective way of improving teacher performance. This is so not only because
the set of work conditions variables was a powerful predictor in all countries,
but also because work conditions are much more easily changed by administrative actions or policy modifications than by teaching roles or practices.
Better work conditions were a very strong predictor of higher job satisfaction, greater dedication to work (work centrality), and reduced stress in all
nine countries. In fact, conditions variables were by far the strongest predictor of overall job satisfaction and the second-strongest predictor of work centrality in every country but the Soviet Union; they were also the strongest
predictor of job-related stress in every country but Singapore (see Tables 7.2,
7.3, and 7.4 for supporting details).

Within the conditions domain, policies that produce more equitable
workloads, increase teacher autonomy, and increase the perceived support of
administrators, colleagues, and parents are most likely to improve teacher
performance. Increases in economic incentives are also likely to have a positive impact, but, surprisingly, this is not likely to be as productive as changes
in the other conditions.

The findings for teacher roles were similar. Extensive involvement in a
wide variety of educational roles was significantly associated with increased
satisfaction and was the strongest predictor of increased dedication to work
(more centrality) in all nine countries. Increased role involvement was also
associated with increased stress in most countries. Although some of the roles
variables (e.g., support for students) might be primarily a measure of individual teacher behavior, three of the stronger predictors—increased teacher
share in school management, participation in education-related activities outside school (increased cosmopoliteness), and opportunities for professional
development—could be affected by changes in policy by the local board and/

or by government agencies. Although the expected effect is somewhat smaller than for improved conditions, policies aimed at improving these factors are also likely to improve teacher performance.

The degree of incongruence between the amount of a condition present and its perceived importance, and to a lesser extent the corresponding incongruence between the amount of role involvement and its importance, are particularly important predictive elements in their respective domains. As explained earlier, the notion of incongruence is represented in two ways in this chapter, which is different than the approach in earlier chapters. Here, the role importance and condition importance means function as a measure of the *algebraic* difference between importance and amount (i.e., the degree of deprivation), while the incongruence mean is the absolute difference in these means (i.e., the total amount of disagreement without considering the direction of the difference). The regression results show that these two incongruence variables were *not* generally significantly associated with job satisfaction in either the roles or conditions domain, but were strongly associated with significantly increased dedication to work (centrality) in both domains in almost every country. Interestingly, increased condition incongruence and, to a lesser extent, increased role incongruence was also associated with increased stress. This seeming paradox is interpreted to mean that a deficit in important conditions is perceived as challenging (i.e., it produces eustress rather than distress), and therefore spurs the teacher to work harder and be more work centered. This interpretation is reinforced by the fact that there was a significant positive correlation, ranging from 0.15 to 0.35, between work centrality and job-related stress in all nine countries (see Table 7.6 for details). The predictive importance of incongruence measures suggests that persons planning interventions aimed at improving work conditions or increasing role involvement would be wise to first consult the faculty involved to see which conditions and roles should be targeted.

Practical Implications. The bottom-line advice is that if one wishes to improve teacher job satisfaction, one should look to policies that improve work conditions. It would be particularly useful to develop policies that produce more equitable workloads, increased autonomy, and increased support from administrators, colleagues, and parents. If one wishes to improve teachers dedication and commitment to their work, look to policies that increase teacher involvement in a variety of roles. Here it would be useful to provide an increased share in decision making, to encourage participation in education-related conferences and meetings outside the school, and to reward teacher support for students. In either case, however, planners should first consult faculty to determine the areas of greatest need.

The *direction* of the relationships found in this study agreed with expectations derived from a review of American research in most instances, and a substantial percentage of the reversals that did occur (e.g., with job-related stress in Singapore) may have been caused by a semantic problem with the interpretation of a single term. This pattern of results provides compelling evidence that teachers' satisfaction, degree of concentration on education (work centrality), and work-related stress are driven by the same broad classes of teaching roles, work conditions, and teaching activities in every country. In particular, this study demonstrates that a strong conceptual frame (derived from one culture) can profitably be used to design and execute cross-cultural investigations.

One omission from this chapter needs to be underlined. Although the direction of influence of major predictors on the three criterion variables was remarkably consistent across countries, there were large differences in the magnitude or strength of predictor influence from country to country. Since our purpose was to compare trends with theoretically expected effects, differences in magnitude were not generally interpreted. A useful sequel to this study would be to develop measures of what Triandis (1996) called cultural syndromes, and test whether the addition of these variables to our database would predict the magnitude as well as the direction of component influence. Syndrome variables might also help explain the *cause* of reverse expectation findings.

There was rather compelling evidence that predictor and/or criterion variables that have skewed distributions reduce the value of multiple R, and, in general, the power of statistical analysis to discover true relationships. Based on this evidence, we strongly advise researchers interested in doing cross-cultural research to make every effort to obtain valid, normally distributed measures of every important variable in your study. These efforts might include, but should not be limited to, the following actions: (1) Use multiple-choice response formats that allow a wide range of responses having both positive and negative valences. (2) Use both positively stated and negatively stated items. (3) Derive all important variables from at least five items. (4) Pretest all items and indexes on a cross-cultural sample before finalizing your instrument.

There was also strong evidence for a two-factor meaning of "stress": eustress and distress. It was suggested that eustress positively influenced satisfaction but had little influence on centrality, and that distress negatively influenced satisfaction but had little influence on centrality. This strongly suggests that future researchers in this area ought to split the stress concept into two separate measures, with one set of items dealing with eustress (challenge) and the other dealing with distress (anxiety). It is hypothesized that roles, conditions, and practices have distinctly different effects on eustress and distress, and that these two stress factors have a differential influence on satisfaction and centrality and/or commitment. A good causal modeling study involving these variables should make an important contribution to our understanding of the influences on the quality of teachers' lives.

A useful avenue of future study derives from the high confirmation rate for work centrality. You will recall that some of the research used to create expectations for work centrality came from studies investigating the antecedents of teacher commitment. This was justified by the observation that the two terms had a job involvement component in common. Since the other components of both centrality and commitment were stable characteristics resistant to the effects of work experiences, it was argued that the two variables should be influenced by the same work-related predictors. The fact that 99.3 percent of the expectations for work centrality were confirmed suggests that this argument was sound. This strongly suggests that our findings regarding predictors of work centrality may apply to teacher commitment as well.

If indeed our findings also apply to teacher commitment, they suggest the possibility of improving it. Improvement of teacher commitment is particularly important because it is one of the few teacher variables that has been firmly linked to student achievement. Firestone and Pennell (1993) reviewed a series of quantitative and qualitative studies and concluded that the better studies clearly demonstrate a positive association between teacher commitment and student achievement. The evidence connecting low commitment with low achievement was particularly compelling, as illustrated by the following quotation:

Low teacher commitment also reduces student achievement. Burned-out teachers are less sympathetic towards students, have a lower tolerance for frustration in the classroom, and feel more anxious and exhausted. They develop fewer plans to improve the academic quality of their instruction and are less likely to challenge authority when faced with rules that keep them from teaching in ways they define as effective (Dworkin, 1987; Farber, 1984). The result can be the treaty or bargain that high school teachers often make with their students, whereby teachers reduce their intellectual demands on students in return for more pleasant social relations and a more orderly classroom. Often teachers and students agree to engage in lessons about ritualistic school knowledge that neither sees as particularly relevant but is easier for all concerned (McNeil, 1988; Powell, Farrar, & Cohen, 1985). The differences between these practices and those advocated by research on teaching for higher order thinking, cited above, are striking. (Firestone & Pennell, 1993, p. 493)

The results of our study suggest that it should be possible to improve teacher commitment. A number of the variables found to have a strong influence on teacher commitment are likely candidates for manipulation by administrators and/or teacher groups. One of the strongest predictors of commitment in our study was more reasonable teacher workloads. Reducing workloads has the added advantage that it will simultaneously reduce stress and increase satisfaction. A number of clever schemes can be used to reduce teacher workload. The author personally favors those that use team-teaching arrangements, in which two or more subjects (e.g., mathematics and physics) are combined, and the responsibility for specific types of content from either subject is delegated to participating teachers according to their interests and competencies. Such arrangements are especially effective because collaboration with other teachers also has a strong positive effect on commitment and a weaker positive effect on satisfaction (Firestone & Pennell, 1993). Collaborative arrangements are also likely to increase the perceived support of colleagues, the perceived amount of teacher autonomy, and the amount of participation in management decisions. Increases in each of these three variables were consistently found to increase centrality, increase satisfaction, and decrease stress in our study. Applied studies that directly assess the effects of collaborative arrangements such as these on centrality and commitment should be an effective tool for improving academic performance.

REFERENCES

Aranya, N.; Kushnir, T.; and Valency, A. (1986). Organizational commitment in a male-dominated profession. *Human Relations, 39* (5), 433–448.

Bateman, T. S.; and Strasser, S. (1984). A longitudinal analysis of the antecedents of organizational commitment. *Academy of Management Journal, 27*, 95–112.

Billingsley, B. S.; and Cross, L. H. (1992). Predictors of commitment, job satisfaction, and the intent to stay in teaching: A comparison of general and special educators. *Journal of Special Education, 25* (4), 453–471.

Cheng, Y. C. (1994). Locus of control as an indicator of Hong Kong teachers' job attitudes and perceptions of organizational characteristics. *Journal of Educational Research, 87* (3), 180–188.

Dubin, R. (1956). Industrial workers' worlds: A study of the central life interest of industrial workers. *Social Problems, 3*, 131.

Dubin, R.; Champoux, J. E.; and Porter, L. W. (1975). Central life interests and organizational commitment of blue collar and clerical workers. *Administrative Science Quarterly, 20* (3), 411–421.

Dworkin, A. G. (1987). *Teacher burnout in the public schools: Structural causes and consequences for children.* Albany: State University of New York Press.

Farber, B. (1984). Stress and burnout in suburban teachers. *Journal of Educational Research, 77*, 325–331.

Firestone, W. A.; and Pennell, J. R. (1993). Teacher commitment, working conditions, and differential policies. *Review of Educational Research, 63* (4), 489–525.

Glisson, C.; and Durick, M. (1988). Predictors of job satisfaction and organizational commitment in human service organizations. *Administrative Science Quarterly, 33*, 61–81.

Grau, L.; Chandler, B.; Burton, B.; and Kolditz, D. (1991). Institutional loyalty and job satisfaction among nurse aides in nursing homes. *Journal of Aging and Health, 3* (1), 47–65.

Hoy, W. K.; and Miskel, C. G. (1987). *Educational administration: Theory research and practice* (3d ed.). New York: Random House.

Jackson, S. E. (1989). Does job control job stress? In S. L. Sauter, J. J. Hurrell, Jr., and C. L. Cooper (Eds.), *Job control and worker health* (pp. 25–53). New York: John Wiley & Sons.

Kahn, R. L.; and Byosiere, R. (1990). Stress in organizations. In M. Dunnette and L. M. Hough (Eds.), *Handbook of industrial and organizational psychology*: Vol. 3. Palo Alto, CA: Consulting Psychologists Press.

Kahn, R. L.; Wolfe, D. M.; Quinn, R. P.; Snoek, J. D.; and Rosenthal, R. A. (1964). *Organizational stress: Studies in role conflict and ambiguity.* New York: John Wiley & Sons.

Khan, S. B.; and Weiss, J. (1973). The teaching of affective responses. In Robert M. W. Travers (Ed.), *Second handbook of research on teaching: A project of the American Educational Research Association* (pp. 759–804). Chicago: Rand McNally.

Knoop, R. (1986). Job involvement: An illusive concept. *Psychological Reports, 59* (2, part 1), 451–456.

Knoop, R. (1995a). Influence of participative decision-making on job satisfaction and organizational commitment of school principals. *Psychological Reports, 76* (2), 379–382.

Knoop, R. (1995b). Relationships among job involvement, job satisfaction, and organizational commitment for nurses. *Journal of Psychology, 129* (6), 643–649.

Lam, P.; Foong, Y. Y.; and Moo, S. N. (1995). Work life, career commitment, and job satisfaction as antecedents of career withdrawal cognition among teacher interns. *Journal of Research and Development in Education, 28* (4), 230–236.

Landy, F.; Quick, J. C.; and Kasl, S. (1994). Work, stress, and well-being. *International Journal of Stress Management, 1* (1), 33–73.

Littrell, P. C.; Billingsley, B. S.; and Cross, L. H. (1994). The effects of principal support on special and general educators' stress, job satisfaction, school commitment, health, and intent to stay in teaching. *Remedial and Special Education, 15* (5), 297–310.

Mannheim, B. (1975). A comparative study of work centrality, job rewards, and satisfaction: Occupational groups in Israel. *Sociology of Work and Occupations, 2* (1), 79–102.

Mannheim, B. (1983). Male and female industrial workers: Job satisfaction, work role centrality, and workplace preference. *Work and Occupations, 10* (4), 413–436.

Mannheim, B. (1993). Gender and the effects of demographics, status, and work values on work centrality. *Work and Occupations, 20* (1), 3–22.

Mannheim, B.; and Angel, O. (1986). Pay systems and work role centrality of industrial workers. *Personnel Psychology, 39* (2), 359–377.

Mannheim, B.; and Cohen, A. (1978). Multivariate analysis of factors affecting work role centrality of occupational categories. *Human Relations, 31* (6), 525–553.

Mannheim, B.; and Dubin, R. (1986). Work role centrality of industrial workers as related to organizational conditions, task autonomy, managerial orientations and personal characteristics. *Journal of Occupational Behavior, 7* (2), 107–124.

Marsh, R. M.; and Mannari, H. (1977). Organizational commitment and turnover: A predictor study. *Administrative Science Quarterly, 22*, 57–75.

McGrath, J. E. (1976). Stress and behavior in organizations. In M. D. Dunnette (Ed.), *Handbook of industrial and organizational psychology.* Chicago: Rand McNally.

McNeil, L. (1988). *Contradictions of control: School structure and school knowledge.* New York: Routledge.

Miskel, C. G.; and Ogawa, R. (1988). In Norman J. Boyan (Ed.), *Handbook of research on educational administration: A project of the American Educational Research Association* (pp. 279–304). New York: Longman.

Moses, J.; and Lyness, K. (1988). Individual and organizational responses to ambiguity. In F. D. Shoorman and B. Schneider (Eds.), *Facilitating work effectiveness.* Lexington, MA: Goodyear.

Munene, J. C.; and Azuka, E. (1991). Some positive outcomes of work participation in Nigeria: A replication. *Journal of Psychology in Africa, 1* (4), 1–16.

Paullay, I. M.; Alliger, G. M.; and Stone-Romero, E. F. (1994). Construct validation of two instruments designed to measure job involvement and work centrality. *Journal of Applied Psychology, 79* (2), 224–228.

Powell, A. G.; Farrar, E.; and Cohen, D. K. (1985). *The shopping mall high school: Winners and losers in the educational marketplace.* Boston: Houghton Mifflin.

Schuler, R. S.; and Jackson, S. E. (1986). Managing stress through PHRM practices: An uncertainty interpretation. *Research in Personnel and Human Resources Management, 4,* 183–224.

Triandis, H. C. (1996). The psychological measurement of cultural syndromes. *American Psychologist, 51* (4), 407–415.

Williams, L. J.; and Hazer, J. T. (1986). Antecedents and consequences of satisfaction and commitment in turnover models: A re-analysis using latent variable structural equation methods. *Journal of Applied Psychology, 71,* 219–231.

Wright, R.; King, S. W.; and Berg, W. E. (1985). Job satisfaction in the workplace: A study of black females in management positions. *Journal of Social Service Research, 8* (3), 65–79.

8

Reflections and Directions

Allen Menlo and Pam Poppleton

In Chapters 1 through 7, several authors have described different parts of this comparative study of phenomena related to the work life of teachers in nine countries. We have reported and discussed the study's results and have considered several of the issues arising in the process of generating them. In this chapter, the two editors, each from their own perspectives and sense of importance, draw closure to this particular research venture. In the first section, Dr. Poppleton provides reflections on the processes, issues, and results of the total study. In the second section, Dr. Menlo provides a series of propositional statements of knowledge derived from study findings and develops implications of the knowledge for improvement of teacher work life across all nine countries.

SECTION I: IMPLICATIONS OF THE STUDY FOR THEORY AND PRACTICE

In this brief overview I will discuss two issues in particular, one practical and one theoretical, that bear upon the stated objectives of the study. The practical issue has to do with the extent to which findings derived from nine countries might be generalizable, and if so, how they may be implemented for the improvement of the secondary teacher's work life. The theoretical issue has to do with the possible existence of a culture of teaching that transcends national boundaries in the sense of "a description of a particular way of life which expresses certain meanings and values, not only in art and learning, but also in institutions and ordinary behavior" (Williams, 1981), and if so, of what nature and significance is it? At the end of these explorations of similarities and differences between countries, we will finally ask if our comparative study tells us anything that we could not have known from single-country studies alone.

The "Inside–Outside" Problem

Both these issues are expressions of the "inside–outside" problem in comparative education, that is, the transfer of ideas, policies, and practices between countries or different settings. The inside–outside dilemma of applying ready-made solutions to pressing educational problems has never been more acute than in the 1990s, as the spread of globalization makes us increasingly aware of "how things are done" elsewhere; of how much we assume, and how little we really know. For example, in addressing problems of the professional development of teachers in relation to practices elsewhere, Terhart (1997) observed, "There is no German word covering the meaning of the English term 'teacher development.' There is just 'teacher education' and then 'ongoing teacher socialization.'" It would be an error, he said, to suppose that all teachers in German schools try to develop their competence to its utmost level or are waiting for developers to do so. "Most of them just do their job and drive home"—a salutary reminder that, in this respect at least, German teachers' actions are determined more by the requirements of their system than by a supposedly universal model of professional development.

What is it then that drives those who are "inside" to seek solutions to their problems from "outside," and equally, how does one develop a process from "outside" when the problem is "inside"? An important step is to inculcate awareness of the outside and to assess how the inside must change for successful transfer to be effective. But in order to be able to take this step, we need to know what is already similar and what is different between inside and outside; which factors are cultural, and which are structural, and how to communicate this information to both sides.

Patterns of Similarities and Differences

The search for similarities and differences in the work lives of teachers in nine countries has sometimes seemed not only ambitious, but presumptuous in the sense that we risked finding the obvious and the stereotypical and overlooking the small, but significant, event or trend. In a study of this kind, it is easier to spot the similarities than the differences, particularly the similarities in the patterns reported in Chapter 7, since it is there that the major interactions are revealed across countries in an analysis that concentrates on bringing all the elements together to identify their relative importance in each country. Table 7.1 shows the rank orders of the demographic, role, condition, and practice domains in contributing to overall job satisfaction, work centrality, and stress. When the rank orders are arranged under "Countries," a remarkable consistency is shown in which overall patterns are similar within countries in each of the four domains, but the order of the conditions, roles, practices, and demographics differed according to the criterion. Conditions of work combined with roles were perceived as most important to overall job satisfaction (except for the Soviet Union); roles and responsibilities followed by conditions and practices combined were most important to work centrality in all cases; and conditions followed by practices and roles combined were most important to the experience of job-related stress in six out of the nine countries (the United States, Germany, and Singapore excepted). In no case did the demographic domain make significant contributions.

Such seeming consistency was not always borne out in the earlier accounts, in which the quality of life domains were treated separately, and it should be noted that there are no systematic accounts of relationships in single countries in this book. This is mainly because the book is a strictly comparative and collaborative effort. Although single-country accounts are necessary in order fully to appreciate the inside–outside problems, some further probing of the similarities and differences revealed by the survey is helpful in order to understand what a high quality work life looks like for teachers in different countries.

First, the psychological conditions of work were more important than the physical ones in contributing to both job satisfaction and work centrality. The highest level of support from colleagues, parents, and community was recorded by Polish teachers, whereas English teachers claimed the highest levels of autonomy and professional support, and Japanese teachers perceived themselves to have the highest morale (esprit de corps).

Singaporean teachers claimed the highest level of physical resources and Canadians the lowest, but the latter recorded the highest level of economic incentives. The gap between the amount and importance of economic incentives was very great for Japanese and Israeli teachers in the direction of deprivation. However, only in England and Canada was the condition associated with the highest levels of stress. Having a reasonable workload was deemed of greatest importance to job satisfaction in England and Singapore, but otherwise, it had variable relationships with job satisfaction, work centrality, and stress. Thus, there is a good deal of variation when condition indexes are shown in country context, distinct from the consistency shown when domains were arranged in rank order of countries.

The same processes have been repeated for the roles and responsibilities domain. When the roles indexes were placed in rank order, there was some evidence of a common culture of teaching in which countries allocated priorities in the same (or similar) order, suggesting that institutional norms operated in the allocation of responsibilities in combination with expressions of teachers' preferred forms of professionality. These processes working together appeared to produce a phenomenon of responsibility enlargement that contributed to generally high levels of work centrality. The overriding factor here is the prominence given to student-support activities that express themselves through different forms of guidance and administrative activities. An exception is that Japanese teachers, who seem to form a special case in the relative narrowness of their role set, recalling "the web of reciprocal obligations in which the social order is enmeshed" (Kudomi, 1992). Other special cases are Poland and the Soviet Union, where the ethical and moral aims of education were not an optional extra for teachers nor were they seen as divorced from academic aims. English teachers showed the highest level of involvement in administrative roles related to school management, running the subject department, and the pastoral–guidance system.

The classroom domain was dominated by overall negative responses to individualized teaching practices in terms of frequency of use, importance to job satisfaction, and level of difficulty. In contrast, the fostering of good teacher–pupil and pupil–pupil relationships was emphasized, and the control of classroom behavior appeared to be a universal aim. Together, both of these aspects contributed most to job satisfaction. Work centrality appeared to be unaffected by the overall difficulty of teaching practices, with the exception of teachers in Singapore and the Soviet Union. It was experienced as stressful across the board, except in Canada and Poland.

The similar patterns revealed by the ranking of the domains across countries is impressive but difficult to interpret because rank orders do not indicate the extent of differences between the ranks. For this we must turn to the ratings which show that ratings of work centrality are consistently greater than those of either job satisfaction or job-related stress, and that, while job satisfaction shows few significant differences between countries, job-related stress is more variable, seeming to be particularly low in Israel and Canada where special conditions must operate. Such conditions arise from different time structures, a wide range of class sizes, and the varying degrees of after-school administrative demands that comprise teachers' work. In addition, the major component of work centrality lies in the roles and responsibilities area and is related to the phenomenon of responsibility enlargement; the major component of overall job satisfaction lies in the conditions area and derives from psychosocial relationships, while the major component of job-related stress comes from workload-related factors. The emphasis on job satisfaction alone as the engine of teacher morale and effort is certainly mistaken, work centrality being the more powerful driving force.

Relationships between the quality-of-life criteria and the four domains are not as simple as they first appeared, since each domain is composed of a number of indexes, each of which may have a different relationship with each of the three criteria. This has been shown in a number of ways. An analysis of the data for the English teachers (Poppleton & Riseborough, 1990) employed a cluster analysis to reveal groups of teachers who had definable characteristics when clustered on sixteen variables, including the three criteria of job satisfaction, work centrality, and stress, plus thirteen value dimensions, which were almost identical to the indexes of this study. The clusters were clearly differentiated by their status on the criterion variables. One cluster (2), comprising 26 percent of the total sample, had the highest mean scores on work centrality and stress and differed from the others by its high profile on aspects of role and classroom practice. This seemed to indicate extended professionality. Cluster 1 members (37%), on the other hand, had the lowest standing of all on job satisfaction with moderately high stress and average work centrality. From their low scores on collegial, pastoral, and pupil relationships, they were called the restricted professionals. Cluster 3 (30%) teachers scored highest of all on job satisfaction and lowest on stress while cluster 4 teachers (7%) were distinguished by the relatively low valuation that its members gave to all aspects of their work lives. Cross-tabulating cluster membership with the demographic variables showed that the groups did not differ from each other in gender or marital status, though cluster 2 tended generally to be younger, and cluster 4 tended to be older than the others.

Sim (1990) employed a causal path analysis in the interpretation of the Singaporean and American data to show that conditions, roles, and practices had both a direct and an indirect impact on teacher job satisfaction and work centrality. "What the path diagram says is that work conditions per se are a necessary but not a sufficient condition for job satisfaction and work centrality. . . . They must be complemented by the presence of certain roles and responsibilities and classroom practices. . . . Taken broadly, the patterns of relationship both in terms of direction and size of impact are remarkably alike for the Singapore and U.S. data, suggesting perhaps, the universality of professional concerns amongst these teachers."

We thus have evidence of the existence of interacting personal perceptions and relationships in determining the nature and quality of the work life, as well as the overlapping of work conditions, roles, responsibilities, and classroom practices in contributing to the impressions of universality in professional concerns. But special relationships keep appearing to emphasize the importance of conditions unique to different countries.

Cultures and Contexts

On the basis of their comparative study of French and English primary school teachers, Broadfoot, Osborn, Gilly, and Paillet (1988) argued that "the national context within which teachers work deeply influences their professional ideology, their perceptions of their professional responsibility, and the way in which they carry out their day to day work." We speak of a national culture in the sense that it is composed of similar beliefs and values held by the majority of a given population about such things as religion, the role of the state, or politics, which may be made explicit in the form of legislation, or in normative practices. But education is, by its very nature, provincial and country-bound. So, if there is a common occupational culture of teaching, of what nature is it?

Judging solely from the evidence presented by this study, the central feature is not job satisfaction or work centrality alone, but the interaction between them, and also, the patterns of work conditions, roles, responsibilities, and classroom practices that we selected to define the teacher's work experiences. The following generalizations define some of the characteristics of the teacher culture as they have emerged from the study.

1. It is an evaluative culture in which all our teachers were able to evaluate the various elements of their work separately from the extent to which they experienced them and to distinguish between those that met their needs and those that did not.

2. Some of the things they valued most highly across countries were psychosocial in nature and some were instrumental. The level of collegial support increased in importance as the demands of the job increased and lack of esprit de corps produced stress. All agreed teaching did not provide strong economic incentives.

3. Although there was evidence of extended (as distinct from restricted) professionality, broadening of the role set and range of responsibilities were judged in terms of incentive power rather than personal satisfaction. Generally, the amount done was greater than its perceived importance. This was especially noticeable in the case of involvement of teacher training, professional development, and concern for the world outside the classroom.

4. Relationships with students and between students were highly valued by all teachers as a source of expressive work centrality. It was also seen as a source of stress for some. The factor most frequently influencing classroom practice, however, was the difficulty of catering to individual differences between students and promoting individualized learning; though apparently, this was not seen to be related to the teacher's job satisfaction or to student learning and development. This is a major finding and has implications of some importance for the proponents of individualization (whatever that term may mean).

In defining the culture of working, the MOW team (1987) distinguished normative beliefs about working as the right to certain work outcomes. Based on an empirical study of occupational samples drawn from eight countries, they were able to show how such beliefs differed between different individuals and occupational groups within and across countries. Teachers across countries assigned much less importance to good pay and more to interpersonal relations and autonomy than other occupational groups. Our data does not include comparisons with other occupations but confirms the high standing of teachers on these dimensions. A tentative summary suggests that the culture of teaching in different settings might be defined by the following normative features.

• Expressive versus instrumental work centrality.

• Extended versus restricted professionality.
• Social obligation versus individual autonomy.

Both "nation" and "occupation" are contextual concepts that have occurred frequently in our study, but we must not forget that the knowledge we have gained about teaching has been derived from teachers' perceptions of their work situations rather than from objective reality. Internal evidence suggests that teachers in some countries see teaching quite simply as classroom instruction, while in others it is seen as a variety of responsibilities that may involve administration and may be based on different conceptions of teaching and learning. It is the sum total of their beliefs and perceptions that define the occupational culture of teaching in terms of the perspectives we sought to uncover. But in order to establish the validity of teachers' perspectives, they have to be tested against evidence drawn from such sources as independent accounts, records, or legislation, which define the macrosocial and economic systems in which the schools are placed. Consequently, in interpreting the data, *we need to take account of the contexts in which the data were gathered as well as the nature of the data itself.*

In this respect, it is not always easy to distinguish between cultural and structural factors, since the existence of the latter will have depended at some point on a complex combination of historical and socioeconomic factors, which may not be accessible to the researcher. This is why Kohn (1989) suggested that we should not seek to determine how or when the structural factors evolved, but accept that "the resultant social structures have a (similar) cross-national impact on people and that the explanation of this impact should be sought in terms of how people experience the social structures, rather than in the historical or cultural processes that shaped them." On the other hand, "where we find differences we should look to those cultural forces for an explanation."

Some of the social–structural factors appearing to produce similarities have already been mentioned. In Chapter 4, two groups of countries were identified from the roles analysis to show the cultural standardization of Poland and the Soviet Union (where teachers were servants of the state) and the organization of the teacher's day and week in Germany and Singapore. In addition, Chapter 6 reports that all teachers experienced difficulties in the use of individualized teaching methods. What might be the structures that bring about this common feature? Insofar as individualized teaching may require a much higher level of resources, both human and material, than other teaching methods, and because units of resource are scarce in state-run comprehensive schools, these may be the causal structures, since the majority of teachers perceive such methods as being desirable for student learning and development. Political, traditional, and economic factors are just three of the many social–structural factors involved.

On the other hand, role diversity between teachers in different countries was interpreted in terms of the cultural uniqueness of Japan (competitiveness, social obligation, and busyness) and the varied programs of secondary schools reflected in the cultural patterns of choice. Chapter 6 reports that "teachers in all countries except Germany cannot seem to get what they want" concerning the amount of workload. The German teachers distinctiveness crops up in every section, which strongly supports the notion of their cultural uniqueness: The MOW study (1987) found instrumentalism to be a strong feature of the West German culture.

Although only three demographic criteria were employed in these analyses, many more factors were available (e.g., characteristics of the schools, the subject(s) taught, number of jobs applied for during the previous year both within and outside teaching, the career pattern, qualifications, changes of school, membership in teacher unions and professional organizations). Not all these factors were available for all countries. All this information is available to researchers who wish to interpret the results of their own surveys more meaningfully and to place them in the macrocontext. *Future work should take greater account of the school context.*

Inside–Outside Revisited

The importance of this study is that the findings can act as a source of information and guidance to teachers, school principals, administrators, and government agencies about their own educational systems in relation to those of others. However, some of the findings are at a very general level. They open up areas for further scrutiny and also point to critical issues, but do not absolve readers from very careful consideration of the findings relating to their own country, and how these findings are embedded in the structural and cultural qualities of their own education systems. Unfortunately, they will not find accounts in this book that are written from single-country perspectives, though nearly all are available in some form (see Poppleton, 1990).

The user of such information may wish to note and "borrow" policies and practices from countries that appear to have a happy and highly motivated teaching force or to have solved similar problems. Comparisons with other countries are frequently invoked in advocating educational reforms in areas such as the acquisition of basic literacy and numeracy, the teaching of science and mathematics, or vocational education, where "the systems elsewhere in Western Europe seem to succeed much better than ours in keeping more of their young people in full-time education and for longer" (Baker, 1987). While one may question the nature of the motivation in the adoption of other countries' solutions, there is no doubt about the value of comparative studies in broadening the ability to see patterns and relationships that are often not visible in the single case. At the end of a comparative study, each participant will take away something different, but the perspective will have changed, leading to a reevaluation of the nature of the problem. In this sense, *our comparative study has told us many things about ourselves, our colleagues, and our partner countries that we could not have known from single-country studies alone.*

But do they enable us to advocate, for example, that Britain should adopt the American system of separating the functions of teaching and administration to reduce burdensome workloads, when there are known to be problems of authority and autonomy, or that Japanese teachers working in a highly competitive culture should look to establishing the more relaxed working environment of the Canadian teachers to reduce job-related stress, or that schools in the West would do well to adopt Eastern teaching methods in mathematics and science, when this would disturb the established relationships between role and subject specialization? Such advocacy smacks of acute anxieties over international competitiveness rather than the careful evaluation of domestic practices in the context of both culture and structure. *What this research shows is that cross-cultural transfer must be supported by appropriate structures to be successful, and comparative study can help to identify these.*

Finally, there is the problem of implementation. If recommendations are made, who is to implement them? Because of the key role of the principal or head teacher in approving recommendations and implementing them, it is unfortunate that an early decision was taken in our study to exclude school heads from the samples. "The Principal in a High School affects faculty morale and can make or break any improvement effort" (Lieberman & Miller, 1992). *The matching of perspectives between principal and staff in the processes of negotiation about transfer is vital and should be a focus of investigation in future studies.*

Our study has recorded what teachers were thinking and feeling during a period of great change when they were under attack in many countries for lowering standards and when they were beginning to leave the profession in large numbers. Today, in Britain at least, the crisis in staffing schools is no longer looming, although it is still present, and a solution has to be sought.

In conclusion, this study has opened up a number of areas for careful scrutiny and further work before irreversible decisions that affect the lives of teachers and schools are taken. The practical and theoretical issues discussed in the comparative research context are vital to the well-being of schools and teachers.

SECTION II: AN APPROACH TO COMMUNICATING RESEARCH FINDINGS

It seems reasonable to expect that researchers who generate findings in the field of education will take the responsibility to address problems and issues of importance in the work lives of educators and then communicate their findings in forms that maximize their potential for being understood and being of interest to relevant professional practitioners. Admittedly, there is some sense of arrogance or naivete to assume that one's work is automatically worthy of attention. Yet, there are academics (Tanner, 1998) who see this kind of responsibility taking as a mandate for educational researchers. I strongly support this mandate. Accordingly, I have taken on the task of presenting several of our study's findings in a form that I have known to contain structural and substantive characteristics promotive of practitioner attention. Personally, I have not noticed this form to have wide usage in the field of education. Therefore, I will explain the rationale behind this kind of presentation before moving ahead with it.

Kennedy (1997), in reviewing reasons for there being a perceived lack of connection between research and practice in education identifies the need for research findings to be translated into an epistemological form that more clearly resembles the real elements of the teaching experience. In addition, she makes the point that the use of findings are enhanced when they are within the conceptual reach of teachers and can influence their thinking.

Another pertinent cognitive condition is described by Renkl, Mandl, and Gruber (1996) in analyzing why some knowledge is inert and without power of movement. Their notion is that such knowledge has a structural deficit that precludes its availability in a form promotive of its application; it is inactive in words and grammar and is in need of empowerment. Other social scientists who have recognized this in past years have recast research findings in the more active form of propositions. Goldstein, Heller, and Sechrest (1966) have done this in the area of psychotherapy, Shaw (1971) in the area of group dynamics, Deutsch (1973) in conflict resolution, Price (1968) in organization development, and Ehrlich (1973) in the area of prejudice. Kunkel (1992) strongly supports the use of propositions in the social sciences in that they possess user-friendly simplicity, consist of units with clear referents, have direct links with empirical data, and are testable and refutable.

Jack Rothman (1974), in an extensive project on knowledge utilization in the field of community organization, developed a procedure for heightening the visibility and understandability of a finding and increasing its potential for action. He transformed a finding into a generalization and then developed a series of action guidelines for logically moving the generalization toward use. The generalization consisted of a statement "about the nature of social phenomena (example: status inconsistency has been found to be associated with a predisposition to participate in social movements)." From the generalization, he constructed a set of derivations intended to translate the generalization into an applied formulation "(example: in seeking participants for social-action programs, the practitioner would be well-advised to recruit from among community residents having characteristics of status inconsistency)." Rothman adds that the action guideline is dependent upon an inference "which moves the generalization one step beyond its immediate scientific formulation." Exercising caution, he then speaks of the action guidelines as "emergent hypotheses" concerning an intervention, and that these hypotheses are also grounded in prior research and can now be tested in the field. It is helpful to recognize that the action guideline, in addition to being advisory on how to put the research finding into motion, also creates a general problem context within which the research finding can be placed. The use of this mechanism is consistent with the conceptually and empirically based perspective of

Robinson (1998), who suggests that practices be treated as solutions to practical problems; that is, research findings are more accurately translated into practice when they relate to a problem in search of a solution.

Building on Rothman's perspective and methodology for translating social science knowledge into practitioner use, and then drawing upon the theoretical considerations of Kennedy, Renkl, Kunkel, and Robinson, a slightly different translation procedure was developed (Menlo, 1991, 1993) for our study. This procedure moves a finding more quickly into the active form of an if . . . then/when . . . then/the more . . . the more type of *proposition*, or propositional statement of knowledge. The proposition restates the finding by moving it from past to present tense and from a multipart statement to one with two symmetrical sections. The proposition is then further activated by a *suggested line of action*, which is a logical extension of the proposition, and is grounded in practitioner experience, relevant social science knowledge, and a "spoonful" of innovative thinking. Both the proposition and the line of action are kept at a midlevel of specificity: enough to provide directionality for action and yet not stray from the finding's original scientific character. The line of action suggests a manipulation of phenomena in the interest of more favorable circumstances for, in our case, teacher work life or education. It represents a cognitive leap from the proposition and calls for the use of inference, conjecture, and imagination. Ideally, the line of action is advisory and not directive. More specificity in action is left to the experiential wisdom of an indigenous planner within the improvement or problem situation. An example of this sequence arising from an actual two-part similarity across all countries in a recent international study on teaching practices is as follows.

Finding: The extent of difficulty teachers had with their practices affected their job satisfaction more than it did the extent to which they used their practices, and the extent to which they used their practices affected the centrality of work in their lives more than it did the extent of difficulty of their practices.

Proposition: The more that teachers engage in their practices and experience mastery over them, the greater will be their sense of job satisfaction and immersion in their work.

Line of Action: To increase teachers' sense of job satisfaction and immersion in their work, there should be plenty of opportunity for them to experience mastery over their practices while fully engaging in their use.

Hopefully, what the reader will have recognized here is the increased power of a built-in predisposition for action and movement, communicated by both a propositional statement and a line of action.

Twenty Findings, Propositions, and Lines of Action

We will now move to the presentation of twenty of our study's findings, which have already been identified in previous chapters, but within contexts more inclusive of other concepts, ideas, and issues that compete for the reader's attention. Each of these findings represents a discovery of the existence of a same condition, pattern, or statistically significant relationship between variables in each of the nine countries. Each finding is a case in which the same thing occurs in all countries when the countries are compared to each other in a side-by-side manner. The findings have emerged from either bivariate or multivariate analyses. Any findings already in existence from prior unicultural studies are now confirmed as having a much broader base of validation. These sets of three-part statements are not intended to be in any particular order of importance or focus, but only to introduce variation in focus and style.

1. *Finding.* For teachers in each of the nine countries, there was either no or very little discrepancy between the perceived importance of their practices as a source of student learning and development and the perceived importance of their practices as a source of job satisfaction (Table 6.1).

Proposition. When teachers perceive their practices as being of a certain value for their students' learning and development, then they are likely to perceive the practices as being of similar value for their own job satisfaction.

Line of Action. Since most teachers' sense of personal power to determine their own job satisfaction can be increased by assisting the teachers in increasing their attributions of power to their own teaching's effect on their students (self-efficacy), school leaders who wish to help teachers feel able to influence their own job satisfaction (self-determination) can initiate and/or encourage teaching activities of a collaborative nature that are known to move teachers toward a general and a personal sense of teacher efficacy.

2. *Finding.* For teachers in each of the nine countries, the two practices cited as most difficult to accomplish were the individualization of lessons for students and motivating them to learn (Table 6.2).

Proposition. The individualizing of instruction and motivation of students are likely to be more difficult for teachers than most of their other practices.

Line of Action. While planners of professional development for teachers may include experiences with several dimensions of skill and knowledge, they would be wise to maintain ongoing opportunities to sharpen competencies at individualizing instruction and motivating students.

3. *Finding.* For teachers in each of the nine countries, only the practice of individualizing instruction was seen as most difficult, indicated as least used, and rated as routinely unimportant for their job satisfaction (Tables 6.2, 6.3, and 6.4).

Proposition. Since the practice of individualizing instruction is the most difficult and least used by teachers, it is likely to be considered by them as less important for their job satisfaction than their other practices.

Line of Action. It is wise for professional-development personnel in schools to be aware that efforts at helping teachers improve their competencies in individualizing instruction are unlikely to have attraction and are likely to be met with little interest and some resistance. Strategies to increase attraction and interest would involve an increase in teachers' perceptions of their potential for mastering the practice and experimenting with its use in their own classrooms under the conditions of joint planning and available assistance.

4. *Finding.* For teachers in each of the nine countries, the difficulty of their combined set of practices was a small but authentic source of both nonsatisfaction and stress with their jobs (Tables 6.9 and 6.11).

Proposition. The more teachers attribute difficulty to their combined set of practices, the more likely they are to have experiences of reduced job satisfaction and increased stress.

Line of Action. Professional development personnel may preclude the buildup of sources of nonsatisfaction and stress for teachers by helping them differentiate the difficulty they attribute to each of their separate practices.

5. *Finding.* For teachers in each of the nine countries, their use of the practice of promoting positive regard with and between their students was a stronger force toward experiencing their work as central to their lives than the use of any of their other practices (Table 6.13).

Proposition. If teachers spend effort and time in developing mutually accepting relationships with and between their students, they are most likely to increase the extent to which they hold work as central in their lives.

Line of Action. School administrators can increase the investment and commitment of teachers to their work in the school by encouraging them to build caring relationships between students and between students and teachers.

6. *Finding.* In each of the nine countries, teachers who rated their practices as being of high importance for both their own job satisfaction and the learning and development of their students also had high work centrality (Tables 6.9 and 6.10).

Proposition. When teachers view the use of their practices as highly important for bringing about both their own job satisfaction and the learning and development of their students, they are likely to have a strong investment in their work.

Line of Action. It appears to be established that teachers can be assisted in maintaining a strong investment and involvement in their work by increasing the power they attribute to their practices for effecting both the learning and development of their students and the sense of satisfaction they derive from their job. What is suggested here, therefore, is the collaborative building of procedures and opportunities for teachers to test and observe the consequences of their teaching plans and actions on their students, to receive feedback and sharpen their skills, to reobserve their efforts, and to discuss their experiences with mutually adventurous colleagues.

7. *Finding.* In each of the nine countries, the perceived support of teachers by colleagues, parents of students, and community contributed significantly to teachers' overall job satisfaction (Tables 5.4 and 7.2).

Proposition. The more teachers experience themselves as recipients of support from colleagues, parents, and community, the more likely they will feel satisfied with their job.

Line of Action. School officials can maintain and increase the job satisfaction of their schools' teachers by working to develop supportive relationships between teachers and their students' parents, teachers, and the community at large, and between teachers themselves.

8. *Finding.* In each of the nine countries, teachers experienced autonomy as one of the conditions most present in their work and viewed professional support as one of the least important conditions for their job satisfaction (Table 5.1).

Proposition. When autonomy is a major condition in teachers' work lives, they tend to place less value upon advisory and technical assistance from others as a source of job satisfaction.

Line of Action. If school leaders wish to increase the use of advisory and technical assistance by teachers, they could help teachers not to view their use of those services as being contrary to the maintenance of their autonomy, but, instead, as responding to the need for teaching success.

9. *Finding.* In each of the nine countries, teachers rated the presence of a cooperative and mutually respectful work relationship between colleagues as a more important condition for generating their feelings of job satisfaction than the availability of advisory, technical, and problem-solving assistance (Table 5.1).

Proposition. A cooperative and mutually respectful relationship between colleagues in a school is more likely to produce job satisfaction for teachers than the availability of advisory, technical, and problem-solving assistance.

Line of Action. School administrators who wish to promote the overall job satisfaction of their schools' teachers will be more successful if they invest their primary efforts and resources in developing interpersonal and intergroup cooperation and respect, rather than in providing for advisory, technical, and problem-solving assistance.

10. *Finding.* Teachers in each of the nine countries indicated that they were less involved in the teacher-education role of supervising student teachers and inducting new teachers into professional responsibilities than their other roles, and that they saw this role as less important for their job satisfaction than their other roles (Figures 4.3, 4.4, and Table 4.1).

Proposition. Teachers are less likely to participate in and view as important for their own job satisfaction the education of future and new teachers in comparison to responsibilities related to their students, their school, and their own development.

Line of Action. To increase the extent to which teachers may be interested and involved in the education of future and new teachers, some means of linking the activity to teacher job satisfaction or the creation of other motives will be required.

11. *Finding.* Teachers in each of the nine countries indicated that the responsibility with which they were either most or second-most involved and which was the most or second-most important for their job satisfaction was giving student support (Table 4.1).

Proposition. Teachers are likely to sense satisfaction with their work when their work concerns the well-being and development of their students moreso than when it concerns other professional issues and responsibilities in their school life.

Line of Action. Administrative and supervisory leadership in schools will be most successful in laying a groundwork for teacher job satisfaction when teachers can view their activities as being in the service of student well-being and development.

12. *Finding.* The overall set of work conditions of teachers in each of the nine countries clearly affected the amount of their job satisfaction, work centrality, and job-related stress. It was their job satisfaction that was most impacted by the totality of the work conditions (Tables 5.4, 5.5, and 5.6).

Proposition. While the teachers' overall sense of their work conditions affect their satisfaction with their job, the centrality of their work in their lives, and any of their job stress, it is their job satisfaction that is the most impacted.

Line of Action. It is possible to especially enhance the satisfaction teachers experience with their job, increase the extent to which their work is central in their lives, and reduce the extent to which their job is a source of stress, by developing and applying considered strategies for overall improvement of their work conditions.

13. *Finding.* For teachers in each of the nine countries, when their perceptions of the importance of either their work conditions or their responsibilities was greater than the presence of the conditions or their involvement in the responsibilities, then their work centrality was increased. When their perceptions of either the importance of their work conditions or their responsibilities was less than the presence or involvement, their work centrality was decreased. (Chapter 4, Predicting the Quality of the Working Life; Chapter 5,

Work Conditions and Work Centrality; and Tables E-9 and F-9 of the *Technical Supplement.*)

Proposition. When good work conditions or teaching responsibilities become more important than available, the centrality of work in teachers' lives rises. When either of them become less important than available, the centrality of work decreases.

Line of Action. Thoughts regarding work tend to be more central to teachers both during and outside school hours when the availability of good conditions and responsibilities fall short of their assessed importance for job satisfaction, and less central when their availability overtakes importance. Therefore, to maintain a highly invested teaching faculty, it would seem advisable to have a sense of challenge to teachers for the improvement of both working conditions and involvement in taking responsibility.

14. *Finding.* When teachers in each of the nine countries experienced high morale and cooperative relationships with their colleagues, their job satisfaction was higher and when they experienced low morale and limited cooperation, their job satisfaction was lower. (Chapter 5, Work Conditions and Overall Job Satisfaction; and Table F-9 of the *Technical Supplement.*)

Proposition. The more that cooperation and good mutual feelings are a part of faculty and staff work life, the more likely it is that teachers will feel satisfied with their jobs.

Line of Action. In order to be successful stimulators of job satisfaction for teachers within a school, administrators are well advised to introduce forces that help faculty and staff work well together and have fulfillment in their relationships.

15. *Finding.* In each of the nine countries, the participation by teachers in activities that can be especially promotive of their own professional development contributed significantly to their treating work as a central part of their lives. (Chapter 5, Work Conditions and Work Centrality; and Table F-9 of the *Technical Supplement.*)

Proposition. The more teachers participate in professional development activities related to education, the more likely it is that they will experience their work as being central to their lives.

Line of Action. The extent to which teachers invest themselves in their work and assign their work a central place in their lives can be increased through their participation in activities that have a high potential for their own professional development. School leaders can assist in making such activities available to teachers, increasing their attractiveness, and encouraging participation in them.

16. *Finding.* Teachers in each of the nine countries who were highly involved in their roles and responsibilities and who experienced an abundance of good work conditions expressed high job satisfaction (Table 7.2).

Proposition. Teachers who have high involvement in their roles and responsibilities and who are in a setting with overall good work conditions will be likely to experience high satisfaction with their job.

Line of Action. School leaders looking to move members of their school faculty toward a stronger sense of job satisfaction can increase the likelihood of bringing this about if they are able to help faculty members extend their motivation for classroom and school responsibility taking and create or enrich the conditions that have been demonstrated to help teachers use their professional expertise.

17. *Finding.* In each of the nine countries, teachers strongly indicated that a reasonable and non-constraining workload and support from colleagues were significant sources of job satisfaction and work centrality. (Chapter 7, Effects of Predictors Identified by Prior Research.)

Proposition. The more that teachers' workloads are reasonable and nonconstraining and the more they receive support from colleagues, the more they experience satisfaction in their job and have investment in their work.

Line of Action. The planners of teacher workload would be wise to have a sensitive understanding of the influence of daily workload and the support of colleagues on the quality of teachers' work lives. It would be most helpful for their planning to be undergirded with information about the ways that such things as class size, free periods, after-school work, and clerical and administrative work, as well as time and arrangements for contact between colleagues, affect teachers' satisfaction with their work. Shared or consultative workload planning can be a positive force.

18. *Finding.* In each of the nine countries, the combined demographic characteristics of teachers had the least or shared-least influence on the extent of teachers' job satisfaction, work centrality, and stress when compared to the influence of their work conditions, roles and responsibilities, and practices (Tables 7.2, 7.3, 7.4, and 7.5).

Proposition. Teachers' age, gender, and marital status are likely to have a smaller effect on the quality of their work lives than will the presence of good work conditions, the opportunity for much responsibility involvement, or their chance to use a wide range of good practices.

Line of Action. School leaders who wish to promote a high quality work life for their teachers that has the best amount and mix of overall job satisfaction, involvement and investment in work, and job-related stress, are well advised to focus their attention on issues other than accommodation of variations in teacher age, gender, or marital status.

19. *Finding.* For teachers in all nine countries, the extent of good working conditions influenced the level of their overall job satisfaction and the level of their job-related stress; the extent of involvement in their roles and responsibilities influenced their level of work centrality; and the extent of their overall use of their teaching practices had no significant influence on their job satisfaction in three countries, no significant influence on their work centrality in five countries, and no significant influence on their job-related stress in seven countries (Tables 7.2, 7.3, and 7.4).

Proposition. The quality of teachers' work lives is more likely to be improved by enriching work conditions and increasing opportunity and support for responsible role taking than by increasing the use of their teaching practices.

Line of Action. While efforts to affect the use of good classroom practices may be a primary force for improving success in teaching, planned programs for improving school work conditions and carefully considered endeavors to augment opportunities for responsible role taking by teachers are primary means to improve the overall quality of teachers' work lives.

20. *Finding.* In all nine countries, the extent of the teachers' overall job satisfaction had a significantly positive relationship with the extent of their work centrality and a significantly negative relationship with the extent of their job-related stress (Table 7.6).

Proposition. Teachers who are highly satisfied with their overall jobs are likely to give more commitment and attention to their work and experience less stress with it than their colleagues who have lower levels of satisfaction.

Line of Action. School leaders who may view the promotion of job satisfaction in teachers as a secondary or tertiary school activity can benefit from the realization that, when achieved, this satisfaction is a strong force toward the best utilization of teachers' professional resources in the service of their students' learning and development.

In addition to serving as a sharing of research-based, advisory information to colleagues in the practice world of teaching and schooling, these twenty statements may also function as an identification of similarities about teaching across several countries, and thus, as one response to the theoretical issue of whether there is a culture of teaching that transcends national boundaries.

REFERENCES

Baker, K. (Secretary of State for Education). (1987). North of England Conference, Rotherham, January 9.

Broadfoot, P.; and Osborn, M.; with Gilly, M.; and Paillet, A. (1988). What professional responsibility means to teachers: National contexts and classroom constants. *British Journal of Sociology of Education, 9* (3), 265–287.

Deutsch, M. (1973). *The resolution of conflict: Constructive and destructive processes.* New Haven: Yale University Press.

Ehrlich, H. J. (1973). *The social psychology of prejudice: A systematic theoretical review and propositional inventory of the American psychological study of prejudice.* New York: John Wiley & Sons.

Goldstein, A. P.; Heller, K.; and Sechrest, L. B. (1966). *Psychotherapy and psychology of behavior change.* New York: John Wiley & Sons.

Kennedy, M. M. (1997). The connection between research and practice. *Educational Researcher, 26* (7), 4–12

Kohn, M. (1989). Cross-national research as an analytic strategy. In M. L. Kohn (Ed.), *Cross-national research in sociology.* Newbury Park, CA: Sage.

Kudomi, Y. (1992). Teachers' culture in Japan: Narrowness of teachers' field. *Hitotsubashi Journal of School Studies, 24* (1), 1–12.

Kunkel, J. H. (1992). The units of unification: Theories or propositions? *American Psychologist, 47* (8), 1058–1059.

Lieberman, A.; and Miller, L. (1992). *Teachers, their world and their work: Implications for school improvement.* New York: Teachers College Press.

Menlo, A. (1991). *The utilization of cross-cultural comparative research for the development of knowledge in education.* Paper presented at the annual meeting of the American Educational Research Association, Chicago, IL, April 3–7.

Menlo, A. (1993). Teachers' development of consensual knowledge through the systematic examination of their teaching experience. Paper presented at the International Conference on Teacher Education: From Practice to Theory, Tel-Aviv, Israel, June 27–July 1.

MOW International Research Team. (1987). *The meaning of working.* Orlando, FL: Academic Press.

Poppleton, P. (1990). The survey data. *Comparative Education, 26* (2–3), 183–210.

Poppleton, P.; and Riseborough, G. (1990) Teaching in the mid-1980s: The centrality of work in secondary teachers' lives. *British Educational Research Journal, 16* (2), 105–124.

Price, J. L. (1968). *Organizational effectiveness: An inventory of propositions.* Homewood, IL: Irwin-Dorsey.

Renkl, A.; Mandl, H.; and Gruber, H. (1996). Inert knowledge: Analyses and remedies. *Educational Psychologist, 31* (2), 115–121.

Robinson, Viviane J. J. (1998). Methodology and the research–practice gap. *Educational Researcher, 27* (1), 17–26.

Rothman, J. (1974). *Planning and organizing for social change: Action principles from social science research.* New York: Columbia University Press.

Shaw, M. E. (1971). *Group dynamics: The psychology of small group behavior.* New York: McGraw-Hill.

Sim, W. K. (1990). Factors associated with job satisfaction and work centrality among Singapore teachers. *Comparative Education, 2* (2–3), 259–276.

Tanner, D. (1998). The social consequences of bad research. *Phi Delta Kappan, 79* (5), 345–349.

Terhart, E. (1997). *Professional development of teachers: The situation in Germany.* Keynote Address, Eighth Biennial Conference of the International Association on Teacher Thinking, Kiel, Germany, October 1–5.

Williams, R. (1981). *Culture.* London: Fontana.